# ENGLISH

## FOR EVERYONE

# EVERYDAY ENGLISH

**Project Editor** Amanda Eisenthal
**Senior Art Editor** Gilda Pacitti
**Editors** Andrea Mills, Laura Sandford, Rona Skene, James Smart
**US Senior Editor** Kayla Dugger
**US Proofreader** Sharon Lucas
**US Executive Editor** Lori Cates Hand
**Designers** Karen Constanti, Ali Scrivens, Anna Scully
**Illustrator** Gus Scott
**Managing Editor** Carine Tracanelli
**Managing Art Editor** Anna Hall
**Jacket Designer** Juhi Sheth
**DTP Designer** Deepak Mittal
**Senior Jackets Coordinator** Priyanka Sharma Saddi
**Jackets Design Development Manager** Sophia MTT
**Senior Production Editor** Andy Hilliard
**Senior Production Controller** Meskerem Berhane
**Publisher** Andrew Macintyre
**Managing Director, DK Learning** Hilary Fine

First American Edition, 2024
Published in the United States by DK Publishing,
a division of Penguin Random House LLC
1745 Broadway, 20th Floor, New York, NY 10019

A catalog record for this book
is available from the Library of Congress.
ISBN 978-0-7440-8499-3

DK books are available at special discounts when purchased
in bulk for sales promotions, premiums, fund-raising,
or educational use.
For details, contact: DK Publishing Special Markets,
1745 Broadway, 20th Floor, New York, NY 10019
SpecialSales@dk.com

Printed and bound in China

**www.dk.com**

# Contents

## ON VACATION

## HEALTH AND MEDICINE

## MEDIA AND COMMUNICATIONS

# How to use this book

*English for Everyone: Everyday English* will help you learn, understand, and practice common and useful American English phrases for a wide range of everyday situations. Most units in the book consist of conversation modules, with illustrated dialogues to place the phrases in context, and practice exercises. Listen to the audio on the website or app, repeat the words and phrases out loud, then complete the exercises to reinforce what you've learned. The answers to the exercises are at the back of the book.

**Unit number** The book is divided into themed units.

**Conversation modules** Conversations are organized into numbered modules covering different scenarios.

**Practice exercises** Most units feature a variety of listening and speaking exercises.

**Exercise number** Each exercise is identified with a unique number, so you can easily locate the audio track.

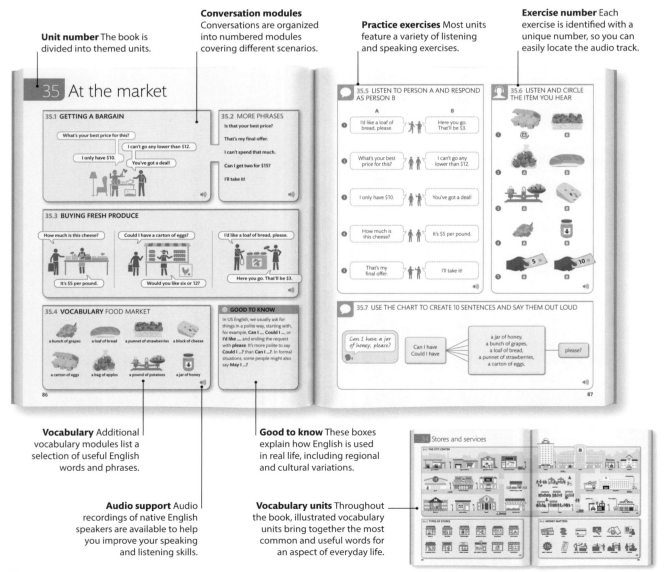

**Vocabulary** Additional vocabulary modules list a selection of useful English words and phrases.

**Audio support** Audio recordings of native English speakers are available to help you improve your speaking and listening skills.

**Good to know** These boxes explain how English is used in real life, including regional and cultural variations.

**Vocabulary units** Throughout the book, illustrated vocabulary units bring together the most common and useful words for an aspect of everyday life.

# Practice exercises

The conversation modules are followed by listening and speaking exercises.
Work through the exercises to test your understanding of the dialogues,
embed the new phrases in your memory, and improve your speaking fluency.
Answers are provided for the speaking exercises and the listening exercises.

**Listening exercise** This symbol indicates that you should listen to an audio track in order to answer the questions in the exercise.

**Listening and speaking exercise** This exercise allows you to simply listen to and repeat the dialogues.

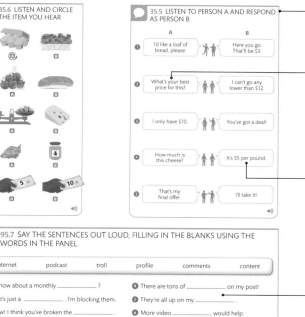

**Listen to Person A**
Listen to the first part of the conversation in the audio track.

**Respond as Person B**
In response to Person A, read the text for Person B out loud. Cover the dialogues to challenge yourself!

**Speaking exercise**
This symbol indicates that you should say your answers out loud.

95.7 SAY THE SENTENCES OUT LOUD, FILLING IN THE BLANKS USING THE WORDS IN THE PANEL

| Internet | podcast | troll | profile | comments | content |

❶ Or how about a monthly _____ ?

❷ That's just a _____ . I'm blocking them.

❸ I saw! I think you've broken the _____ .

❹ There are tons of _____ on my post!

❺ They're all up on my _____ .

❻ More video _____ would help.

**Fill in the blanks** In these speaking exercises, the blanks are a prompt to find the missing word from the panel and say the whole phrase out loud.

# Audio

This book offers extensive supporting audio resources. Each word and phrase in the conversation and vocabulary modules is recorded and can be played, paused, and repeated as often as you like.

**SUPPORTING AUDIO**
This symbol indicates that extra audio material to support a module or exercise is available for you to listen to.

**LISTENING EXERCISES**
This symbol indicates that you should listen to an audio track in order to answer the questions in the exercise.

**FREE AUDIO**
website and app
**www.dkefe.com**

To access the audio, download the app or go online, then choose the **American English** option when prompted.

# Answers

Answers are provided for most of the exercises, so you can see how well you have understood and remembered the phrases and expressions you have learned.

**Answers** The answers to the exercises are at the back of the book.

**Exercise numbers**
Match these numbers to the unique module number at the top-left corner of each exercise.

**Audio** This symbol indicates that the answers can also be listened to.

# 01 Greetings

## 1.1 INFORMAL GREETINGS

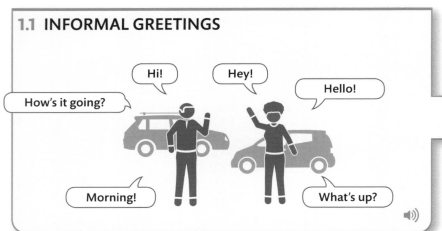

How's it going?

Hi!

Hey!

Hello!

Morning!

What's up?

## 1.2 MORE PHRASES

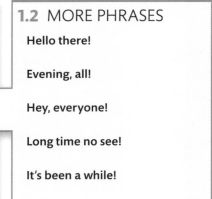

Hello there!

Evening, all!

Hey, everyone!

Long time no see!

It's been a while!

## 1.3 FORMAL GREETINGS

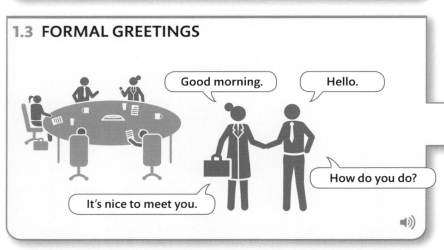

Good morning.

Hello.

How do you do?

It's nice to meet you.

## 1.4 MORE PHRASES

Good afternoon.

Good evening.

It's a pleasure to meet you.

It's nice to meet you all.

It's great to meet face to face!

## 1.5 EXCHANGING GREETINGS

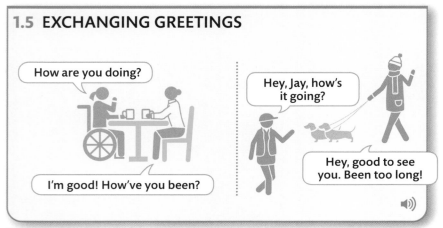

How are you doing?

I'm good! How've you been?

Hey, Jay, how's it going?

Hey, good to see you. Been too long!

### 🌐 GOOD TO KNOW

In informal English, you will often hear greetings in their abbreviated form, such as **How've you been?**, which flows more naturally than its long form, **How have you been?** It's also common to omit **It's** before phrases like **Great to see you**, **Nice to meet you**, and **Been too long!**

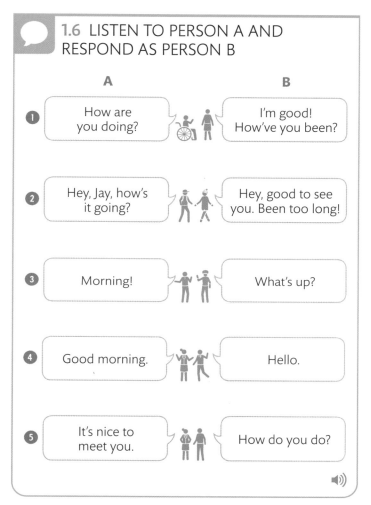

## 1.6 LISTEN TO PERSON A AND RESPOND AS PERSON B

**A**        **B**

**1**   How are you doing?    I'm good! How've you been?

**2**   Hey, Jay, how's it going?    Hey, good to see you. Been too long!

**3**   Morning!    What's up?

**4**   Good morning.    Hello.

**5**   It's nice to meet you.    How do you do?

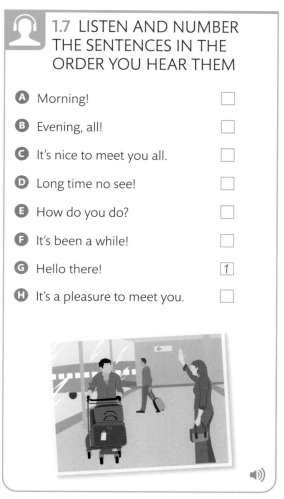

## 1.7 LISTEN AND NUMBER THE SENTENCES IN THE ORDER YOU HEAR THEM

**A** Morning! ☐

**B** Evening, all! ☐

**C** It's nice to meet you all. ☐

**D** Long time no see! ☐

**E** How do you do? ☐

**F** It's been a while! ☐

**G** Hello there! ☐ 1

**H** It's a pleasure to meet you. ☐

## 1.8 SAY THE SENTENCES OUT LOUD, FILLING IN THE BLANKS USING THE WORDS IN THE PANEL

| doing | afternoon | time | meet | Hey | going | Good | do |

**1** How do you _____ ?

**2** _____ evening.

**3** It's nice to _____ you.

**4** Good _____ .

**5** Hey, Jay, how's it _____ ?

**6** _____ , everyone!

**7** How are you _____ ?

**8** Long _____ no see!

11

# Making introductions

## 2.1 INTRODUCING YOURSELF INFORMALLY

Hey, I'm Tao.

How's it going? I'm Joe.

Hi, my name's Karim.

I'm Eva. Great to meet you.

You, too!

I don't think we've met. I'm Sofia.

I'm Jasmine, a friend of Jack's.

So nice to meet you.

## 2.2 INTRODUCING YOURSELF FORMALLY

Hello, I'm Daniyal Ali.

It's a pleasure to meet you, Mr. Ali.

Good morning! My name's Levi.

Pleased to meet you. I'm Maria.

Wonderful to meet you, Maria.

We have a new employee! Would you like to introduce yourself?

Of course. I'm Samantha, but you can call me Sam.

## 2.3 INTRODUCING OTHER PEOPLE

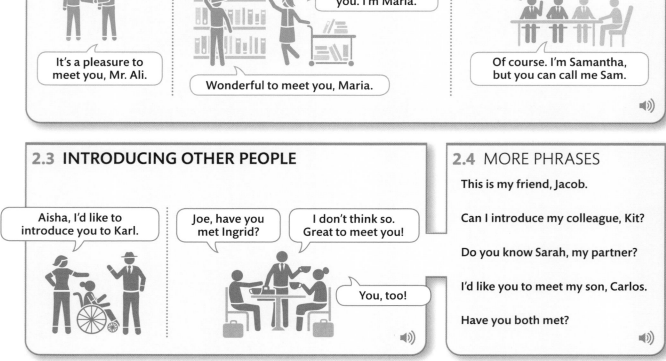

Aisha, I'd like to introduce you to Karl.

Joe, have you met Ingrid?

I don't think so. Great to meet you!

You, too!

## 2.4 MORE PHRASES

This is my friend, Jacob.

Can I introduce my colleague, Kit?

Do you know Sarah, my partner?

I'd like you to meet my son, Carlos.

Have you both met?

## 2.5 LISTEN TO PERSON A AND RESPOND AS PERSON B

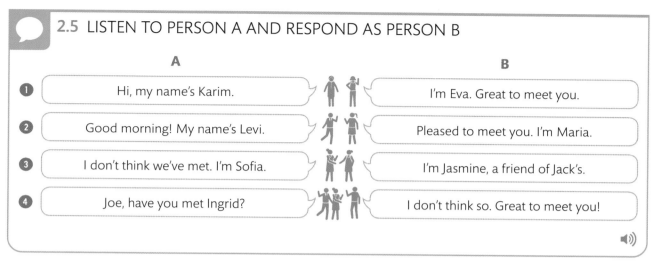

|  | A |  | B |
|---|---|---|---|
| 1 | Hi, my name's Karim. | | I'm Eva. Great to meet you. |
| 2 | Good morning! My name's Levi. | | Pleased to meet you. I'm Maria. |
| 3 | I don't think we've met. I'm Sofia. | | I'm Jasmine, a friend of Jack's. |
| 4 | Joe, have you met Ingrid? | | I don't think so. Great to meet you! |

## 2.6 USE THE CHART TO CREATE NINE SENTENCES AND SAY THEM OUT LOUD

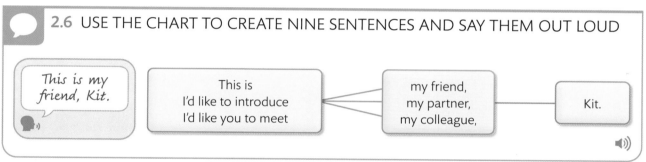

*This is my friend, Kit.*

| This is | | |
| I'd like to introduce | my friend, | Kit. |
| I'd like you to meet | my partner, | |
| | my colleague, | |

## 2.7 RESPOND OUT LOUD TO THE AUDIO, FILLING IN THE BLANKS USING THE WORDS IN THE PANEL

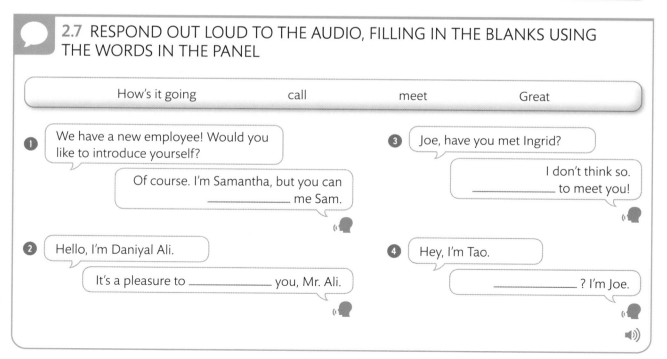

How's it going        call        meet        Great

1 We have a new employee! Would you like to introduce yourself?

Of course. I'm Samantha, but you can _____ me Sam.

2 Hello, I'm Daniyal Ali.

It's a pleasure to _____ you, Mr. Ali.

3 Joe, have you met Ingrid?

I don't think so. _____ to meet you!

4 Hey, I'm Tao.

_____ ? I'm Joe.

## GOOD TO KNOW

Short "filler" words and phrases can appear at the start, middle, or end of a sentence. They ease the flow of conversation and can help your English sound more natural. They might be useful for giving you time to think about a question before answering it, for showing interest, or for getting attention.

## 3.1 STARTING A SENTENCE

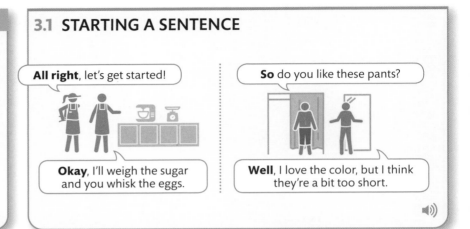

**All right**, let's get started!

**Okay**, I'll weigh the sugar and you whisk the eggs.

**So** do you like these pants?

**Well**, I love the color, but I think they're a bit too short.

## 3.2 IN THE MIDDLE OF A SENTENCE

What did you think of the play?

I **kind of** liked it, but it was a bit long.

How's the new puppy?

He's, **like**, really cute but super naughty!

You must be disappointed with the result.

Yeah, but, **you know**, the team did their best.

## 3.3 AT THE END OF A SENTENCE

How was your pasta?

It was okay, **I guess**.

I hate rush hour! I'm thinking of moving to the countryside.

That's not a bad idea, **actually**.

Are you coming to Sam's party tonight?

I'm a bit too tired, **to be honest**.

## 3.4 TAG QUESTIONS

George plays the guitar, **doesn't he?**

You haven't seen my keys, **have you?**

He's really upset, **isn't he?**

Yeah, **he does**.

No, **I haven't**, sorry.

Yeah, **he is**.

## 3.5 SHOWING YOU'RE LISTENING

So we've just been to Paris.

Really?

Yes, we saw all the sights.

Uh huh ...

We went up the Eiffel Tower ...

Okay ...

... but it poured rain!

Oh no!

Then we saw the Mona Lisa ...

Wow!

... and caught a show at the Moulin Rouge.

Sounds cool!

## 3.6 LISTEN TO PERSON A AND RESPOND AS PERSON B

| | A | B |
|---|---|---|
| 1 | All right, let's get started! | Okay, I'll weigh the sugar and you whisk the eggs. |
| 2 | What did you think of the play? | I kind of liked it, but it was a bit long. |
| 3 | You must be disappointed with the result. | Yeah, but, you know, the team did their best. |
| 4 | Are you coming to Sam's party tonight? | I'm a bit too tired, to be honest. |
| 5 | You haven't seen my keys, have you? | No, I haven't, sorry. |

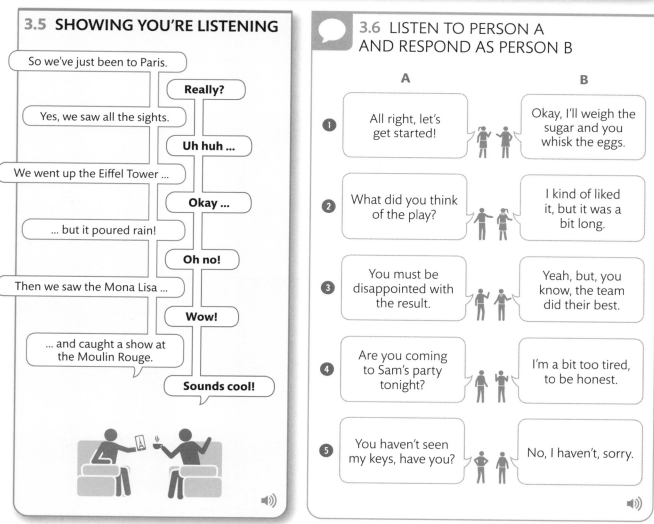

# 04 Saying you don't understand

## 4.1 WAYS TO SAY YOU DON'T UNDERSTAND

Sorry, I'm not following you.

Sorry, I don't understand. My English isn't great.

I'm not quite sure what you mean.

## 4.2 SAYING YOU CAN'T HEAR SOMEONE

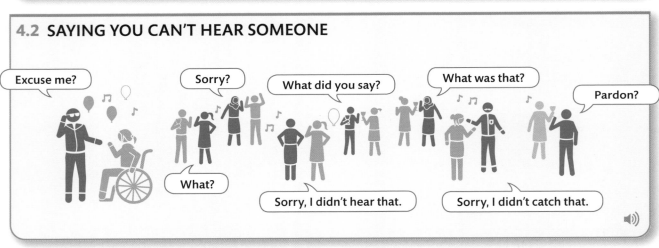

Excuse me?

Sorry?

What did you say?

What was that?

Pardon?

What?

Sorry, I didn't hear that.

Sorry, I didn't catch that.

## 4.3 ASKING SOMEONE TO REPEAT

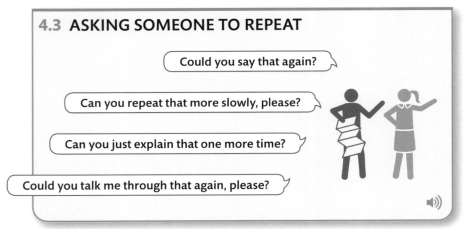

Could you say that again?

Can you repeat that more slowly, please?

Can you just explain that one more time?

Could you talk me through that again, please?

### 🌐 GOOD TO KNOW

Saying **What?** is a simple way to ask someone to repeat what they just said. However, it can sound blunt to English speakers, so it is best saved for friends. **Excuse me?** or **Sorry, I didn't catch that** are more polite alternatives when speaking to someone you don't know well.

## 4.4 LISTEN AND NUMBER THE SENTENCES IN THE ORDER YOU HEAR THEM

**A** Sorry, I didn't hear that. ☐

**B** Sorry? ☐

**C** Excuse me? ☐ 1

**D** Sorry, I'm not following you. ☐

**E** What was that? ☐

**F** Pardon? ☐

**G** What? ☐

**H** What did you say? ☐

## 4.5 MATCH THE SENTENCES AND SAY THEM OUT LOUD

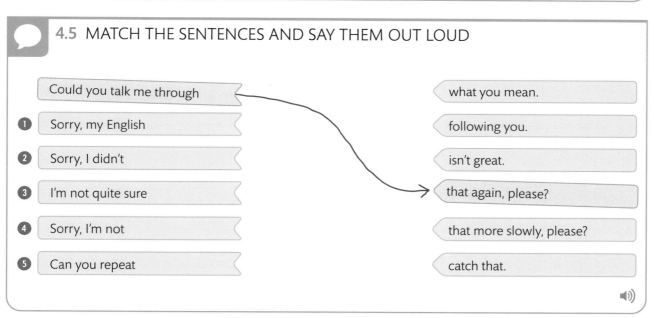

Could you talk me through

**1** Sorry, my English

**2** Sorry, I didn't

**3** I'm not quite sure

**4** Sorry, I'm not

**5** Can you repeat

what you mean.

following you.

isn't great.

that again, please?

that more slowly, please?

catch that.

## 4.6 USE THE CHART TO CREATE 12 SENTENCES AND SAY THEM OUT LOUD

*Sorry? Could you say that again, please?*

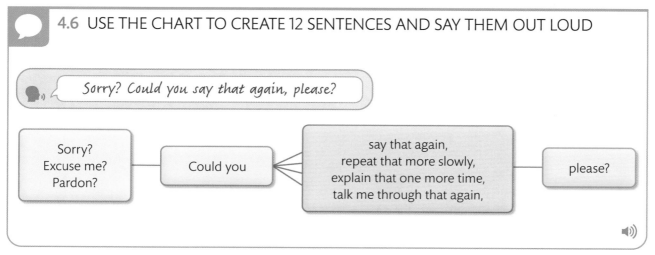

| Sorry?<br>Excuse me?<br>Pardon? | Could you | say that again,<br>repeat that more slowly,<br>explain that one more time,<br>talk me through that again, | please? |

# 05 Opinions and preferences

## 5.1 SAYING WHAT YOU LIKE

I really like these boots. What do you think?

I absolutely love them!

This soup is great, isn't it?

Yeah, it's pretty good!

Are you going hiking again?

Yes, I'm really into it right now!

## 5.2 SAYING WHAT YOU DON'T LIKE

Interested in going out for sushi tonight?

Hmm ... I'm not much of a sushi fan.

We're heading to the skate park—wanna come?

No, I'm good. Skateboarding isn't really my thing.

Are you into horror movies?

No way! I can't stand them.

## 5.3 MORE PHRASES

I'm a big fan!

It's so my thing!

I've always loved it.

I'm just not really into it.

I'm not that excited about it.

I couldn't think of anything worse!

## 🌐 GOOD TO KNOW

We can use **No way!** to object to something. If someone says, **Do you like oysters?** you could reply, **No way! They're gross!** The phrase can also be used to express surprise: **No way! I can't believe he said that!**

## 5.4 LISTEN TO PERSON A AND RESPOND AS PERSON B

| | A | | B |
|---|---|---|---|
| ❶ | I really like these boots. What do you think? | | I absolutely love them! |
| ❷ | Are you going hiking again? | | Yes, I'm really into it right now! |
| ❸ | Are you into horror movies? | | No way! I can't stand them. |
| ❹ | Interested in going out for sushi tonight? | | Hmm … I'm not much of a sushi fan. |

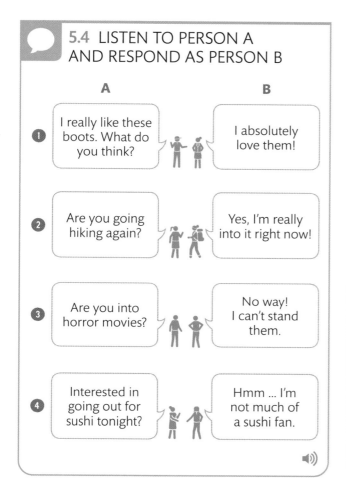

🔊

## 5.5 SAY THE SENTENCES OUT LOUD, FILLING IN THE BLANKS USING THE WORDS IN THE PANEL

> think     fan     great     into
> always     love     thing     pretty

❶ Yes, I'm really _____ it right now!

❷ I absolutely _____ them!

❸ I've _____ loved it.

❹ I'm a big _____ !

❺ Yeah, it's _____ good!

❻ It's so my _____ !

❼ This soup is _____ , isn't it?

❽ What do you _____ ?

🔊

## 5.6 MATCH THE SENTENCES AND SAY THEM OUT LOUD

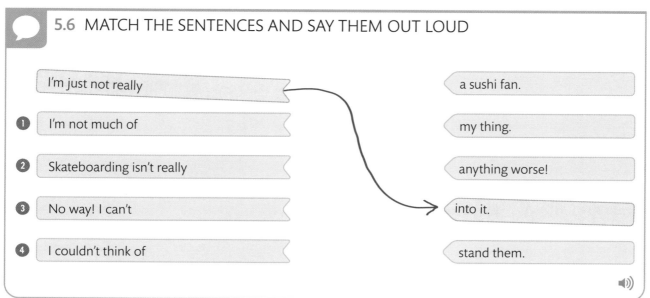

I'm just not really ——————→ into it.

❶ I'm not much of                a sushi fan.

❷ Skateboarding isn't really     my thing.

❸ No way! I can't                anything worse!

❹ I couldn't think of             stand them.

🔊

## 5.7 GIVING OPINIONS FORMALLY

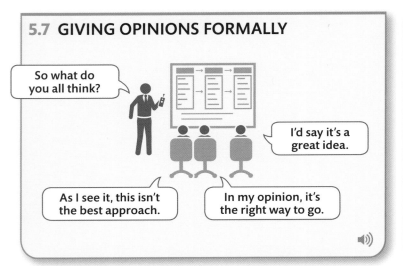

## 5.8 MORE PHRASES

What's your view?

What's your opinion on this?

How do you feel about it?

I feel like ...

As far as I'm concerned ...

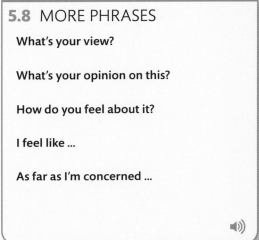

## 5.9 EXPRESSING PREFERENCES

## 5.10 EXPRESSING INDIFFERENCE

## 5.11 LISTEN TO PERSON A AND RESPOND AS PERSON B

**A** **B**

1. So what do you all think? — I'd say it's a great idea.

2. How do you feel about it? — As I see it, this isn't the best approach.

3. What do you want? Pizza or tacos? — I don't mind tacos, but I'd prefer pizza.

4. I'd much rather have tacos. — I'd rather have tacos, too.

5. Where would you rather go—bowling or ice-skating? — I don't really mind. Happy either way.

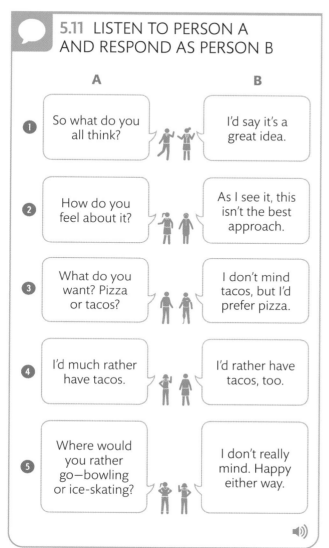

## 5.12 LISTEN AND NUMBER THE SENTENCES IN THE ORDER YOU HEAR THEM

Ⓐ What's your opinion on this? ☐

Ⓑ I'd say it's a great idea. ☐

Ⓒ I don't really mind. ☐

Ⓓ What's your view? 1

Ⓔ I'd definitely go for pizza. ☐

Ⓕ How do you feel about it? ☐

Ⓖ In my opinion, it's the right way to go. ☐

Ⓗ As far as I'm concerned ... ☐

Ⓘ I don't care. Both are okay with me. ☐

Ⓙ As I see it, this isn't the best approach. ☐

## 5.13 USE THE CHART TO CREATE EIGHT SENTENCES AND SAY THEM OUT LOUD

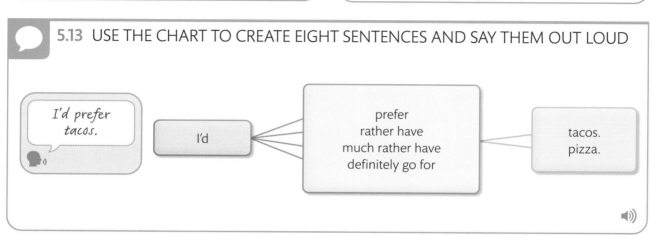

*I'd prefer tacos.*

I'd → prefer / rather have / much rather have / definitely go for → tacos. / pizza.

21

## 6.1 AGREEING WITH OPINIONS

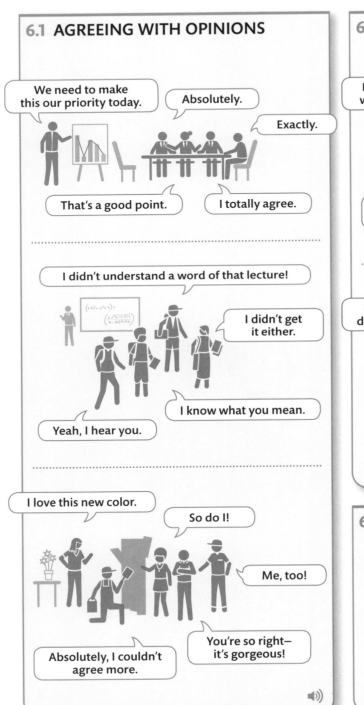

We need to make this our priority today.

Absolutely.

Exactly.

That's a good point.

I totally agree.

I didn't understand a word of that lecture!

I didn't get it either.

I know what you mean.

Yeah, I hear you.

I love this new color.

So do I!

Me, too!

You're so right—it's gorgeous!

Absolutely, I couldn't agree more.

## 6.2 DISAGREEING WITH OPINIONS

I thought this book was really inspiring.

Sorry, I'm not with you on this one.

I'm not convinced, to be honest ...

Nah, it didn't do it for me.

Well, I think she did the right thing.

Do you? I'm not so sure ...

I don't think so either.

No way!

Come on! She was way out of line!

## 6.3 AGREEING TO DISAGREE

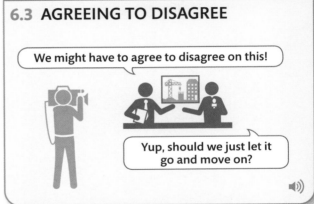

We might have to agree to disagree on this!

Yup, should we just let it go and move on?

## 6.4 LISTEN TO PERSON A AND RESPOND AS PERSON B

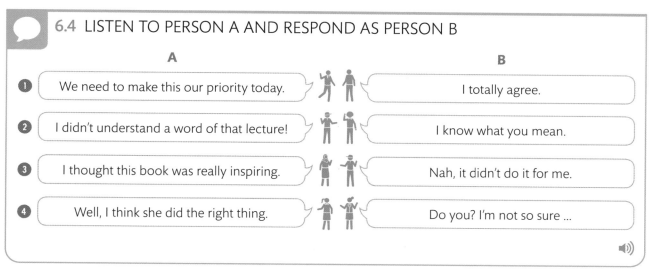

| | A | | B |
|---|---|---|---|
| 1 | We need to make this our priority today. | | I totally agree. |
| 2 | I didn't understand a word of that lecture! | | I know what you mean. |
| 3 | I thought this book was really inspiring. | | Nah, it didn't do it for me. |
| 4 | Well, I think she did the right thing. | | Do you? I'm not so sure … |

## 6.5 USE THE CHART TO CREATE 12 SENTENCES AND SAY THEM OUT LOUD

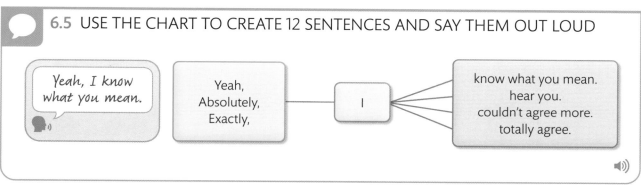

Yeah, I know what you mean.

Yeah, Absolutely, Exactly,

I

know what you mean.
hear you.
couldn't agree more.
totally agree.

## 6.6 MATCH THE SENTENCES AND SAY THEM OUT LOUD

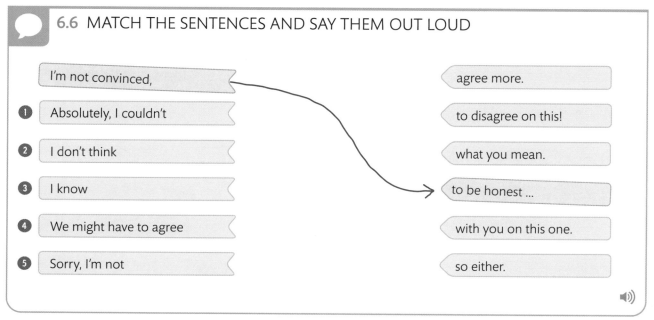

| | | | |
|---|---|---|---|
| | I'm not convinced, | | agree more. |
| 1 | Absolutely, I couldn't | | to disagree on this! |
| 2 | I don't think | | what you mean. |
| 3 | I know | | to be honest … |
| 4 | We might have to agree | | with you on this one. |
| 5 | Sorry, I'm not | | so either. |

23

# Making suggestions

## 7.1 MAKING PLANS

It's such a nice day! Should we go somewhere?

Okay! We could go for a walk by the river.

How about hitting the beach?

I know! Let's go swimming!

Why don't we bike to the park?

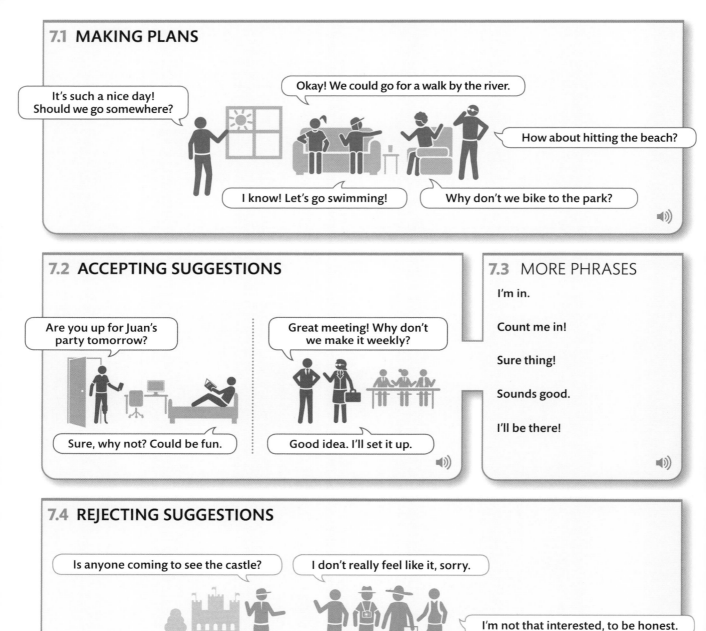

## 7.2 ACCEPTING SUGGESTIONS

Are you up for Juan's party tomorrow?

Sure, why not? Could be fun.

Great meeting! Why don't we make it weekly?

Good idea. I'll set it up.

## 7.3 MORE PHRASES

I'm in.

Count me in!

Sure thing!

Sounds good.

I'll be there!

## 7.4 REJECTING SUGGESTIONS

Is anyone coming to see the castle?

I don't really feel like it, sorry.

I'm not that interested, to be honest.

I think I'll give it a pass.

Hmm ... I'd rather not, thanks.

## 7.5 LISTEN TO PERSON A AND RESPOND AS PERSON B

| | A | B |
|---|---|---|
| 1 | It's such a nice day! Should we go somewhere? | Okay! We could go for a walk by the river. |
| 2 | Are you up for Juan's party tomorrow? | Sure, why not? Could be fun. |
| 3 | Great meeting! Why don't we make it weekly? | Good idea. I'll set it up. |
| 4 | Is anyone coming to see the castle? | I'm not that interested, to be honest. |
| 5 | Why don't we bike to the park? | I know! Let's go swimming. |

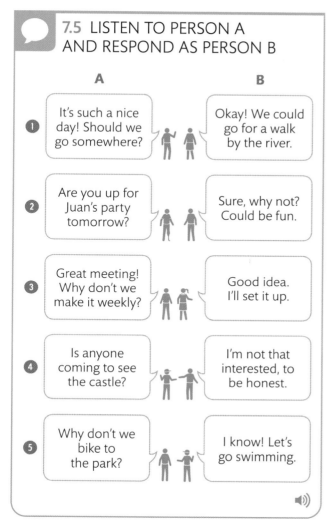

## 7.6 SAY THE SENTENCES OUT LOUD, FILLING IN THE BLANKS USING THE WORDS IN THE PANEL

| feel | think | Why | interested |
|---|---|---|---|
| Sounds | Count | Let's | Sure |

1 _____ don't we bike to the park?

2 I _____ I'll give it a pass.

3 _____ me in!

4 I know! _____ go swimming!

5 _____ thing!

6 I'm not that _____ , to be honest.

7 _____ good.

8 I don't really _____ like it, sorry.

## 7.7 USE THE CHART TO CREATE NINE SENTENCES AND SAY THEM OUT LOUD

*Is anyone going to Juan's party tomorrow?*

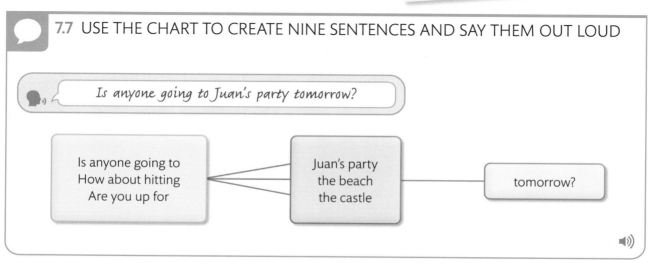

| Is anyone going to<br>How about hitting<br>Are you up for | Juan's party<br>the beach<br>the castle | tomorrow? |
|---|---|---|

# 08 Saying thank you

## 8.1 WAYS TO THANK PEOPLE

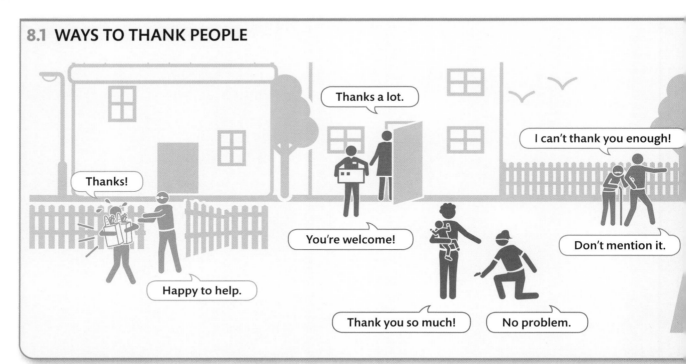

## 8.3 LISTEN TO PERSON A AND RESPOND AS PERSON B

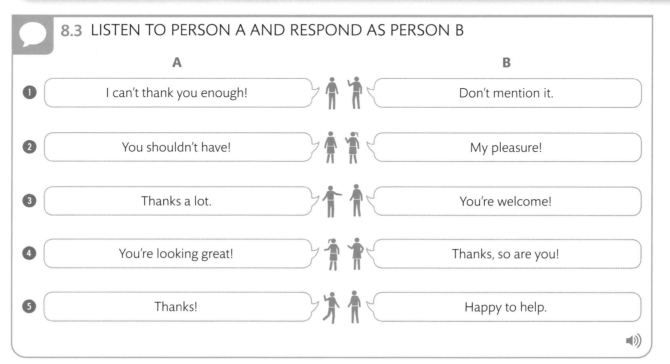

You shouldn't have!

My pleasure!

You're looking great!

Thanks, so are you!

## 8.2 MORE PHRASES

Thanks a million!

Thank you, I really appreciate it.

That's so kind!

I owe you one!

Thanks for having me over!

Have a nice day.

Anytime!

No worries!

## 8.4 LISTEN AND NUMBER THE SENTENCES IN THE ORDER YOU HEAR THEM

Ⓐ Have a nice day. ☐

Ⓑ Anytime! ☐

Ⓒ No problem. ☐1

Ⓓ You shouldn't have! ☐

Ⓔ Thanks a million! ☐

Ⓕ No worries! ☐

Ⓖ I owe you one! ☐

Ⓗ That's so kind! ☐

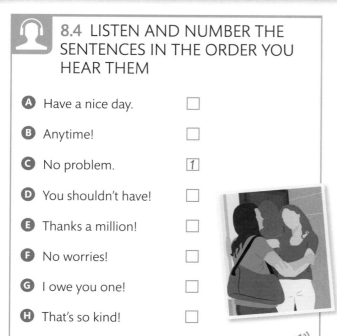

## 8.5 SAY THE SENTENCES OUT LOUD, FILLING IN THE BLANKS USING THE WORDS IN THE PANEL

| enough | pleasure | much |
| --- | --- | --- |
| | appreciate | mention |

❶ Don't _____ it.

❷ Thank you so _____ !

❸ My _____ !

❹ I can't thank you _____ !

❺ Thank you, I really _____ it.

# Saying sorry

## 9.1 MAKING AND ACCEPTING APOLOGIES

Oops! Sorry!

No worries!

I'm really sorry I forgot your birthday!

No big deal!

Oh no, I stained your top! Sorry!

It's okay. It'll come out in the wash.

## 9.2 MORE PHRASES

My bad!

I'm sorry to bother you.

I owe you an apology.

I feel awful.

That's okay, it was nothing.

No problem, I'm happy to help.

You don't have to apologize!

Thank you, that means a lot.

## 9.3 EXPRESSING SYMPATHY

I was sorry to hear you've been in the hospital.

Thank you. I'm feeling much better now.

I'm sorry for your loss.

Thanks, I appreciate you saying that.

### GOOD TO KNOW

**Sorry** is a word with many uses. In US English, people sometimes say **sorry** instead of **excuse me**. You might say **sorry** to ask someone to move in a crowded place or to apologize for bumping into them. US English also uses **sorry** to ask someone to repeat what they just said: **Sorry? I didn't quite catch that ...**

## 9.4 LISTEN TO PERSON A AND RESPOND AS PERSON B

**A**            **B**

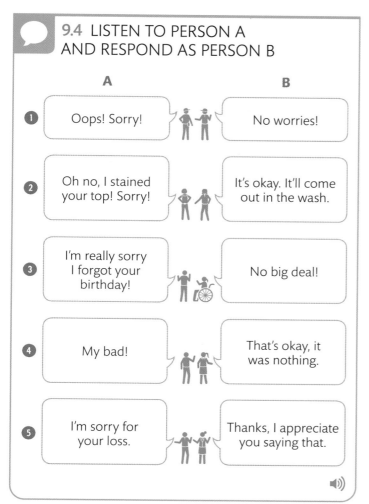

**1**   Oops! Sorry!     No worries!

**2**   Oh no, I stained your top! Sorry!     It's okay. It'll come out in the wash.

**3**   I'm really sorry I forgot your birthday!     No big deal!

**4**   My bad!     That's okay, it was nothing.

**5**   I'm sorry for your loss.     Thanks, I appreciate you saying that.

## 9.5 LISTEN AND NUMBER THE SENTENCES IN THE ORDER YOU HEAR THEM

**A** I'm sorry for your loss. ☐

**B** I owe you an apology. ☐

**C** I was sorry to hear you've been in the hospital. ☐ 1

**D** I feel awful. ☐

**E** Thank you. I'm feeling much better now. ☐

**F** No problem, I'm happy to help. ☐

**G** I'm sorry to bother you. ☐

**H** You don't have to apologize! ☐

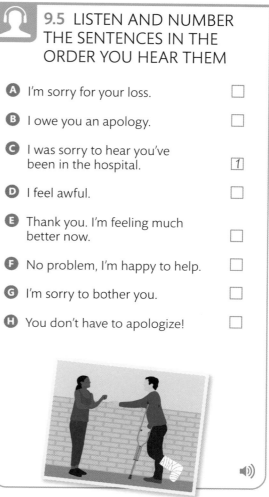

## 9.6 MATCH THE SENTENCES AND SAY THEM OUT LOUD

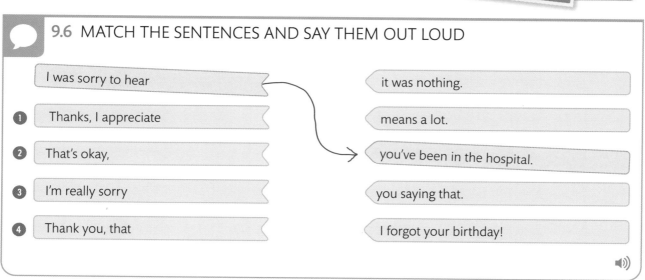

I was sorry to hear    →   you've been in the hospital.

it was nothing.

**1** Thanks, I appreciate     means a lot.

**2** That's okay,     you saying that.

**3** I'm really sorry     I forgot your birthday!

**4** Thank you, that

# 10 Saying goodbye

## 10.1 INFORMAL GOODBYES

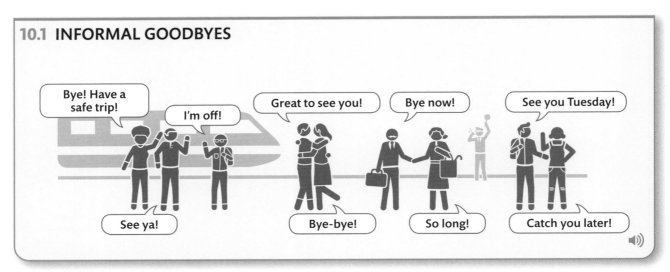

## 10.2 FORMAL GOODBYES

## 10.3 MAKING FUTURE PLANS

### 🌐 GOOD TO KNOW

When it comes to saying goodbye, English has many regional and cultural variations. **I should head out** is often used in the Midwest, while **Later!** or **I'm out!** are common among younger speakers.

## 10.4 LISTEN AND NUMBER THE SENTENCES IN THE ORDER YOU HEAR THEM

**A** Goodbye. ☐

**B** See you Tuesday! ☐1

**C** Speak to you soon. ☐

**D** See ya! ☐

**E** All the best. ☐

**F** I'm off! ☐

**G** Catch you later! ☐

**H** Bye now! ☐

## 10.5 MATCH THE SENTENCES AND SAY THEM OUT LOUD

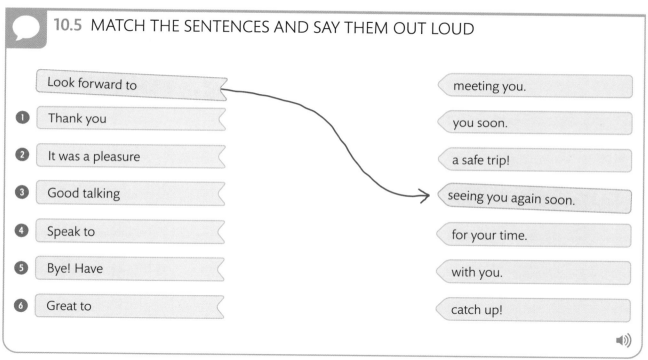

Look forward to — seeing you again soon.

meeting you.

**1** Thank you

you soon.

**2** It was a pleasure

a safe trip!

**3** Good talking

for your time.

**4** Speak to

with you.

**5** Bye! Have

catch up!

**6** Great to

## 10.6 USE THE CHART TO CREATE NINE SENTENCES AND SAY THEM OUT LOUD

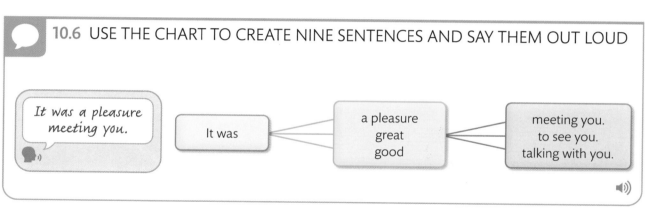

*It was a pleasure meeting you.*

It was | a pleasure / great / good | meeting you. / to see you. / talking with you.

31

# 11 Dates, time, and weather

## 11.1 DISCUSSING DATES

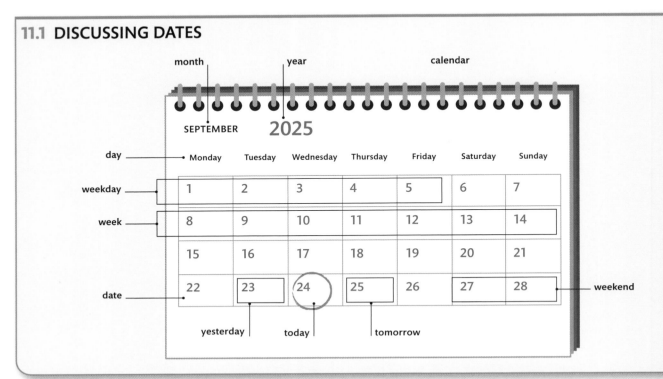

## 11.2 TELLING THE TIME

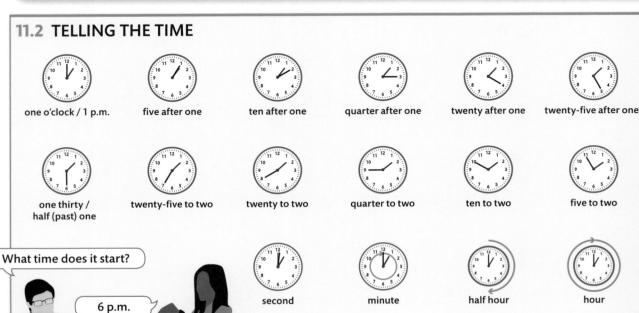

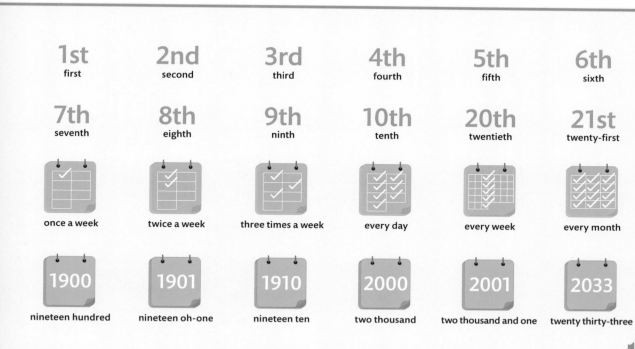

| 1st first | 2nd second | 3rd third | 4th fourth | 5th fifth | 6th sixth |
|---|---|---|---|---|---|

| 7th seventh | 8th eighth | 9th ninth | 10th tenth | 20th twentieth | 21st twenty-first |
|---|---|---|---|---|---|
| once a week | twice a week | three times a week | every day | every week | every month |
| 1900 nineteen hundred | 1901 nineteen oh-one | 1910 nineteen ten | 2000 two thousand | 2001 two thousand and one | 2033 twenty thirty-three |

## 11.3 DESCRIBING THE WEATHER

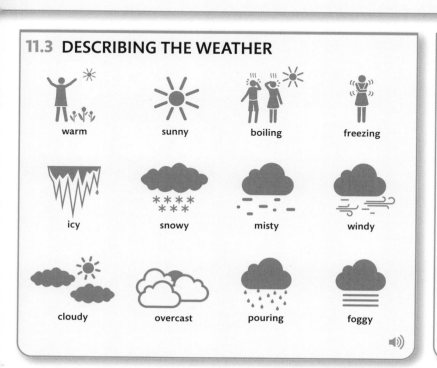

| warm | sunny | boiling | freezing |
|---|---|---|---|
| icy | snowy | misty | windy |
| cloudy | overcast | pouring | foggy |

## 11.4 EXTREME WEATHER

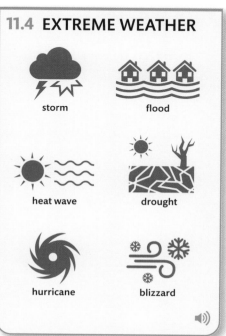

| storm | flood |
|---|---|
| heat wave | drought |
| hurricane | blizzard |

33

# 12 Making arrangements

## 12.1 TIMES

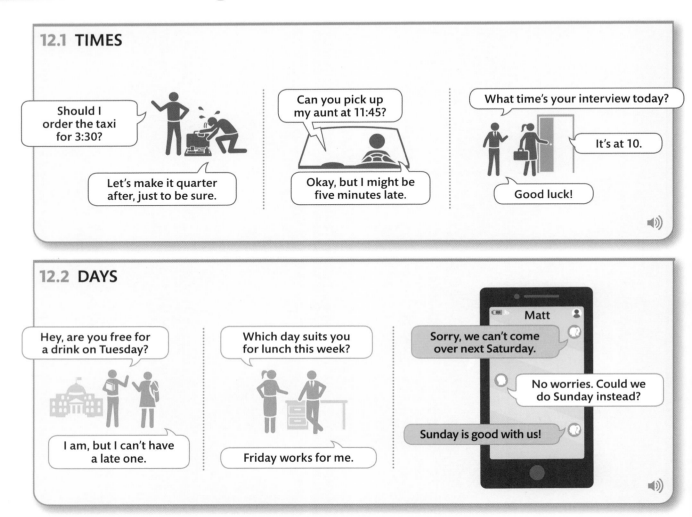

Should I order the taxi for 3:30?

Let's make it quarter after, just to be sure.

Can you pick up my aunt at 11:45?

Okay, but I might be five minutes late.

What time's your interview today?

It's at 10.

Good luck!

## 12.2 DAYS

Hey, are you free for a drink on Tuesday?

I am, but I can't have a late one.

Which day suits you for lunch this week?

Friday works for me.

Matt

Sorry, we can't come over next Saturday.

No worries. Could we do Sunday instead?

Sunday is good with us!

## 12.3 DATES

So when's the big day?

We've set the date for May 31st of next year!

Keep it free!

### 🌐 GOOD TO KNOW

US English uses different language to talk about dates depending on whether it is written or spoken. Written English usually expresses a date as a month followed by a cardinal number (e.g. **May 31**), but spoken English would express this date as **May 31st** or **the 31st of May**.

## 12.4 LISTEN TO THE AUDIO AND MATCH THE CORRECT RESPONSE

Can you pick up my aunt at 11:45?

Could we do Sunday instead?

1 Sorry, we can't come over next Saturday.

Let's make it quarter after, just to be sure.

2 Should I order the taxi for 3:30?

It's at 10.

3 Which day suits you for lunch this week?

Okay, but I might be five minutes late.

4 What time's your interview today?

Friday works for me.

## 12.5 LISTEN TO PERSON A AND RESPOND AS PERSON B

A                                  B

1 Hey, are you free for a drink on Tuesday?    I am, but I can't have a late one.

2 Which day suits you for lunch this week?    Friday works for me.

3 So when's the big day?    We've set the date for May 31st of next year!

4 What time's your interview today?    It's at 10.

## 12.6 SAY THE SENTENCES OUT LOUD, FILLING IN THE BLANKS USING THE WORDS IN THE PANEL

works        on Tuesday        next        good
        May 31st        free        suits

1 Which day _____ you for lunch this week?

2 Friday _____ for me.

3 Sunday is _____ with us!

4 Hey, are you free for a drink _____ ?

5 Sorry, we can't come over _____ Saturday.

6 Keep it _____ !

7 We've set the date for _____ of next year!

35

# 13 Talking about the weather

## 13.1 DESCRIBING THE WEATHER

What's the weather like out there?

It's boiling! Over 90 degrees every day.

How was the weather on your vacation?

A bit mixed—the usual sunshine and showers!

It's a little chilly today, isn't it?

Yes, the weather's turned, hasn't it?

## 13.2 MORE PHRASES

What's the temperature like?

It's freezing outside!

It's really windy!

Lovely weather, isn't it?

It's very overcast out there.

It's absolutely pouring!

## 13.3 THE WEATHER FORECAST

Here's the forecast for tomorrow.

It will be mainly cloudy ...

... with a few sunny spells ...

... and a slight chance of showers ...

... with temperatures a little below normal.

## 13.4 MORE PHRASES

Today, we'll see scattered showers.

Mist and fog will form later.

There'll be plenty of warm sunshine.

Snow is expected.

Temperatures are above average for this time of year.

## 13.5 LISTEN TO PERSON A AND RESPOND AS PERSON B

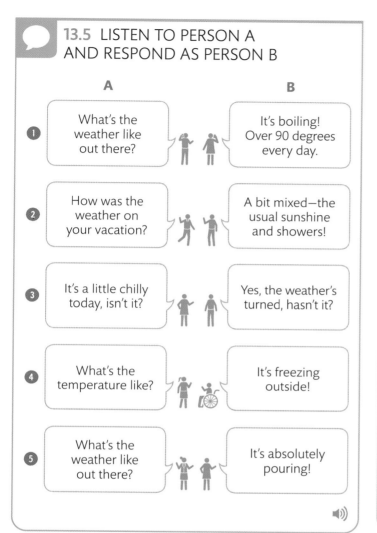

**A**

① What's the weather like out there?

② How was the weather on your vacation?

③ It's a little chilly today, isn't it?

④ What's the temperature like?

⑤ What's the weather like out there?

**B**

It's boiling! Over 90 degrees every day.

A bit mixed—the usual sunshine and showers!

Yes, the weather's turned, hasn't it?

It's freezing outside!

It's absolutely pouring!

## 13.6 LISTEN AND NUMBER THE PICTURES IN THE ORDER THEY ARE DESCRIBED

Ⓐ ☐   Ⓑ 1

Ⓒ ☐   Ⓓ ☐

Ⓔ ☐   Ⓕ ☐

Ⓖ ☐   Ⓗ ☐

## 13.7 USE THE CHART TO CREATE 10 SENTENCES AND SAY THEM OUT LOUD

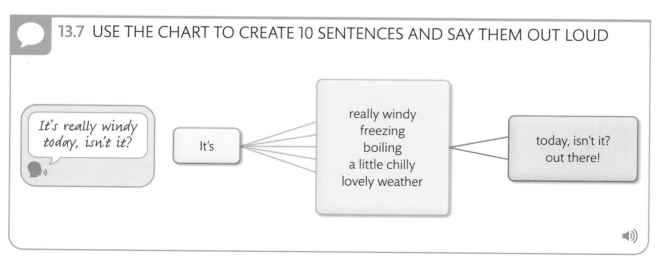

It's really windy today, isn't it?

It's

really windy
freezing
boiling
a little chilly
lovely weather

today, isn't it?
out there!

# 14 Family and relationships

## 14.1 MY FAMILY

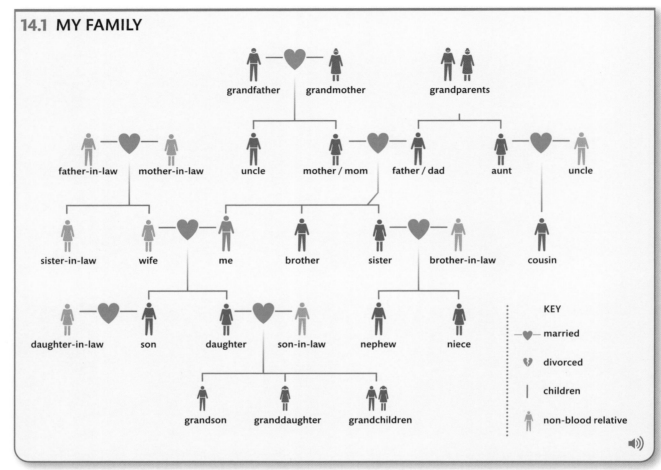

KEY
- ❤— married
- 💔 divorced
- | children
- non-blood relative

## 14.2 MY STEPFAMILY

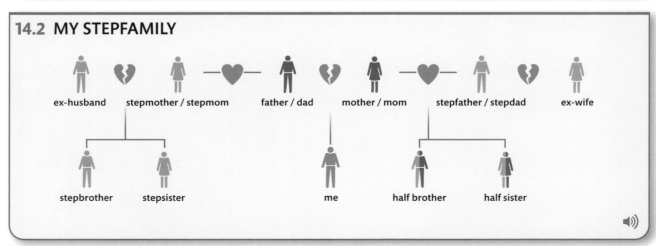

## 14.3 RELATIONSHIPS

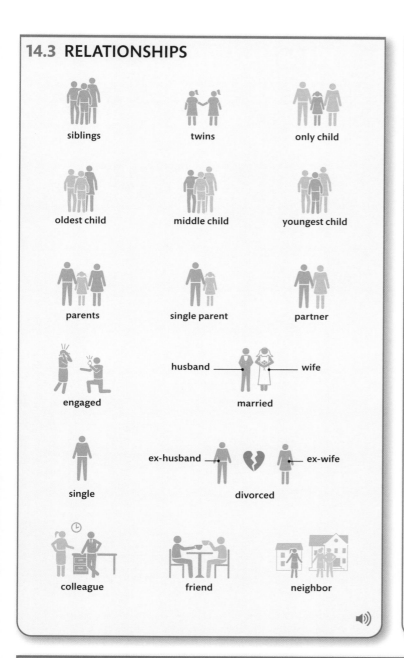

siblings

twins

only child

oldest child

middle child

youngest child

parents

single parent

partner

engaged

husband — married — wife

single

ex-husband — divorced — ex-wife

colleague

friend

neighbor

## 14.4 LIFE EVENTS

birth

birthday

graduation

first job

promotion

falling in love

wedding

vacation

divorce

new home

retirement

funeral

## 14.5 GROWING UP

baby

toddler

girl    boy

children

teenagers

woman    man

adults

senior citizens

## 15.1 IMMEDIATE FAMILY

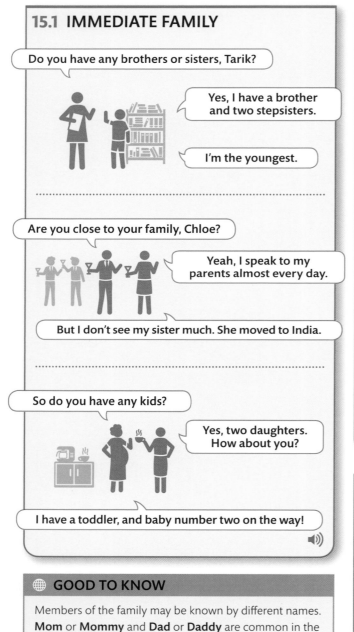

Do you have any brothers or sisters, Tarik?

Yes, I have a brother and two stepsisters.

I'm the youngest.

Are you close to your family, Chloe?

Yeah, I speak to my parents almost every day.

But I don't see my sister much. She moved to India.

So do you have any kids?

Yes, two daughters. How about you?

I have a toddler, and baby number two on the way!

### 🌐 GOOD TO KNOW

Members of the family may be known by different names. **Mom** or **Mommy** and **Dad** or **Daddy** are common in the US, while in some regions, **Mama** or **Ma** and **Papa**, **Pop**, or **Pa** may be used. **Grandma** and **Grandpa** are common names for grandparents.

## 15.2 EXTENDED FAMILY

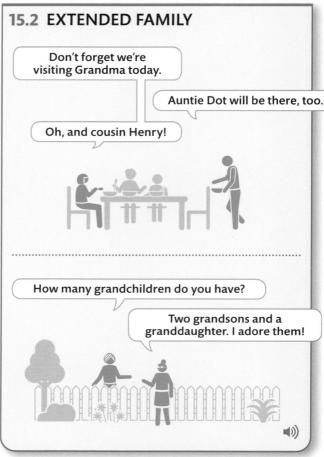

Don't forget we're visiting Grandma today.

Auntie Dot will be there, too.

Oh, and cousin Henry!

How many grandchildren do you have?

Two grandsons and a granddaughter. I adore them!

## 15.3 MORE PHRASES

I'm the oldest.

I'm the middle child.

I'm an only child.

I have two younger sisters.

We grew up in Springfield.

## 15.4 LISTEN AND NUMBER THE PICTURES IN THE ORDER THEY ARE DESCRIBED

A ☐

B 1

C ☐

D ☐

E ☐

F ☐

## 15.5 LISTEN TO PERSON A AND RESPOND AS PERSON B

A | B
---|---
1 | Do you have any brothers or sisters, Tarik? | Yes, I have a brother and two stepsisters.
2 | Don't forget we're visiting Grandma today. | Auntie Dot will be there, too.
3 | So do you have any kids? | Yes, two daughters. How about you?
4 | Are you close to your family, Chloe? | Yeah, I speak to my parents almost every day.
5 | How many grandchildren do you have? | Two grandsons and a granddaughter. I adore them!

## 15.6 MATCH THE SENTENCES AND SAY THEM OUT LOUD

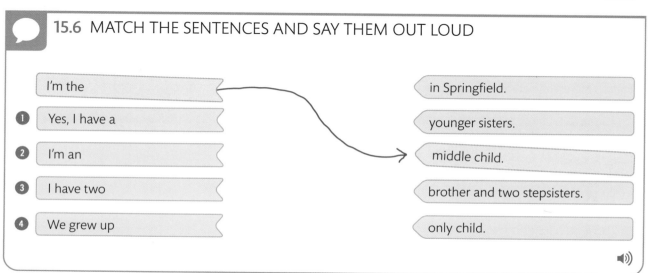

I'm the → middle child.

in Springfield.

1 Yes, I have a — younger sisters.

2 I'm an — only child.

3 I have two — brother and two stepsisters.

4 We grew up

# 16 Life events

## 16.1 CELEBRATIONS

Happy birthday!

What presents did you get?

I hear congratulations are in order?

Yes, I got the promotion!

Here's to the newlyweds!

Thanks, everyone!

## 16.2 MILESTONES

Congrats on the birth of your baby boy!

Isn't he beautiful!

Well done!

Happy graduation!

We're really proud of you!

Welcome to my new home!

Your very own place at last!

## 16.3 OTHER EVENTS

Happy anniversary! Here's to another 30 years!

Oh, they're gorgeous! Thank you!

All the best for your retirement.

I'll miss you all!

I'm so sorry for your loss.

Let me know if there's anything I can do.

## 16.4 LISTEN TO PERSON A AND RESPOND AS PERSON B

**A** **B**

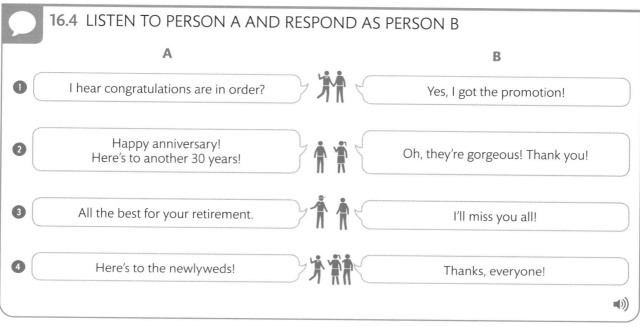

1. I hear congratulations are in order? — Yes, I got the promotion!

2. Happy anniversary! Here's to another 30 years! — Oh, they're gorgeous! Thank you!

3. All the best for your retirement. — I'll miss you all!

4. Here's to the newlyweds! — Thanks, everyone!

---

## 16.5 LISTEN AND NUMBER THE SENTENCES IN THE ORDER YOU HEAR THEM

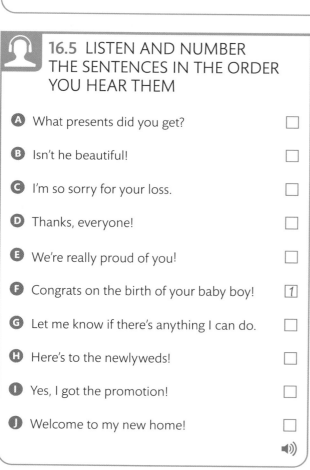

A What presents did you get? ☐

B Isn't he beautiful! ☐

C I'm so sorry for your loss. ☐

D Thanks, everyone! ☐

E We're really proud of you! ☐

F Congrats on the birth of your baby boy! ☐ 1

G Let me know if there's anything I can do. ☐

H Here's to the newlyweds! ☐

I Yes, I got the promotion! ☐

J Welcome to my new home! ☐

---

## 16.6 SAY THE SENTENCES OUT LOUD, FILLING IN THE BLANKS USING THE WORDS IN THE PANEL

| proud | miss | done |
| Happy | best | congratulations |

1. _____ birthday!

2. I hear _____ are in order?

3. We're really _____ of you!

4. All the _____ for your retirement.

5. Well _____ !

6. I'll _____ you all!

43

# 17 Socializing

## 17.1 AT A PARTY

## 17.3 LISTEN TO THE AUDIO AND MATCH THE CORRECT RESPONSE

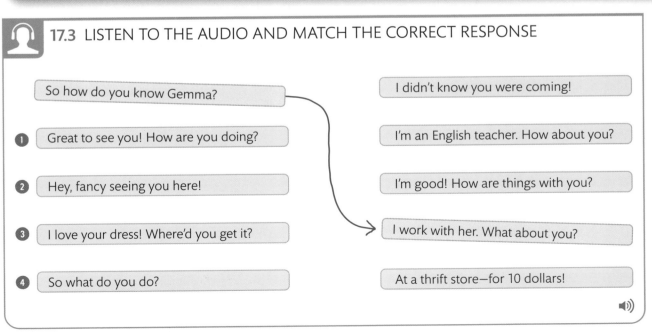

So how do you know Gemma?

I work with her. How about you?

We're old school friends.

I love your dress! Where'd you get it?

At a thrift store— for 10 dollars!

## 17.2 MORE PHRASES

How have you been?

How's it going?

What have you been up to?

Not bad. How are you?

I'm really well!

We used to work together.

Long time no see!

You look great!

Thanks so much for coming!

## 17.4 LISTEN TO PERSON A AND RESPOND AS PERSON B

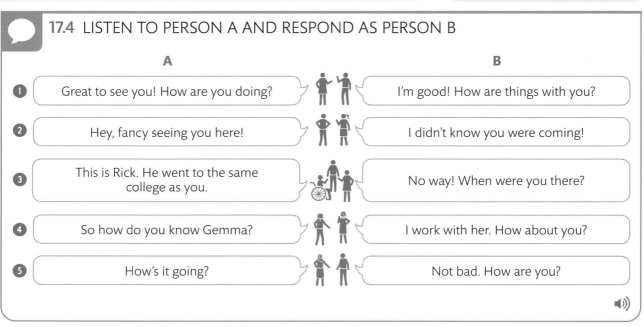

| A | B |
|---|---|
| ❶ Great to see you! How are you doing? | I'm good! How are things with you? |
| ❷ Hey, fancy seeing you here! | I didn't know you were coming! |
| ❸ This is Rick. He went to the same college as you. | No way! When were you there? |
| ❹ So how do you know Gemma? | I work with her. How about you? |
| ❺ How's it going? | Not bad. How are you? |

# 18 Dating and romance

## 18.1 ASKING SOMEONE ON A DATE

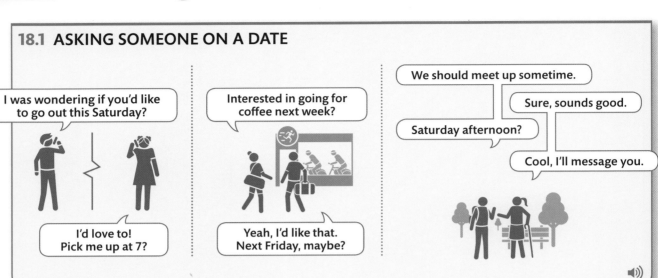

I was wondering if you'd like to go out this Saturday?

I'd love to! Pick me up at 7?

Interested in going for coffee next week?

Yeah, I'd like that. Next Friday, maybe?

We should meet up sometime.

Sure, sounds good.

Saturday afternoon?

Cool, I'll message you.

## 18.2 MORE WAYS TO SAY YES

Sounds great!

That would be really nice.

Sure, let's meet up.

I was hoping you'd ask me.

You took your time!

I thought you'd never ask!

## 18.3 TURNING DOWN A DATE

I'd love to take you out tonight.

That's really kind, but I already have plans.

Another night, maybe?

Thanks, but I'm not dating right now.

## 18.4 MORE WAYS TO SAY NO

I'm not looking for a relationship, sorry.

I just like you as a friend.

Thanks, but I'm actually already seeing someone.

It was nice to meet you, but I'm not really feeling a connection.

## 18.5 LISTEN TO PERSON A AND RESPOND AS PERSON B

A B

1 Interested in going for coffee next week? Yeah, I'd like that. Next Friday, maybe?

2 We should meet up sometime. Sure, sounds good.

3 I'd love to take you out tonight. That's really kind, but I already have plans.

4 Another night, maybe? Thanks, but I'm not dating right now.

## 18.6 USE THE CHART TO CREATE 12 SENTENCES AND SAY THEM OUT LOUD

*Interested in going for coffee this Saturday?*

| Interested in going
I was wondering if you'd like to go | for coffee
out | this Saturday?
next Friday?
sometime? |

## 18.7 MATCH THE SENTENCES AND SAY THEM OUT LOUD

I'm not looking — for a relationship, sorry.

1 I was hoping — you'd ask me.

2 You took — as a friend.

3 That would be — your time!

4 I just like you — really nice.

47

## 18.8 ON A FIRST DATE

Hey! Nice to see you.

You, too. You look great.

Thanks, so do you. Should we get a coffee first?

Sounds good!

I can't lie, I'm a little nervous.

So am I. I haven't been on a date for ages!

Me neither!

Have you been on the app a while?

What kind of things are you into?

How long have you been single?

Are you looking for something serious?

## 18.9 ENDING THE DATE

Thanks so much for tonight. I had a really great time.

Same here. Let's do it again soon.

Yeah, definitely. I'll message you.

That was great. Do you wanna meet up again?

Maybe. I'll call you.

How are you getting home?

I'm just booking a ride.

## 18.10 MORE PHRASES

Thanks for a fun night.

It was nice to hang out with you.

Can I call you?

I'd really like to see you again.

I'd better head off. Early start tomorrow!

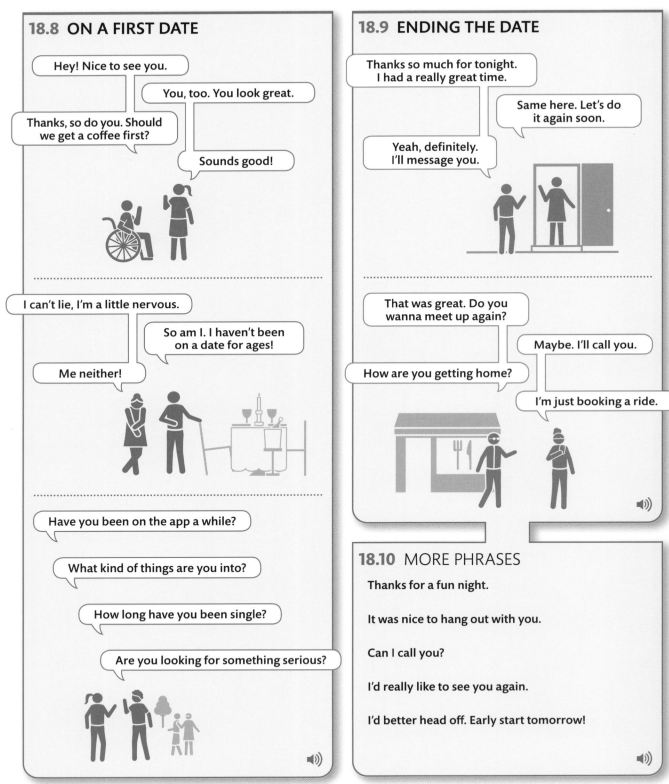

## 18.11 LISTEN TO PERSON A AND RESPOND AS PERSON B

| | A | | B |
|---|---|---|---|
| ① | Hey! Nice to see you. | | You, too. You look great. |
| ② | I can't lie, I'm a little nervous. | | So am I. I haven't been on a date for ages! |
| ③ | How are you getting home? | | I'm just booking a ride. |
| ④ | Thanks so much for tonight. I had a really great time. | | Same here. Let's do it again soon. |

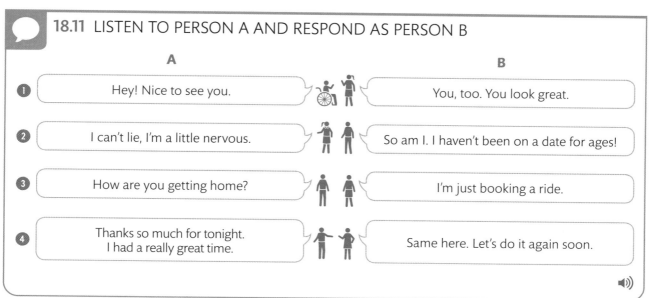

## 18.12 LISTEN AND NUMBER THE SENTENCES IN THE ORDER YOU HEAR THEM

Ⓐ Can I call you? ☐

Ⓑ Thanks, so do you. Should we get a coffee first? ☐1

Ⓒ Are you looking for something serious? ☐

Ⓓ Thanks for a fun night. ☐

Ⓔ Have you been on the app a while? ☐

Ⓕ Yeah, definitely. I'll message you. ☐

Ⓖ That was great. Do you wanna meet up again? ☐

Ⓗ I can't lie, I'm a little nervous. ☐

Ⓘ Maybe. I'll call you. ☐

Ⓙ How long have you been single? ☐

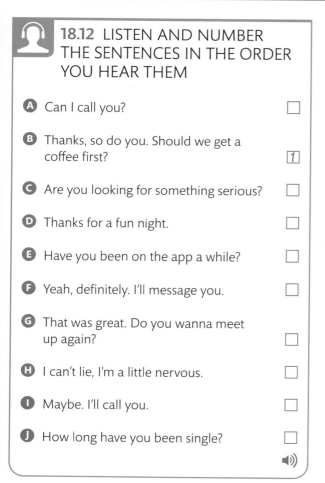

## 18.13 SAY THE SENTENCES OUT LOUD, FILLING IN THE BLANKS USING THE WORDS IN THE PANEL

| single | again | into |
|---|---|---|
| booking | head | hang |

① It was nice to _____ out with you.

② What kind of things are you _____ ?

③ I'd really like to see you _____ .

④ I'd better _____ off. Early start tomorrow!

⑤ How long have you been _____ ?

⑥ I'm just _____ a ride.

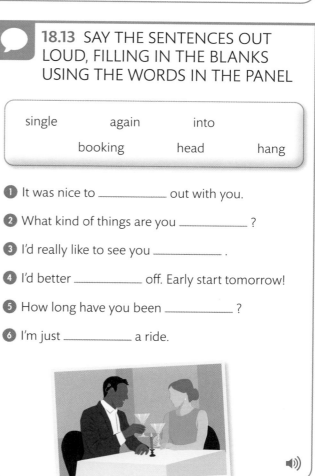

# 19 Showing support

## 19.1 BEING ENCOURAGING

I'm so stressed. My exams are in two weeks!

Hang in there, sweetheart. I know you can do it!

We're never going to finish on time.

Come on, we've got this!

I don't know whether to try out for the team.

Go on, it's worth a shot!

Yeah, you're a great player!

## 19.2 OFFERING SUPPORT

I know things are tough, but we're here for you.

Thanks, guys, you're the best!

You can talk to me anytime. My door's always open.

Thank you, I really appreciate it.

It's good to have you back! Anything you need, just ask.

That's really sweet. I will!

## 19.3 MORE PHRASES

Let me know if I can do anything.

I know this hasn't been easy.

We've got your back.

You've been a lot of help.

That means a lot.

I'm very grateful.

## 19.4 LISTEN AND NUMBER THE SENTENCES IN THE ORDER YOU HEAR THEM

A We've got your back. ☐

B Thank you, I really appreciate it. ☐1

C I know things are tough, but we're here for you. ☐

D You can talk to me anytime. My door's always open. ☐

E That means a lot. ☐

F I'm very grateful. ☐

G Go on, it's worth a shot! ☐

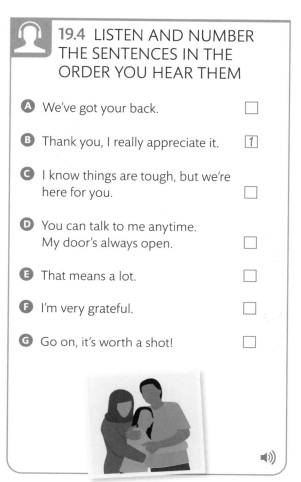

## 19.5 LISTEN TO PERSON A AND RESPOND AS PERSON B

| A | B |
|---|---|

1 I'm so stressed. My exams are in two weeks! → Hang in there, sweetheart. I know you can do it!

2 We're never going to finish on time. → Come on, we've got this!

3 I know things are tough, but we're here for you. → Thanks, guys, you're the best!

4 I don't know whether to try out for the team. → Go on, it's worth a shot!

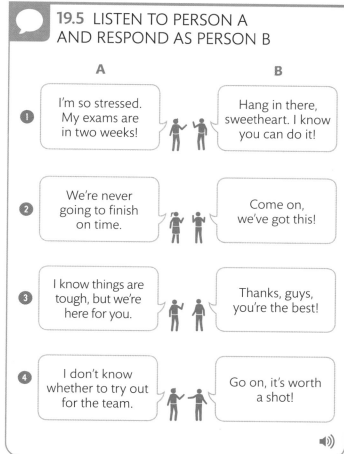

## 19.6 SAY THE SENTENCES OUT LOUD, FILLING IN THE BLANKS USING THE WORDS IN THE PANEL

| sweet | tough | help | appreciate |
|---|---|---|---|
| easy | ask | grateful | anything |

1 Anything you need, just _____ .

2 Let me know if I can do _____ .

3 I know things are _____ , but we're here for you.

4 You've been a lot of _____ .

5 That's really _____ . I will!

6 I'm very _____ .

7 I know this hasn't been _____ .

8 Thank you, I really _____ it.

# 20 Eating and drinking

## 20.1 COFFEES, TEAS, AND SOFT DRINKS

black coffee • coffee with milk • espresso • cappuccino • latte • iced coffee

tea • herbal tea • iced tea • hot chocolate • milkshake • orange juice

oat milk • skim milk • soy milk • cola • sparkling water • mineral water

whole milk • almond milk • reusable cup • sugar

## 20.2 VERBS

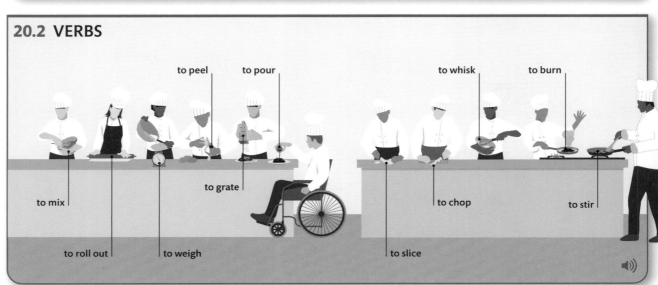

to peel • to pour • to whisk • to burn

to mix • to grate • to chop • to stir

to roll out • to weigh • to slice

## 20.3 KITCHEN EQUIPMENT

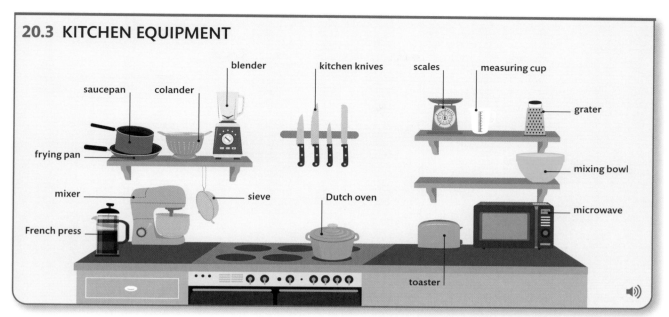

saucepan · colander · blender · kitchen knives · scales · measuring cup · grater · frying pan · mixing bowl · mixer · sieve · Dutch oven · microwave · French press · toaster

## 20.4 FOOD PREPARATION

fried · stir-fried · deep-fried

poached · boiled · stewed

roasted · baked · grilled

marinated · steamed · smoked

## 20.5 EATING OUT

appetizer · entrée · side order

dessert · to book a table · to order

check · to split the check · gluten-free

vegan · vegetarian · dairy-free

53

# 21 Cafés and coffee shops

## 21.1 AT THE COFFEE SHOP

## 21.2 MORE PHRASES

An iced coffee to go, please.

Could I have a skinny latte?

I brought my own cup.

Any milk or sugar?

Do you have a loyalty card?

Regular or large?

Take a seat and I'll bring your drinks over to you.

## 21.3 LISTEN AND CIRCLE THE ITEM YOU HEAR

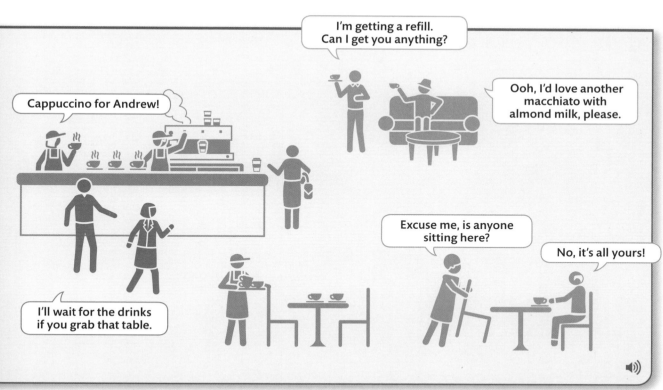

## 21.4 LISTEN TO PERSON A AND RESPOND AS PERSON B

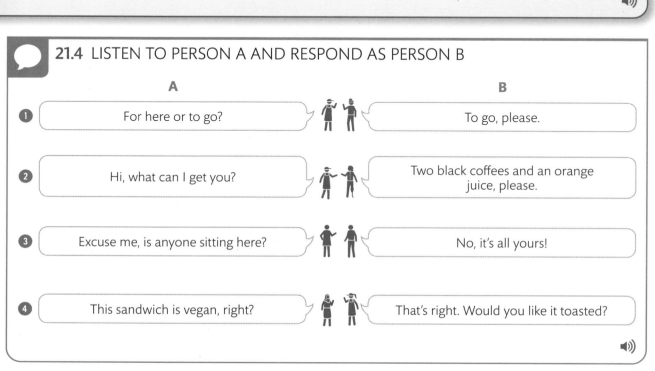

# 22 Takeout and delivery

## 22.1 GETTING TAKEOUT

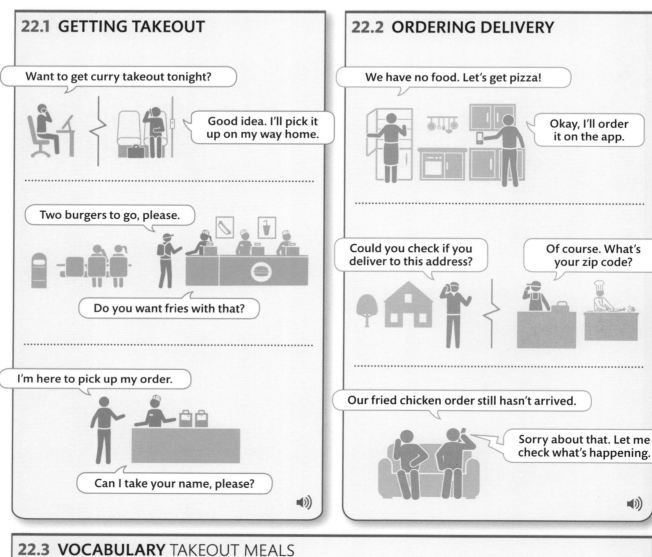

Want to get curry takeout tonight?

Good idea. I'll pick it up on my way home.

Two burgers to go, please.

Do you want fries with that?

I'm here to pick up my order.

Can I take your name, please?

## 22.2 ORDERING DELIVERY

We have no food. Let's get pizza!

Okay, I'll order it on the app.

Could you check if you deliver to this address?

Of course. What's your zip code?

Our fried chicken order still hasn't arrived.

Sorry about that. Let me check what's happening.

## 22.3 VOCABULARY TAKEOUT MEALS

curry

noodles

pizza

sushi

tacos

kebab

burgers

fried chicken

fries

nachos

takeout

delivery

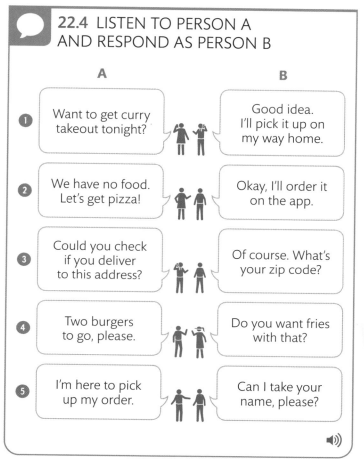

## 22.4 LISTEN TO PERSON A AND RESPOND AS PERSON B

**A**

**B**

1. Want to get curry takeout tonight?

Good idea. I'll pick it up on my way home.

2. We have no food. Let's get pizza!

Okay, I'll order it on the app.

3. Could you check if you deliver to this address?

Of course. What's your zip code?

4. Two burgers to go, please.

Do you want fries with that?

5. I'm here to pick up my order.

Can I take your name, please?

## 22.5 LISTEN AND NUMBER THE PICTURES IN THE ORDER THEY ARE DESCRIBED

A ☐
B ☐ 1
C ☐
D ☐
E ☐
F ☐

## 22.6 SAY THE SENTENCES OUT LOUD, FILLING IN THE BLANKS USING THE WORDS IN THE PANEL

want    go    arrived    pick
order    check    takeout    Let's

1. Want to get curry _____ tonight?

2. Two burgers to _____ , please.

3. I'll _____ it up on my way home.

4. Okay, I'll _____ it on the app.

5. We have no food. _____ get pizza!

6. Our fried chicken order still hasn't _____ .

7. Let me _____ what's happening.

8. Do you _____ fries with that?

# 23 Bars and pubs

## 23.1 BUYING DRINKS

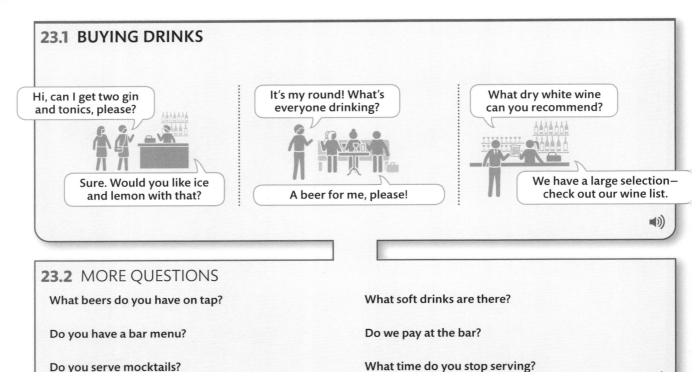

Hi, can I get two gin and tonics, please?

Sure. Would you like ice and lemon with that?

It's my round! What's everyone drinking?

A beer for me, please!

What dry white wine can you recommend?

We have a large selection—check out our wine list.

## 23.2 MORE QUESTIONS

What beers do you have on tap?

Do you have a bar menu?

Do you serve mocktails?

What soft drinks are there?

Do we pay at the bar?

What time do you stop serving?

## 23.3 LAST CALL

Last call! We close in 10 minutes.

Can we have the same again, please?

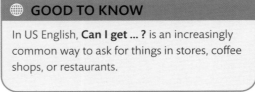

### 🌐 GOOD TO KNOW

In US English, **Can I get ... ?** is an increasingly common way to ask for things in stores, coffee shops, or restaurants.

## 23.4 VOCABULARY DRINKS

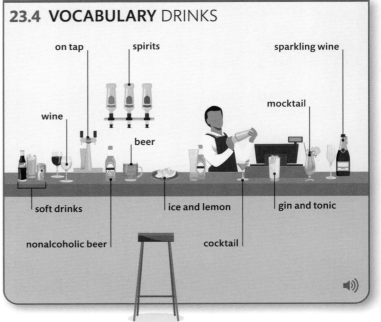

on tap

spirits

sparkling wine

mocktail

wine

beer

soft drinks

ice and lemon

gin and tonic

nonalcoholic beer

cocktail

## 23.5 LISTEN TO PERSON A AND RESPOND AS PERSON B

| A | | B |
|---|---|---|
| ❶ Last call! We close in 10 minutes. | 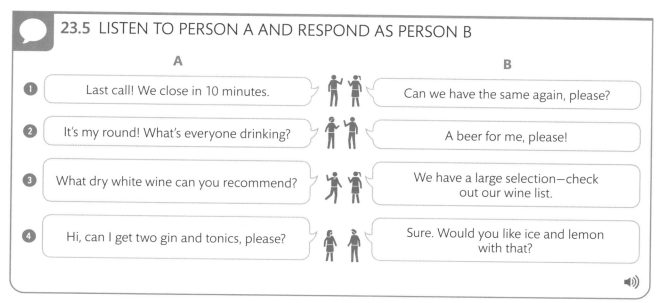 | Can we have the same again, please? |
| ❷ It's my round! What's everyone drinking? | | A beer for me, please! |
| ❸ What dry white wine can you recommend? | | We have a large selection—check out our wine list. |
| ❹ Hi, can I get two gin and tonics, please? | | Sure. Would you like ice and lemon with that? |

## 23.6 LISTEN AND NUMBER THE SENTENCES IN THE ORDER YOU HEAR THEM

Ⓐ Do you have a bar menu? ☐

Ⓑ What time do you stop serving? ☐

Ⓒ Hi, can I get two gin and tonics, please? ☐

Ⓓ It's my round! What's everyone drinking? ☐ 1

Ⓔ Can we have the same again, please? ☐

Ⓕ We have a large selection—check out our wine list. ☐

Ⓖ What beers do you have on tap? ☐

Ⓗ Do we pay at the bar? ☐

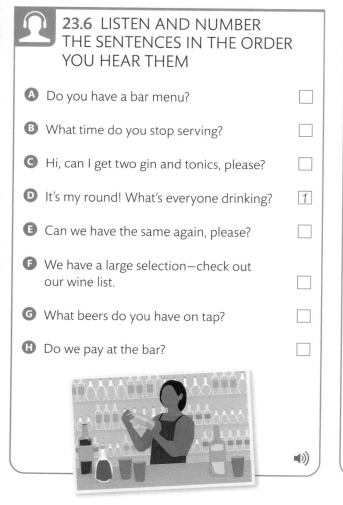

## 23.7 SAY THE SENTENCES OUT LOUD, REPLACING THE PICTURES WITH WORDS

❶ Can I get a [picture], please?

❷ Do you serve [picture]?

❸ A glass of [picture] for me, please!

❹ What [picture] can you recommend?

❺ What [picture] are there?

# 24 At the restaurant

## 24.1 BOOKING A TABLE

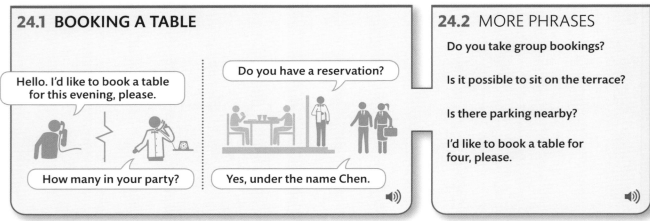

Hello. I'd like to book a table for this evening, please.

How many in your party?

Do you have a reservation?

Yes, under the name Chen.

## 24.2 MORE PHRASES

Do you take group bookings?

Is it possible to sit on the terrace?

Is there parking nearby?

I'd like to book a table for four, please.

## 24.3 ORDERING YOUR MEAL

Are you ready to order?

I think I'll go for the salad, too.

I'll have the fish, please.

I'd like the salad, please.

Could I have the steak?

## 24.4 MORE PHRASES

Does anyone have any allergies?

Yes, I'm allergic to nuts.

I'll bring you the wine list.

Could you bring us another fork, please?

## 24.5 VOCABULARY A RESTAURANT TABLE

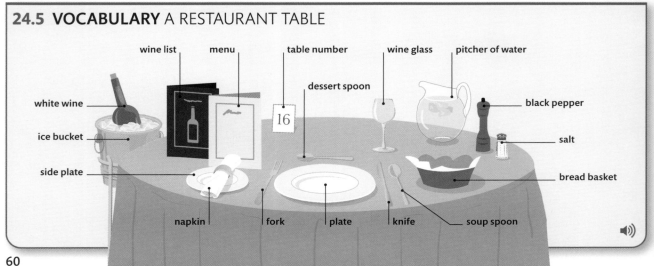

wine list · menu · table number · wine glass · pitcher of water · dessert spoon · white wine · black pepper · ice bucket · salt · side plate · bread basket · napkin · fork · plate · knife · soup spoon

## 24.6 LISTEN TO PERSON A AND RESPOND AS PERSON B

**A**

**B**

1. Do you have a reservation? — Yes, under the name Chen.

2. I'd like to book a table for this evening, please. — How many in your party?

3. Are you ready to order? — I'll have the fish, please.

4. Does anyone have any allergies? — Yes, I'm allergic to nuts.

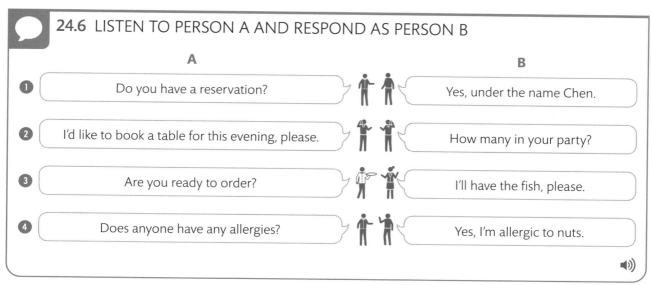

## 24.7 LISTEN AND NUMBER THE PICTURES IN THE ORDER THEY ARE DESCRIBED

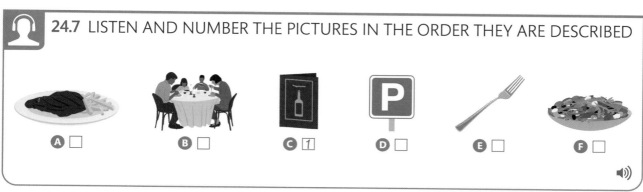

Ⓐ ☐   Ⓑ ☐   Ⓒ 1   Ⓓ ☐   Ⓔ ☐   Ⓕ ☐

## 24.8 SAY THE SENTENCES OUT LOUD, REPLACING THE PICTURES WITH WORDS

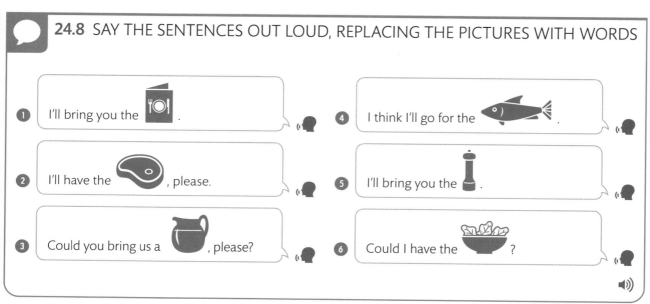

1. I'll bring you the 🍽 .

2. I'll have the 🥩 , please.

3. Could you bring us a 🧴 , please?

4. I think I'll go for the 🐟 .

5. I'll bring you the 🧂 .

6. Could I have the 🥗 ?

## 24.9 DISCUSSING YOUR MEAL

How's your soup?

Really tasty. How's yours?

It's really good. Want to try some?

Your chicken looks delicious.

It's a bit too salty, actually.

How's your steak?

Nothing special, to be honest. I should've ordered the salad!

## 24.10 MAKING COMPLAINTS

Excuse me,

... this pasta is a bit cold.

... I didn't order red wine. I ordered white.

... this glass is dirty.

## 24.11 PAYING THE CHECK

Would you like to see the dessert menu?

Not for me, thanks. I'm done!

Just the check, please.

Should we split the check?

No, I'll get this. It's your birthday, after all!

### 🌐 GOOD TO KNOW

We often use **actually** or **to be honest** at the beginning or end of a sentence to give an opinion, show we disagree with someone, or correct a misunderstanding.

## 24.12 MORE PHRASES

| | |
|---|---|
| How would you like to pay? | Let's each pay half. |
| Can we pay in cash? | Let's split it three ways. |
| Would you like a receipt? | It's on me! |

## 24.13 LISTEN AND CIRCLE THE ITEM YOU HEAR

① Ⓐ B

② A B

③ A B

④ A B

## 24.14 RESPOND OUT LOUD TO THE AUDIO, FILLING IN THE BLANKS USING THE WORDS IN THE PANEL

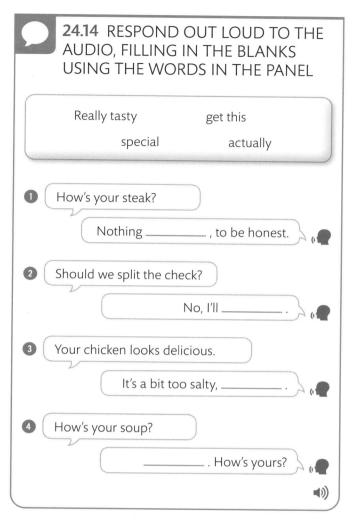

Really tasty     get this

special     actually

① How's your steak?

Nothing _____ , to be honest.

② Should we split the check?

No, I'll _____ .

③ Your chicken looks delicious.

It's a bit too salty, _____ .

④ How's your soup?

_____ . How's yours?

## 24.15 USE THE CHART TO CREATE EIGHT SENTENCES AND SAY THEM OUT LOUD

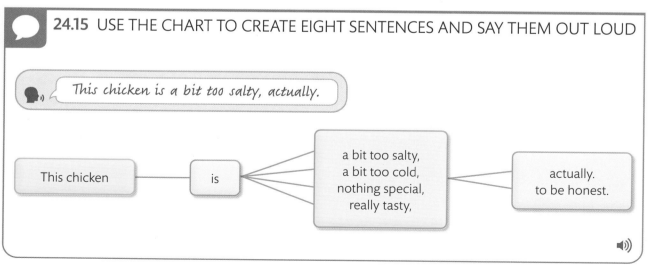

This chicken is a bit too salty, actually.

| This chicken | is | a bit too salty, a bit too cold, nothing special, really tasty, | actually. to be honest. |

# 25 Cooking and eating

## 25.1 FOLLOWING A RECIPE

What are you making?

I'm trying a new recipe for brownies. Wanna help?

Sure, love to! I'll start weighing the flour.

How long does the bread need in the oven?

It says to check it after 30 minutes.

Okay, I'll set the timer!

So what do we do next?

Let's see ... Peel and slice the apples.

## 25.2 MORE RECIPE PHRASES

Chop the butter into cubes.

Mix the ingredients together.

Stir the cheese into the sauce.

Preheat the oven to 475°F (250°C).

## 25.3 COOKING METHODS

How are you cooking the broccoli?

I'm steaming it to keep the flavor.

I've brought the soup to a boil. What next?

Turn it down and simmer for 20 minutes.

Want eggs for breakfast? Poached or scrambled?

Poached for me.

I'll have scrambled!

## 25.4 MORE WAYS TO COOK

Fry the onions for five minutes.

Should I grill or fry the fish?

I'm roasting a chicken for lunch.

I've baked you a birthday cake!

## 25.5 LISTEN AND NUMBER THE PICTURES IN THE ORDER THEY ARE DESCRIBED

A ☐    B ☐    C ☑ 1    D ☐    E ☐    F ☐

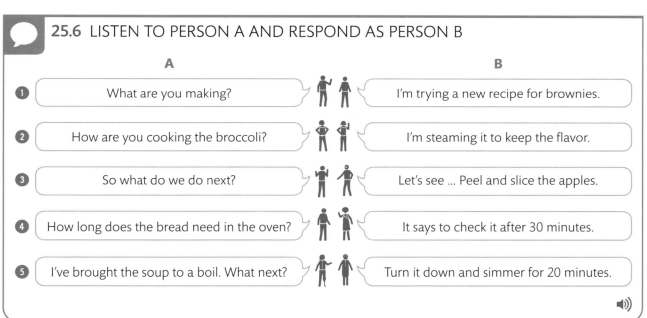

## 25.6 LISTEN TO PERSON A AND RESPOND AS PERSON B

| A | | B |
| --- | --- | --- |
| ① What are you making? | | I'm trying a new recipe for brownies. |
| ② How are you cooking the broccoli? | | I'm steaming it to keep the flavor. |
| ③ So what do we do next? | | Let's see ... Peel and slice the apples. |
| ④ How long does the bread need in the oven? | | It says to check it after 30 minutes. |
| ⑤ I've brought the soup to a boil. What next? | | Turn it down and simmer for 20 minutes. |

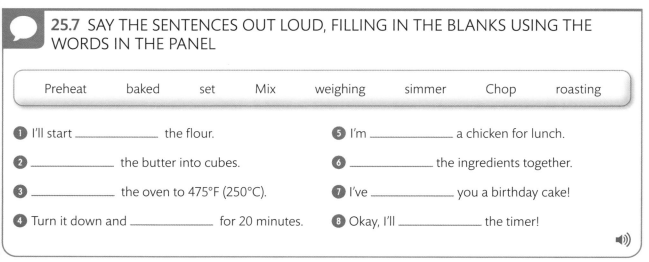

## 25.7 SAY THE SENTENCES OUT LOUD, FILLING IN THE BLANKS USING THE WORDS IN THE PANEL

| Preheat | baked | set | Mix | weighing | simmer | Chop | roasting |
| --- | --- | --- | --- | --- | --- | --- | --- |

① I'll start _____ the flour.

② _____ the butter into cubes.

③ _____ the oven to 475°F (250°C).

④ Turn it down and _____ for 20 minutes.

⑤ I'm _____ a chicken for lunch.

⑥ _____ the ingredients together.

⑦ I've _____ you a birthday cake!

⑧ Okay, I'll _____ the timer!

## 25.8 COOKING TOGETHER

Who's cooking tonight?

It's my turn. I'm doing veggie lasagna.

Great! I love the way you make it.

Should I make some garlic bread to go with it?

## 25.9 ENJOYING FOOD

This is so delicious.

It tastes amazing!

It's really tasty.

This is absolutely fantastic!

That was yummy.

## 25.10 HAVING A COOKOUT

Can I get anyone a drink?

Food's ready! Grab a plate.

Can I have one of those hot dogs?

I think I'll start with a mushroom kebab.

Ooh, what have you got?

I'd love a bit of everything!

## 25.11 COOKING FOR FRIENDS

Thanks for having us over. Something smells good!

I've made a Thai green curry. Hope you like it!

## 25.12 DIETARY REQUIREMENTS

Is there anything you don't eat?

I don't eat pork.

I can't have things that contain gluten.

I'm vegetarian / vegan / pescatarian.

I'm allergic to shellfish.

I don't really like peppers.

**25.13 LISTEN AND NUMBER THE SENTENCES IN THE ORDER YOU HEAR THEM**

**A** Food's ready! Grab a plate. ☐

**B** This is so delicious. ☐

**C** Who's cooking tonight? ☐ 1

**D** Can I get anyone a drink? ☐

**E** I've made a Thai green curry. ☐

**F** Is there anything you don't eat? ☐

**G** I can't have things that contain gluten. ☐

**H** Ooh, what have you got? ☐

**25.14 MATCH THE SENTENCES AND SAY THEM OUT LOUD**

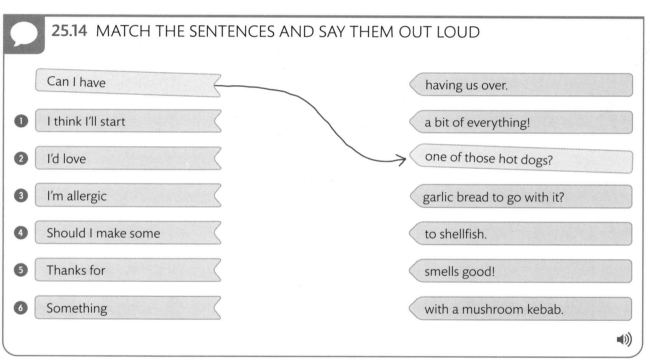

Can I have — having us over.

**1** I think I'll start — a bit of everything!

**2** I'd love — one of those hot dogs?

**3** I'm allergic — garlic bread to go with it?

**4** Should I make some — to shellfish.

**5** Thanks for — smells good!

**6** Something — with a mushroom kebab.

**25.15 USE THE CHART TO CREATE 12 SENTENCES AND SAY THEM OUT LOUD**

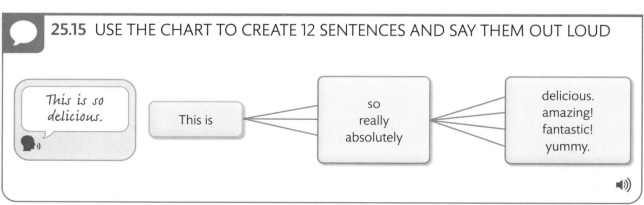

*This is so delicious.*

This is | so / really / absolutely | delicious. / amazing! / fantastic! / yummy.

# 26 Free time and hobbies

## 26.1 OUTDOOR ACTIVITIES

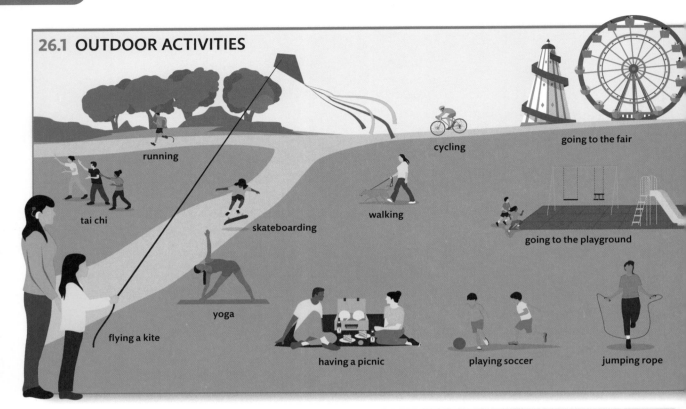

running

cycling

going to the fair

tai chi

skateboarding

walking

going to the playground

yoga

flying a kite

having a picnic

playing soccer

jumping rope

## 26.2 GAMES

darts

board game

jigsaw puzzle

cards

gaming

dominoes

chess

chess pieces

chessboard

## 26.3 CREATIVE HOBBIES

painting

drawing

crafting

knitting

sewing

photography

pottery

baking

gardening

mountain biking

snowboarding

skiing

climbing

sailing

fishing

hiking

quad biking

swimming

orienteering

foraging

camping

horseback riding

bird-watching

## 26.4 ENTERTAINMENT

theater

movie theater

nightclub

ballet

concert

festival

band

orchestra

choir

## 26.5 MUSIC GENRES

pop

rock

country

hip-hop

dance

bhangra

jazz

classical

opera

# 27 At the movies

## 27.1 GETTING TICKETS

What time is the next screening?

It's at 2 p.m. We're just in time!

Three tickets for the 2 p.m. screening, please.

## 27.2 OTHER QUESTIONS

How long is the movie?

Which screen is it showing at?

Is there time to get popcorn?

Is the next screening sold out?

Can we have seats at the back?

## 27.3 ASKING QUESTIONS ABOUT ACCESS

Is the movie okay for kids under 10?

It's PG, so it's fine for all ages!

Can I get to Screen 2 this way?

Yes, just follow the ramps.

Is this the subtitled screening?

You need to go to Screen 5, down the hall.

## 27.4 DISCUSSING THE MOVIE

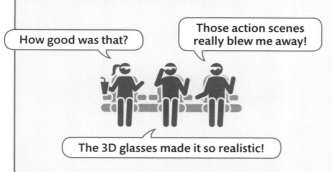

How good was that?

Those action scenes really blew me away!

The 3D glasses made it so realistic!

That was way too long!

The acting was terrible.

I wasn't happy about the ending.

## 27.5 LISTEN TO PERSON A AND RESPOND AS PERSON B

**A**

**B**

1. What time is the next screening?

   It's at 2 p.m. We're just in time!

2. Is the movie okay for kids under 10?

   It's PG, so it's fine for all ages!

3. Can I get to Screen 2 this way?

   Yes, just follow the ramps.

4. How good was that?

   Those action scenes really blew me away!

## 27.6 LISTEN AND NUMBER THE PICTURES IN THE ORDER THEY ARE DESCRIBED

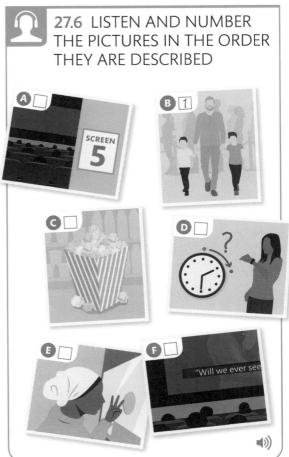

A ☐

B 1

C ☐

D ☐

E ☐

F ☐ "Will we ever see

## 27.7 SAY THE SENTENCES OUT LOUD, FILLING IN THE BLANKS USING THE WORDS IN THE PANEL

| movie | happy | 3D glasses | popcorn |
| kids | subtitled | seats | screen |

1. The _____ made it so realistic!

2. Which _____ is it showing at?

3. Can we have _____ at the back?

4. I wasn't _____ about the ending.

5. Is there time to get _____ ?

6. How long is the _____ ?

7. Is this the _____ screening?

8. Is the movie okay for _____ under 10?

# 28 At the theater

## 28.1 AT THE BOX OFFICE

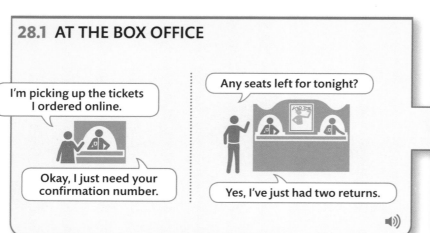

I'm picking up the tickets I ordered online.

Okay, I just need your confirmation number.

Any seats left for tonight?

Yes, I've just had two returns.

## 28.2 MORE PHRASES

When is opening night?

I've booked seats in the front row.

Is tonight's performance sold out?

Is there an intermission?

Where is the cloakroom?

## 28.3 BEFORE THE PERFORMANCE

Can I see your tickets, please?

Follow me. You're in the front row.

Please turn off your cell phones. The show is about to start.

## 28.4 INTERMISSION

How long is the intermission?

It's 20 minutes. Time for a drink at the bar!

## 28.5 VOCABULARY INSIDE THE THEATER

seat

performer

box

front row

audience

curtain

prop

set

stage

back row

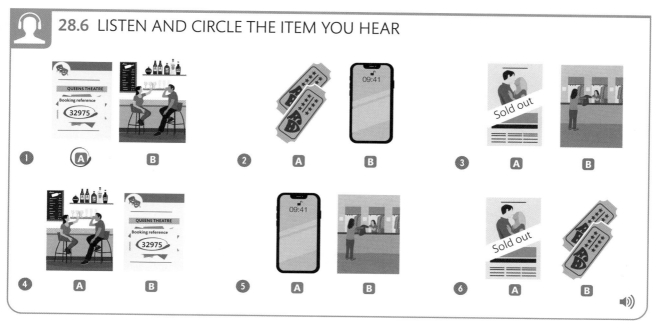

## 28.6 LISTEN AND CIRCLE THE ITEM YOU HEAR

1. Ⓐ | B
2. A | B
3. A | B
4. A | B
5. A | B
6. A | B

## 28.7 MATCH THE SENTENCES AND SAY THEM OUT LOUD

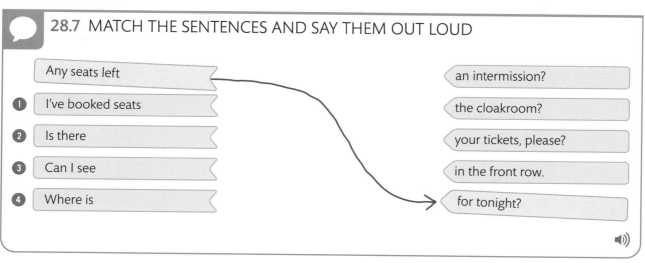

Any seats left — for tonight?

1. I've booked seats — in the front row.
2. Is there — an intermission?
3. Can I see — your tickets, please?
4. Where is — the cloakroom?

## 28.8 USE THE CHART TO CREATE SIX SENTENCES AND SAY THEM OUT LOUD

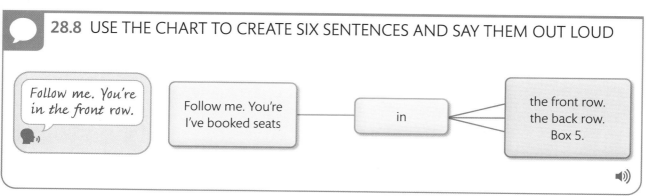

Follow me. You're in the front row.

| Follow me. You're / I've booked seats | in | the front row. / the back row. / Box 5. |

# 29 Concerts and festivals

## 29.1 AT A CONCERT

What time does the headliner start?

9 p.m., but the opening band has just come on.

Have your bags ready for inspection, please.

Sorry, you can't take bottles in.

Let's find the concession stand. I'm thirsty!

I'll meet you back in the main arena.

## 29.2 AT AN OPEN-AIR FESTIVAL

Who's playing on the main stage tonight?

Here's the lineup for the whole weekend. Enjoy!

## 29.3 MORE PHRASES

Is the campsite open yet?

I can't find my tent.

Can I see your wristband, please?

That food truck sells great burgers.

The bathroom line is too long!

## 29.4 AT A CLASSICAL CONCERT

There's a free classical concert at the park tonight.

Do we have to reserve tickets?

No, we can just turn up.

That was really impressive!

What an amazing performance!

Encore! Encore!

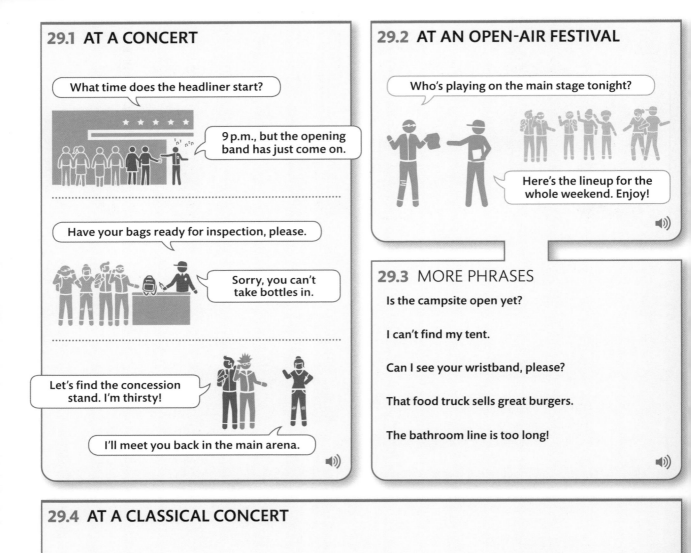

**29.5 LISTEN AND NUMBER THE PICTURES IN THE ORDER THEY ARE DESCRIBED**

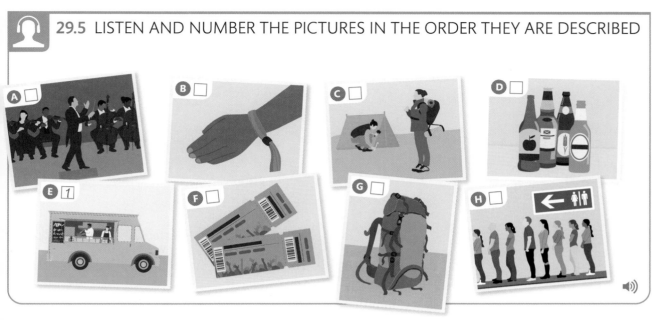

**29.6 RESPOND OUT LOUD TO THE AUDIO, FILLING IN THE BLANKS USING THE WORDS IN THE PANEL**

turn up    the lineup

come on    performance

the main arena

1. Who's playing on the main stage tonight?

Here's _____ for the whole weekend.

2. Let's find the concession stand. I'm thirsty!

I'll meet you back in _____ .

3. Do we have to reserve tickets?

No, we can just _____ .

4. What time does the headliner start?

9 p.m., but the opening band has just _____ .

5. That was really impressive!

What an amazing _____ !

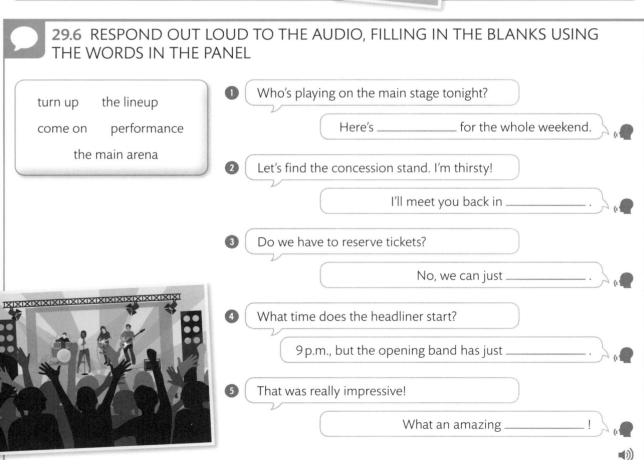

# 30 At the gym

## 30.1 JOINING A GYM

How much does it cost to join?

Here's our list of membership options.

Can I have a tour?

Yes, I'll show you around now.

So what do you think?

It all looks great. Sign me up!

## 30.2 OTHER QUESTIONS TO ASK

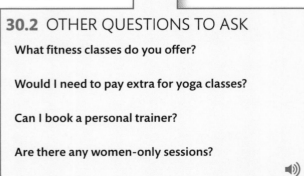

What fitness classes do you offer?

Would I need to pay extra for yoga classes?

Can I book a personal trainer?

Are there any women-only sessions?

## 30.3 ATTENDING A CLASS

Have you been to this fitness class before?

Yes, a few times. It's super fun!

Hi, I'm here for the spin class.

Great. Grab a free bike and join in!

## 30.4 VOCABULARY AT THE GYM

personal trainer

to work out

weight training

spin class

yoga

Pilates

fitness class

HIIT

dance class

## 30.5 LISTEN TO PERSON A AND RESPOND AS PERSON B

**A**       **B**

1. How much does it cost to join? — Here's our list of membership options.

2. Have you been to this fitness class before? — Yes, a few times. It's super fun!

3. Can I have a tour? — Yes, I'll show you around now.

4. So what do you think? — It all looks great. Sign me up!

5. Hi, I'm here for the spin class. — Great. Grab a free bike and join in!

## 30.6 LISTEN AND NUMBER THE SENTENCES IN THE ORDER YOU HEAR THEM

- **A** Can I have a tour? ☐
- **B** It all looks great. Sign me up! ☐
- **C** Can I book a personal trainer? [1]
- **D** Here's our list of membership options. ☐
- **E** What fitness classes do you offer? ☐
- **F** How much does it cost to join? ☐
- **G** Are there any women-only sessions? ☐
- **H** Would I need to pay extra for yoga classes? ☐

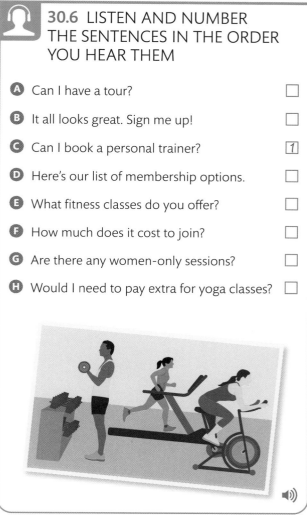

## 30.7 USE THE CHART TO CREATE FIVE SENTENCES AND SAY THEM OUT LOUD

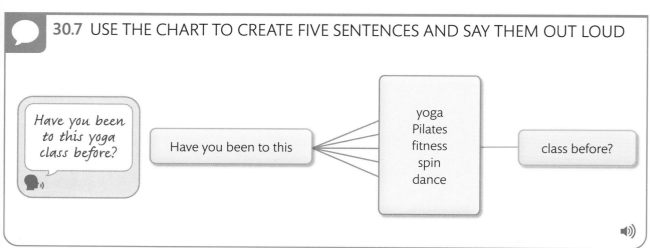

*Have you been to this yoga class before?*

Have you been to this

yoga
Pilates
fitness
spin
dance

class before?

# 31 Sports activities

## 31.1 TEAM SPORTS

Wanna join us for a game of baseball?

Yeah, I'm up for that.

Are you coming to basketball practice?

No, I sprained my ankle last week!

Pass it!

Over here!

Shoot!

Man on!

## 31.2 AT THE SPORTS CENTER

Hi, do you give tennis lessons here?

Yes, we run them on Saturdays.

Can I reserve a lane for swimming?

Of course. What time would you like?

You look lost. Do you need any help?

I'm looking for the badminton court.

## 31.3 VOCABULARY SPORTS

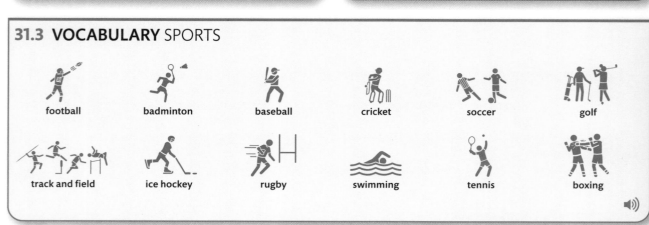

football

badminton

baseball

cricket

soccer

golf

track and field

ice hockey

rugby

swimming

tennis

boxing

## 31.4 LISTEN TO THE AUDIO AND MATCH THE CORRECT RESPONSE

Wanna join us for a game of baseball?

Of course. What time would you like?

**1** Hi, do you give tennis lessons here?

No, I sprained my ankle last week!

**2** Can I reserve a lane for swimming?

Yes, we run them on Saturdays.

**3** Pass it!

Yeah, I'm up for that.

**4** Are you coming to basketball practice?

Over here!

## 31.5 LISTEN TO PERSON A AND RESPOND AS PERSON B

A | B

**1** Can I reserve a lane for swimming? | Of course. What time would you like?

**2** Are you coming to basketball practice? | No, I sprained my ankle last week!

**3** You look lost. Do you need any help? | I'm looking for the badminton court.

**4** Wanna join us for a game of baseball? | Yeah, I'm up for that.

## 31.6 SAY THE SENTENCES OUT LOUD, REPLACING THE PICTURES WITH WORDS

**1** Wanna join us for a game of ___ ?

**2** Are you coming to ___ practice?

**3** Do you give ___ lessons here?

**4** I'd like to book a ___ lesson, please.

**5** We run ___ practice on Mondays.

# 32 Sporting events

## 32.1 BUYING TICKETS

Want to go to the golf tournament?

Yes! When do tickets go on sale?

Tonight. I think they'll sell out fast!

Any seats left for the tennis final today?

Yes, there are a few. You're just in time!

## 32.2 OTHER QUESTIONS TO ASK

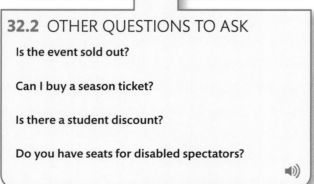

Is the event sold out?

Can I buy a season ticket?

Is there a student discount?

Do you have seats for disabled spectators?

## 32.3 WATCHING SPORTS

Are you watching track and field?

You bet! It starts in half an hour.

Are you showing the soccer game here?

Yes, we are. Tonight at 8.

Come on, guys!

You can do it!

Go, Tigers!

Keep going!

Keep it up!

## 32.4 LISTEN TO PERSON A AND RESPOND AS PERSON B

| A | | B |
|---|---|---|
| **1** Want to go to the golf tournament? | | Yes! When do tickets go on sale? |
| **2** Are you showing the soccer game here? | | Yes, we are. Tonight at 8. |
| **3** Any seats left for the tennis final today? | | Yes, there are a few. You're just in time! |
| **4** Are you watching track and field? | | You bet! It starts in half an hour. |
| **5** Come on, guys! | | You can do it! |

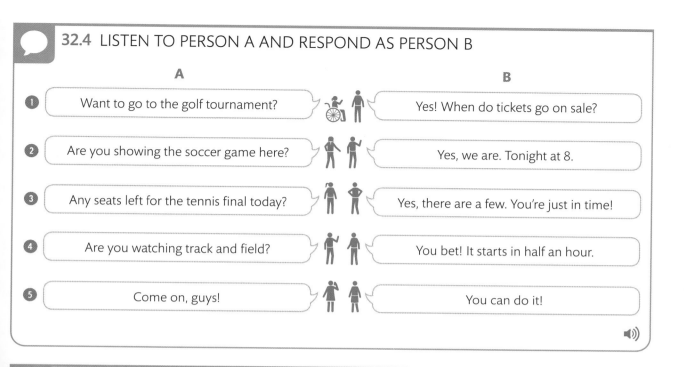

## 32.5 LISTEN AND NUMBER THE PICTURES IN THE ORDER THEY ARE DESCRIBED

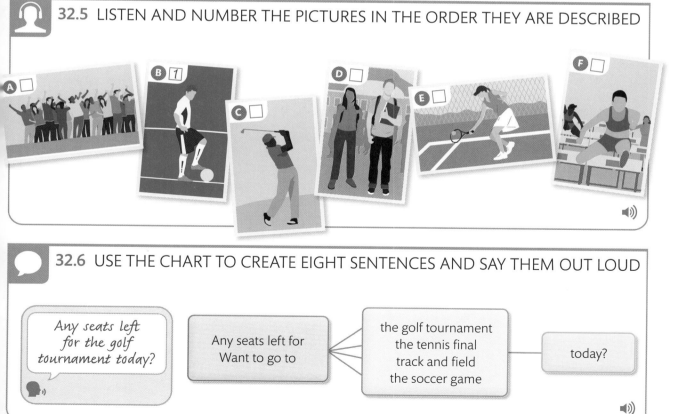

## 32.6 USE THE CHART TO CREATE EIGHT SENTENCES AND SAY THEM OUT LOUD

*Any seats left for the golf tournament today?*

| Any seats left for / Want to go to | the golf tournament / the tennis final / track and field / the soccer game | today? |
|---|---|---|

# 33 Hobbies

## 33.1 STARTING A NEW HOBBY

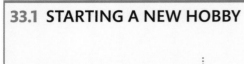

Guess what? I've just started doing karate!

No way! Good for you!

Check this out ... I'm giving knitting a try!

Wow! Maybe I'll try it, too!

I've taken up pottery recently.

That sounds fun— I might join you.

## 33.2 ASKING ABOUT HOBBIES

Do you have any hobbies?

Yeah, I play tennis and I'm learning the guitar.

So what do you normally do in your free time?

I usually go swimming on weekends. How about you?

What do you do outside of work?

Gaming, mostly. And I'm writing a blog.

## 33.3 TALKING ABOUT HOBBIES

So how long have you all been playing?

The piano? Since I was 11.

How about you?

I've been playing the sax for 10 years!

I only started learning the bass guitar three years ago.

## 33.4 LISTEN AND CIRCLE THE ITEM YOU HEAR

1. A / **B**
2. A / B
3. A / B
4. A / B
5. A / B

## 33.5 SAY THE SENTENCES OUT LOUD, REPLACING THE PICTURES WITH WORDS

1. I'm giving [picture] a try!
2. I've taken up [picture] recently.
3. I only started learning [picture] a year ago.
4. I usually play [picture] on weekends.
5. I've just started learning the [picture].
6. I've been playing the [picture] for six years.

## 33.6 USE THE CHART TO CREATE EIGHT SENTENCES AND SAY THEM OUT LOUD

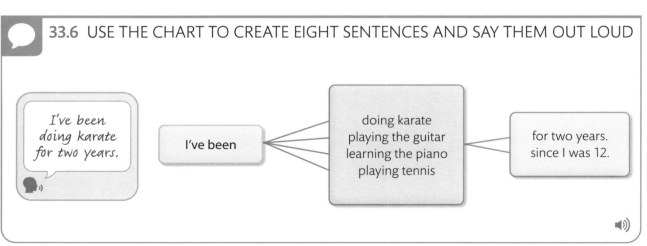

I've been doing karate for two years.

| I've been | doing karate<br>playing the guitar<br>learning the piano<br>playing tennis | for two years.<br>since I was 12. |

# 34 Stores and services

## 34.1 THE CITY CENTER

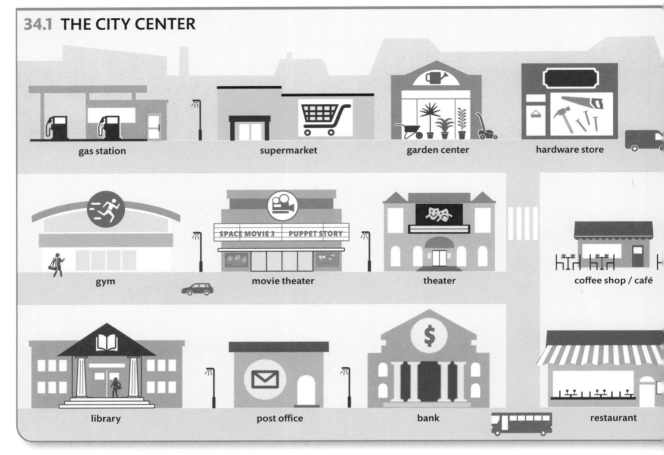

gas station

supermarket

garden center

hardware store

gym

movie theater

SPACE MOVIE 3    PUPPET STORY

theater

coffee shop / café

library

post office

bank

restaurant

## 34.2 TYPES OF STORES

bakery

butcher

fishmonger

produce store

boutique

shoe store

antiques store

florist

vision center

hair salon / barber

newsstand

bookstore

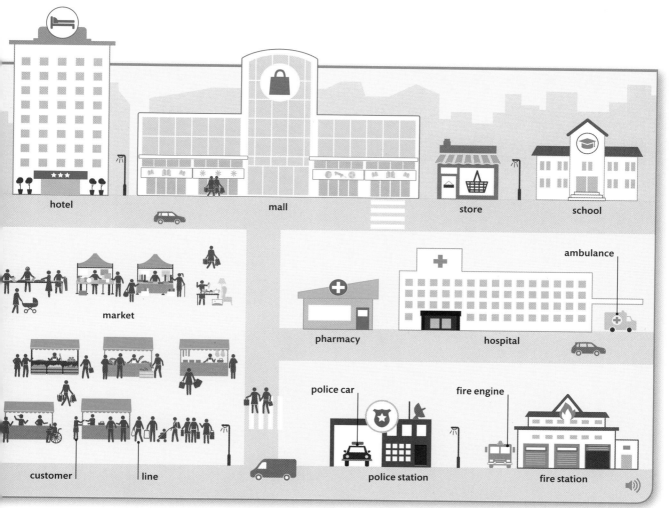

hotel

mall

store

school

market

pharmacy

hospital

ambulance

customer

line

police car

fire engine

police station

fire station

## 34.3 MONEY MATTERS

bills

coins

debit card

loyalty card

contactless payment

ATM

sale / reduced

receipt

pay (for something)

return goods

exchange

refund

# 35 At the market

## 35.1 GETTING A BARGAIN

What's your best price for this?

I can't go any lower than $12.

I only have $10.

You've got a deal!

## 35.2 MORE PHRASES

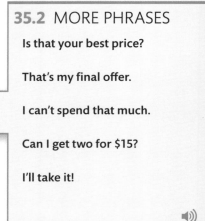

Is that your best price?

That's my final offer.

I can't spend that much.

Can I get two for $15?

I'll take it!

## 35.3 BUYING FRESH PRODUCE

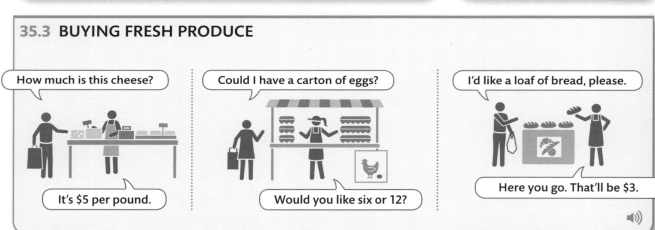

How much is this cheese?

It's $5 per pound.

Could I have a carton of eggs?

Would you like six or 12?

I'd like a loaf of bread, please.

Here you go. That'll be $3.

## 35.4 VOCABULARY FOOD MARKET

a bunch of grapes

a loaf of bread

a punnet of strawberries

a block of cheese

a carton of eggs

a bag of apples

a pound of potatoes

a jar of honey

### ⊕ GOOD TO KNOW

In US English, we usually ask for things in a polite way, starting with, for example, **Can I ...**, **Could I ...**, or **I'd like ...**, and ending the request with **please**. It's more polite to say **Could I ...?** than **Can I ...?**. In formal situations, some people might also say **May I ...?**

## 35.5 LISTEN TO PERSON A AND RESPOND AS PERSON B

**A** **B**

1. I'd like a loaf of bread, please. → Here you go. That'll be $3.

2. What's your best price for this? → I can't go any lower than $12.

3. I only have $10. → You've got a deal!

4. How much is this cheese? → It's $5 per pound.

5. That's my final offer. → I'll take it!

## 35.6 LISTEN AND CIRCLE THE ITEM YOU HEAR

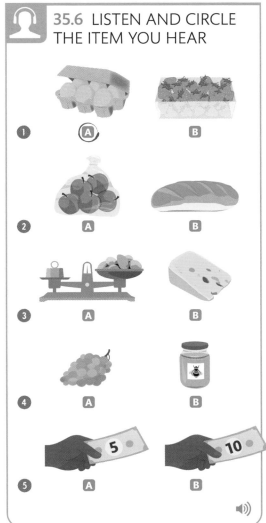

1. (A) B

2. A B

3. A B

4. A B

5. A B

## 35.7 USE THE CHART TO CREATE 10 SENTENCES AND SAY THEM OUT LOUD

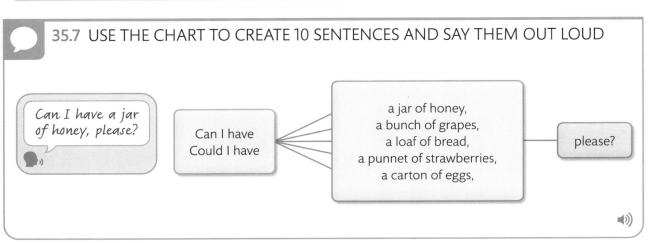

Can I have a jar of honey, please?

Can I have / Could I have → a jar of honey, a bunch of grapes, a loaf of bread, a punnet of strawberries, a carton of eggs, → please?

# 36 At the supermarket

## 36.1 ASKING FOR THINGS

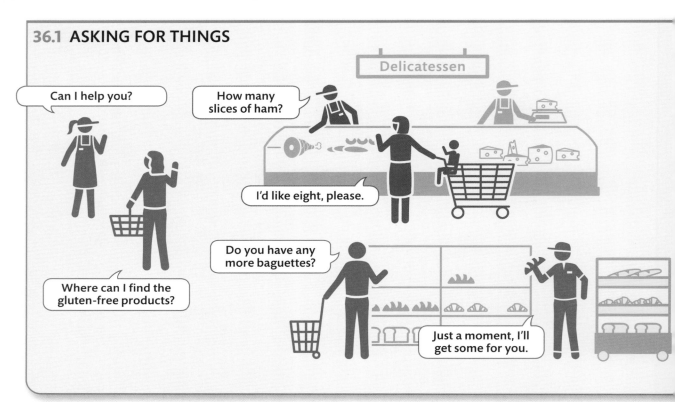

Can I help you?

How many slices of ham?

Delicatessen

I'd like eight, please.

Where can I find the gluten-free products?

Do you have any more baguettes?

Just a moment, I'll get some for you.

## 36.2 LISTEN AND NUMBER THE SENTENCES IN THE ORDER YOU HEAR THEM

**A** You'll find it in aisle 10. ☐

**B** I can't find the pet food. ☐

**C** Can I help you? 1

**D** How many slices of ham? ☐

**E** Do you have oat milk here? ☐

**F** I'd like eight, please. ☐

## 36.3 LISTEN AND CIRCLE THE ITEM YOU HEAR

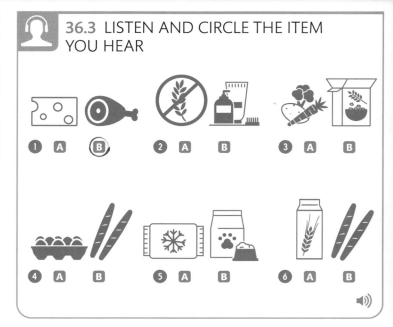

**1** A (B)  **2** A B  **3** A B

**4** A B  **5** A B  **6** A B

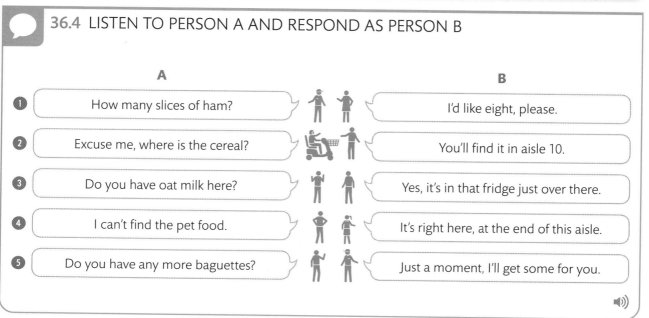

## 36.4 LISTEN TO PERSON A AND RESPOND AS PERSON B

| | A | | B |
|---|---|---|---|
| ❶ | How many slices of ham? | | I'd like eight, please. |
| ❷ | Excuse me, where is the cereal? | | You'll find it in aisle 10. |
| ❸ | Do you have oat milk here? | | Yes, it's in that fridge just over there. |
| ❹ | I can't find the pet food. | | It's right here, at the end of this aisle. |
| ❺ | Do you have any more baguettes? | | Just a moment, I'll get some for you. |

## 36.5 AT THE CHECKOUT

Do you need a bag?

No, I've brought my own, thanks.

That's $45.20. Do you have a loyalty card?

Yes, just a second ...

That's all gone through. Would you like a receipt?

No, that's fine, thanks.

## 36.7 USING THE SELF-CHECKOUT

Excuse me, this milk carton is leaking.

No problem. I'll go and get another one.

This barcode won't scan.

Here, I'll give it a try.

Please tap or insert your card into the payment device.

## 36.8 VOCABULARY AISLES

bakery

fruit

vegetables

dairy products

meat and poultry

frozen food

gluten-free products

cereals

household products

pet food

health and beauty

baby products

deli

checkout

self-checkout

Would you like to use the self-checkout?

No, thanks. I'm happy to wait.

## 36.6 MORE PHRASES

Do you take cash?

How much is it for a bag?

Could I have a receipt, please?

Could you scan my loyalty card, please?

I don't have my loyalty card with me.

Can I use these coupons?

## 36.9 LISTEN AND NUMBER THE SENTENCES IN THE ORDER YOU HEAR THEM

**A** Do you need a bag? ☐

**B** This barcode won't scan. ☐

**C** Would you like to use the self-checkout? ☐ 1

**D** No, thanks. I'm happy to wait. ☐

**E** That's $45.20. Do you have a loyalty card? ☐

**F** Can I use these coupons? ☐

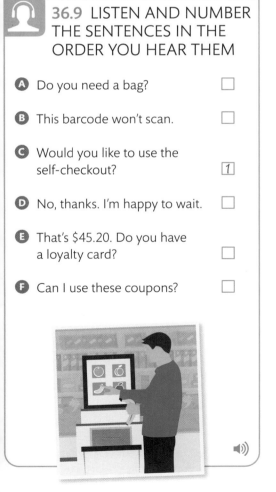

## 36.10 SAY THE SENTENCES OUT LOUD, REPLACING THE PICTURES WITH WORDS

**1** Excuse me, where's the [image] aisle?

**2** Would you like to use the [image] ?

**3** Where can I find the [image] ?

**4** Do you have [image] here?

**5** I can't find the [image] and [image] .

# At the garden center

## 37.1 BUYING PLANTS

Hello, how can I help?

We need some advice on starting a vegetable garden.

What kind of houseplants are you looking for?

I don't really mind, but my apartment doesn't get much light.

## 37.2 PLANT CARE

When is the best time to plant these seeds?

How much sunlight do they need?

How often do they need watering?

How tall will the plant grow?

## 37.3 MORE QUESTIONS

How often should I feed it?

Does it need much looking after?

Will it survive the winter?

What's a good compost to use?

How do I get rid of weeds?

## 37.4 VOCABULARY GARDENING

herb garden

houseplant

outdoor plants

seeds

bulbs

compost

wheelbarrow

spade

watering can

trowel

shears

fork

## 37.5 LISTEN AND NUMBER THE PICTURES IN THE ORDER THEY ARE DESCRIBED

A ☐   B 1

C ☐   D ☐

E ☐   F ☐

## 37.6 SAY THE SENTENCES OUT LOUD, FILLING IN THE BLANKS USING THE WORDS IN THE PANEL

| seeds | feed | sunlight |
|---|---|---|
| | weeds | survive | looking |

1 Will it _____ the winter?

2 When is the best time to plant these _____ ?

3 How much _____ do they need?

4 Does it need much _____ after?

5 How often should I _____ it?

6 How do I get rid of _____ ?

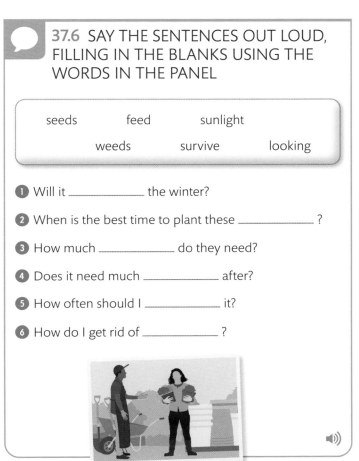

## 37.7 MATCH THE SENTENCES AND SAY THEM OUT LOUD

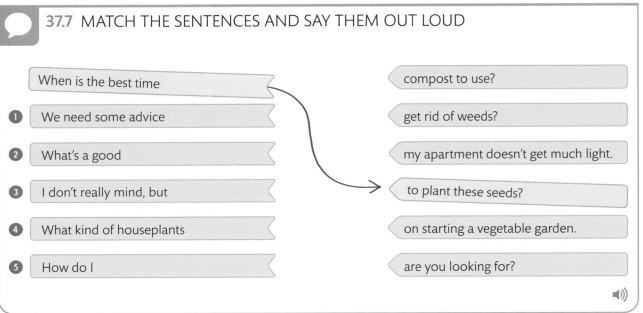

When is the best time ————————————→ to plant these seeds?

1 We need some advice          compost to use?

2 What's a good          get rid of weeds?

3 I don't really mind, but          my apartment doesn't get much light.

4 What kind of houseplants          on starting a vegetable garden.

5 How do I          are you looking for?

# 38 At the hardware store

## 38.1 ASKING FOR ADVICE

What would you recommend for sanding a table?

What do I need for tiling my bathroom?

What's best for plastering walls?

What do you have for filling a crack?

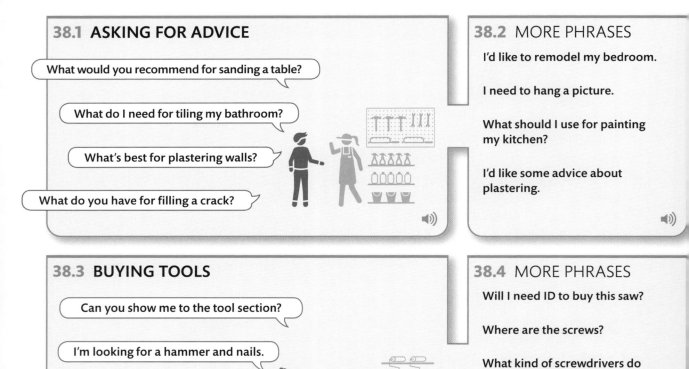

## 38.2 MORE PHRASES

I'd like to remodel my bedroom.

I need to hang a picture.

What should I use for painting my kitchen?

I'd like some advice about plastering.

## 38.3 BUYING TOOLS

Can you show me to the tool section?

I'm looking for a hammer and nails.

Where can I find a saw?

Who can I ask about drills?

## 38.4 MORE PHRASES

Will I need ID to buy this saw?

Where are the screws?

What kind of screwdrivers do you sell?

Do you have any cordless power tools?

## 38.5 VOCABULARY TOOLS AND HOME IMPROVEMENTS

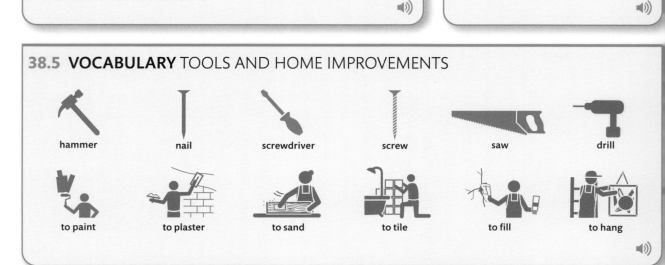

| hammer | nail | screwdriver | screw | saw | drill |
|---|---|---|---|---|---|

| to paint | to plaster | to sand | to tile | to fill | to hang |
|---|---|---|---|---|---|

## 38.6 LISTEN AND NUMBER THE SENTENCES IN THE ORDER YOU HEAR THEM

**A** What's best for plastering walls? ☐

**B** What do I need for tiling my bathroom? ☐

**C** What should I use for painting my kitchen? ☐ 1

**D** Where can I find a saw? ☐

**E** What do you have for filling a crack? ☐

**F** Who can I ask about drills? ☐

**G** Will I need ID to buy this saw? ☐

**H** I need to hang a picture. ☐

**I** I'm looking for a hammer and nails. ☐

**J** I'd like some advice about plastering. ☐

## 38.7 SAY THE SENTENCES OUT LOUD, REPLACING THE PICTURES WITH WORDS

**1** I'm looking for a ___ .

**2** Where can I find a ___ ?

**3** Do you have any ___ ?

**4** Who can I ask about ___ ?

**5** What kind of ___ do you sell?

**6** Where are the ___ ?

## 38.8 USE THE CHART TO CREATE NINE SENTENCES AND SAY THEM OUT LOUD

*What do I need for plastering walls?*

| | | |
|---|---|---|
| What do I need<br>What would you recommend<br>What's best | for | plastering walls?<br>tiling my bathroom?<br>filling a crack? |

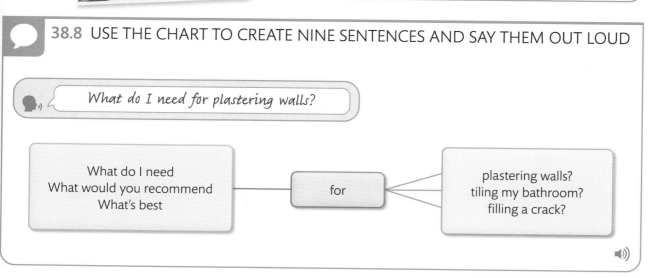

# Buying clothes and shoes

## 39.1 AT THE CLOTHES STORE

Do you have this shirt in a larger size?

Let me go check.

Can I try these dresses on, please?

Yes, you can take up to four items in.

These pants feel too big.

I'll go and get you the next size down.

## 39.2 AT THE SHOE STORE

Do you have these sneakers in a size 10?

I don't think so, but I'll just check for you.

Your website says you have these sandals in stock.

Yes, they came in yesterday.

Are these boots part of the sale?

SALE

Sorry, no. All the sale items are on this shelf.

## 39.3 VOCABULARY CLOTHES AND SHOES

pants

skirt

dress

jacket

coat

shorts

suit

sweater

shirt

T-shirt

sandals

sneakers

boots

socks

## 39.4 LISTEN AND NUMBER THE PICTURES IN THE ORDER THEY ARE DESCRIBED

A [1]
B [ ]
C [ ]
D [ ]
E [ ]
F [ ]

## 39.5 LISTEN TO PERSON A AND RESPOND AS PERSON B

| | A | B |
|---|---|---|
| 1 | Can I try these dresses on, please? | Yes, you can take up to four items in. |
| 2 | These pants feel too big. | I'll go and get you the next size down. |
| 3 | Do you have these sneakers in a size 10? | I don't think so, but I'll just check for you. |
| 4 | Do you have this shirt in a larger size? | Let me go check. |

## 39.6 USE THE CHART TO CREATE 12 SENTENCES AND SAY THEM OUT LOUD

Do you have this sweater in a size 10, please?

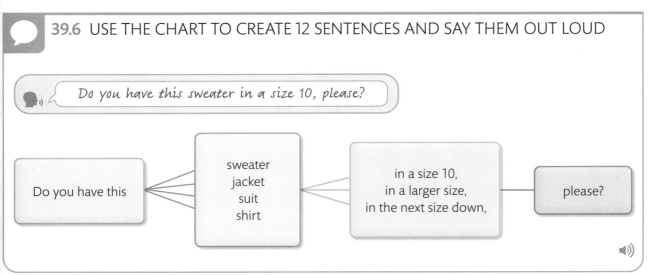

| Do you have this | sweater jacket suit shirt | in a size 10, in a larger size, in the next size down, | please? |

# 40 Returning goods

## 40.1 EXPLAINING THE PROBLEM

Where can I return this bag?
I bought the wrong color.

Our returns desk is on the second floor.

I need to return these pants.

Can I ask what the problem is?

They're too big.

**RETURNS**

## 40.2 MORE PHRASES

I bought the wrong size.

The lamp isn't working properly.

The shoes are too tight.

The dress doesn't fit right.

The vase is broken.

## 40.3 REFUNDS AND EXCHANGES

I have to return this, but I lost my receipt.

Without a receipt, we can only
offer an exchange, I'm afraid.

I'm returning this hat. I just don't like it!

Do you have a receipt?

No, it was a gift.

Don't worry, I'll give
you store credit.

I bought this online. Can I get a refund?

Yes, I just need your order number.

## 40.4 LISTEN TO PERSON A AND RESPOND AS PERSON B

**A**           **B**

1. I bought this online. Can I get a refund?    Yes, I just need your order number.

2. Where can I return this bag? I bought the wrong color.    Our returns desk is on the second floor.

3. I need to return these pants.    Can I ask what the problem is?

4. Do you have a receipt?    No, it was a gift.

5. Can I ask what the problem is?    They're too big.

## 40.5 SAY THE SENTENCES OUT LOUD, REPLACING THE PICTURES WITH WORDS

1. The [boots] are too tight.

2. Where can I return these [heels]?

3. This [dress] is too small.

4. I have to return this, but I lost my [receipt].

5. The [pants] don't fit right.

6. I need to return this [purse].

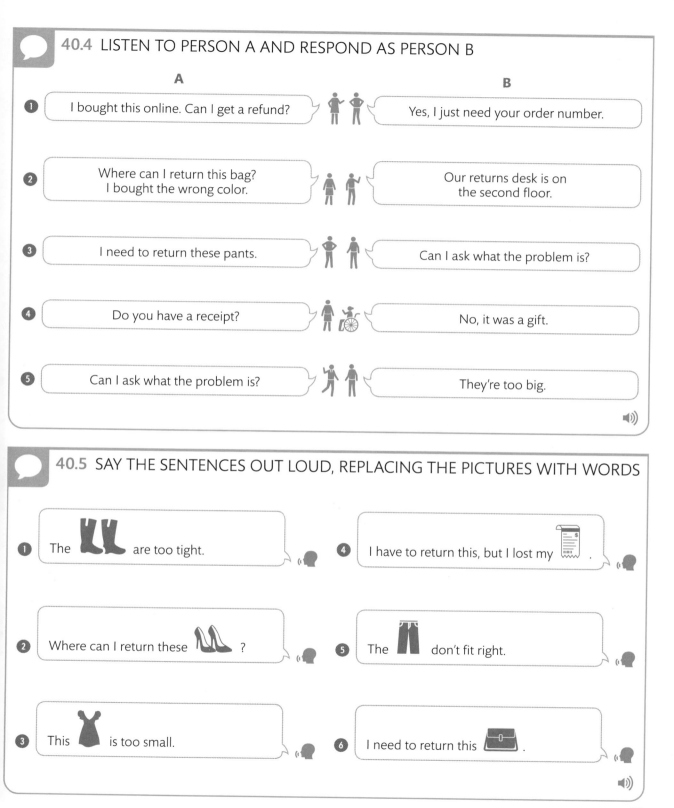

## 41.1 MAKING AN APPOINTMENT

Would you like to make an appointment?

Yes, please. Can you do Thursday at 3 p.m.?

Sorry, we're fully booked on Thursday.

How about Friday morning?

Friday is fine. Is 9:30 okay?

## 41.2 MORE QUESTIONS

Would you like a wash and cut?

Have you been to this salon before?

Who normally does your hair?

Can you come in on Monday?

Is Saturday afternoon any good?

What's the earliest you could fit me in?

Would you like to make another appointment?

## 41.3 AT THE BARBERSHOP

I just need a quick trim. Can you fit me in?

Could you wait 20 minutes? There's one person ahead of you.

Not too much off the top, please.

Sure. No problem.

## 41.4 VOCABULARY HAIR AND BEAUTY

hairdresser

barber

beautician

beard trim

cut

blow-dry

highlights

bangs

facial

manicure

pedicure

waxing

## 41.5 LISTEN TO PERSON A AND RESPOND AS PERSON B

**A**

**B**

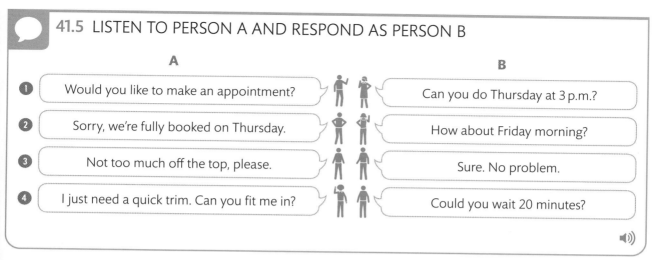

1. Would you like to make an appointment? / Can you do Thursday at 3 p.m.?

2. Sorry, we're fully booked on Thursday. / How about Friday morning?

3. Not too much off the top, please. / Sure. No problem.

4. I just need a quick trim. Can you fit me in? / Could you wait 20 minutes?

## 41.6 MATCH THE SENTENCES AND SAY THEM OUT LOUD

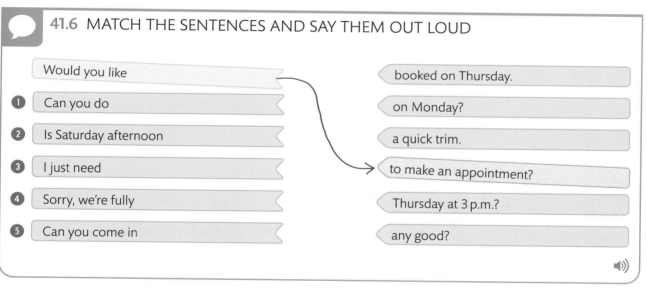

Would you like — to make an appointment?

1. Can you do — booked on Thursday.

2. Is Saturday afternoon — on Monday?

3. I just need — a quick trim.

4. Sorry, we're fully — Thursday at 3 p.m.?

5. Can you come in — any good?

## 41.7 USE THE CHART TO CREATE EIGHT SENTENCES AND SAY THEM OUT LOUD

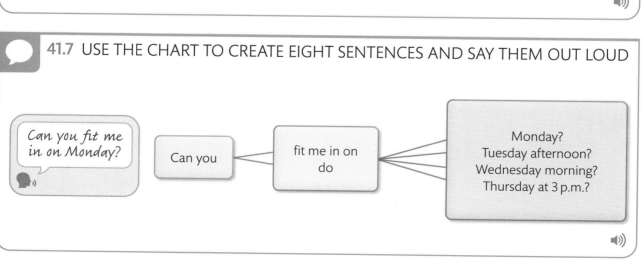

*Can you fit me in on Monday?*

Can you — fit me in on / do — Monday? / Tuesday afternoon? / Wednesday morning? / Thursday at 3 p.m.?

101

## 41.8 CONSULTING THE STYLIST

So what are we doing today?

Just my usual, I think.

I feel like a change, but I don't know what to go for.

Have a look through these styles to get some ideas.

I was thinking of something like this ...

I think a shorter style would really suit you.

## 41.9 MORE PHRASES

What color would be best for me?

Could you cut it a bit shorter at the sides?

Leave it longer on top, please.

Could you cut the bangs a bit more?

I'll have some gel on it, please.

Do you think I should go for highlights?

## 41.10 BEAUTY AND GROOMING

I'd like a manicure, please.

Okay. Have a look at these colors and take your pick.

I booked a back wax for 4 p.m.

Could I take your name, please?

So you're having the aromatherapy facial today?

Yes, that's right.

## 41.11 LISTEN AND NUMBER THE SENTENCES IN THE ORDER YOU HEAR THEM

**A** I'd like a manicure, please. ☐

**B** What color would be best for me? ☐ 1

**C** Do you think I should go for highlights? ☐

**D** Could you cut it a bit shorter at the sides? ☐

**E** Leave it longer on top, please. ☐

**F** Could you cut the bangs a bit more? ☐

**G** So you're having the aromatherapy facial today? ☐

**H** I feel like a change, but I don't know what to go for. ☐

**I** I'll have some gel on it, please. ☐

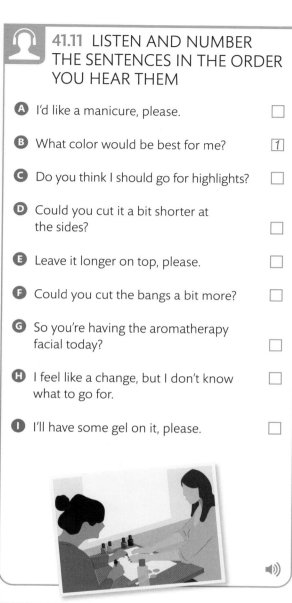

## 41.12 SAY THE SENTENCES OUT LOUD, FILLING IN THE BLANKS USING THE WORDS IN THE PANEL

> a bit more    suit you    go for    best
> my usual    gel    on top

**1** I feel like a change, but I don't know what to _____ .

**2** Just _____ , I think.

**3** I'll have some _____ on it, please.

**4** What color would be _____ for me?

**5** Could you cut the bangs _____ ?

**6** I think a shorter style would really _____ .

**7** Leave it longer _____ , please.

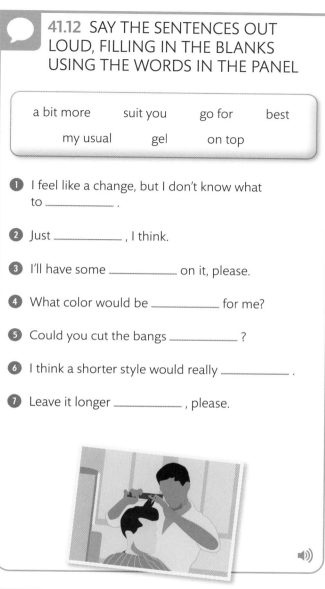

## 41.13 USE THE CHART TO CREATE NINE SENTENCES AND SAY THEM OUT LOUD

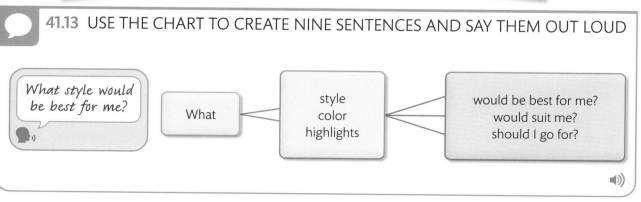

*What style would be best for me?*

| What | style / color / highlights | would be best for me? / would suit me? / should I go for? |

# 42 Sending and receiving

## 42.1 AT THE POST OFFICE

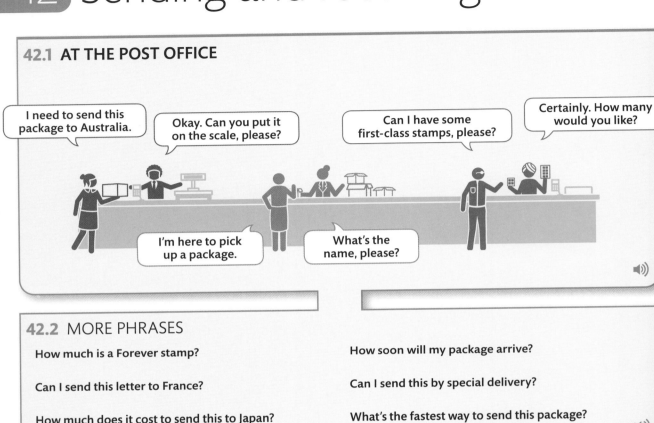

I need to send this package to Australia.

Okay. Can you put it on the scale, please?

Can I have some first-class stamps, please?

Certainly. How many would you like?

I'm here to pick up a package.

What's the name, please?

## 42.2 MORE PHRASES

How much is a Forever stamp?

Can I send this letter to France?

How much does it cost to send this to Japan?

How soon will my package arrive?

Can I send this by special delivery?

What's the fastest way to send this package?

## 42.3 COURIER SERVICE

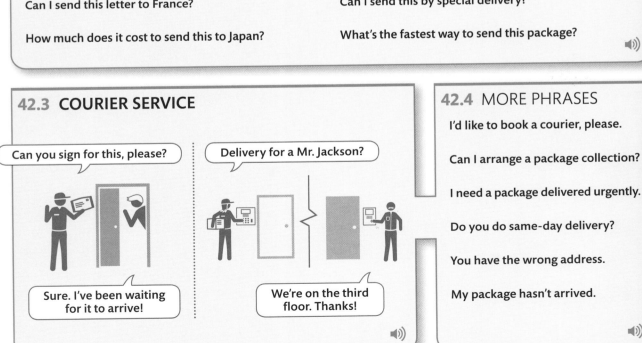

Can you sign for this, please?

Delivery for a Mr. Jackson?

Sure. I've been waiting for it to arrive!

We're on the third floor. Thanks!

## 42.4 MORE PHRASES

I'd like to book a courier, please.

Can I arrange a package collection?

I need a package delivered urgently.

Do you do same-day delivery?

You have the wrong address.

My package hasn't arrived.

## 42.5 LISTEN TO PERSON A AND RESPOND AS PERSON B

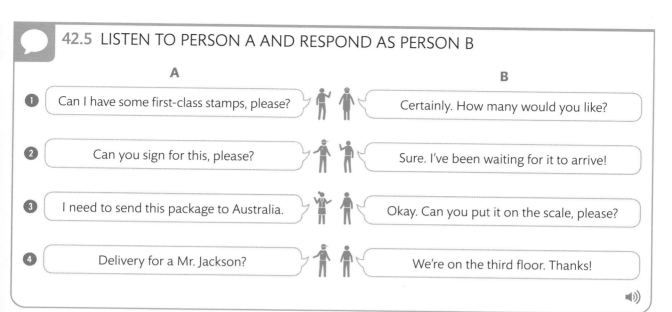

**A**

**B**

1. Can I have some first-class stamps, please? — Certainly. How many would you like?

2. Can you sign for this, please? — Sure. I've been waiting for it to arrive!

3. I need to send this package to Australia. — Okay. Can you put it on the scale, please?

4. Delivery for a Mr. Jackson? — We're on the third floor. Thanks!

## 42.6 LISTEN AND NUMBER THE PICTURES IN THE ORDER THEY ARE DESCRIBED

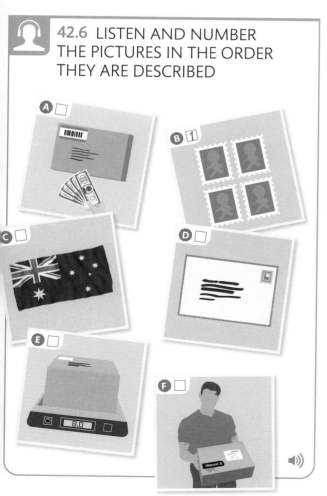

A ☐   B ☐1

C ☐   D ☐

E ☐   F ☐

## 42.7 SAY THE SENTENCES OUT LOUD, FILLING IN THE BLANKS USING THE WORDS IN THE PANEL

| cost | send | like | put |
|------|------|------|-----|
| waiting | pick up | sign | arrive |

1. How many would you _____ ?

2. Can you _____ it on the scale, please?

3. How much does it _____ to send this to Japan?

4. I'm here to _____ a package.

5. Can you _____ for this, please?

6. How soon will my package _____ ?

7. Can I _____ this letter to France?

8. Sure. I've been _____ for it to arrive!

105

## 43.1 OPENING A BANK ACCOUNT

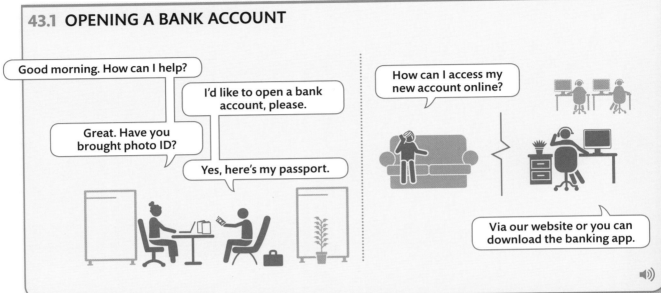

Good morning. How can I help?

I'd like to open a bank account, please.

Great. Have you brought photo ID?

Yes, here's my passport.

How can I access my new account online?

Via our website or you can download the banking app.

## 43.2 MAKING PAYMENTS AND WITHDRAWALS

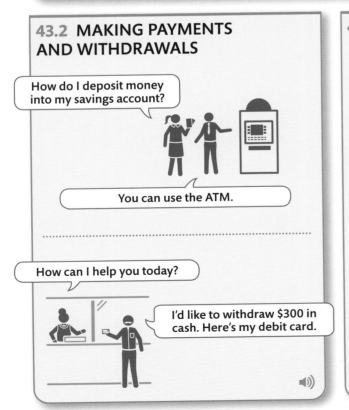

How do I deposit money into my savings account?

You can use the ATM.

How can I help you today?

I'd like to withdraw $300 in cash. Here's my debit card.

## 43.3 VOCABULARY AT THE BANK

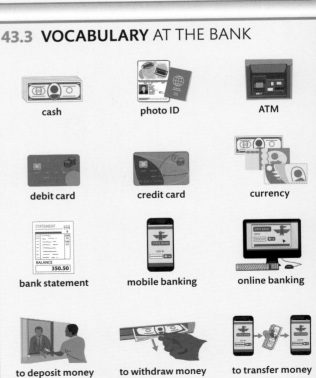

cash

photo ID

ATM

debit card

credit card

currency

bank statement

mobile banking

online banking

to deposit money

to withdraw money

to transfer money

## 43.4 LISTEN TO PERSON A AND RESPOND AS PERSON B

| A | B |
|---|---|
| ① Good morning. How can I help? | I'd like to open a bank account, please. |
| ② Great. Have you brought photo ID? | Yes, here's my passport. |
| ③ How do I deposit money into my savings account? | You can use the ATM. |
| ④ How can I access my new account online? | Via our website or you can download the banking app. |

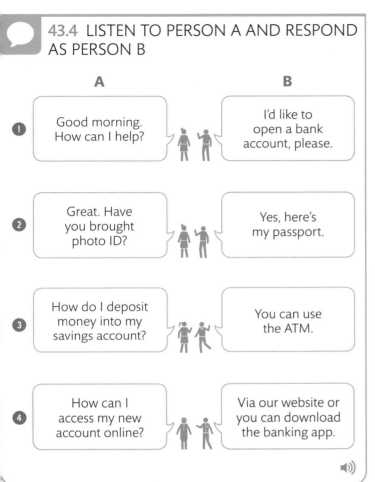

## 43.5 LISTEN AND CIRCLE THE ITEM YOU HEAR

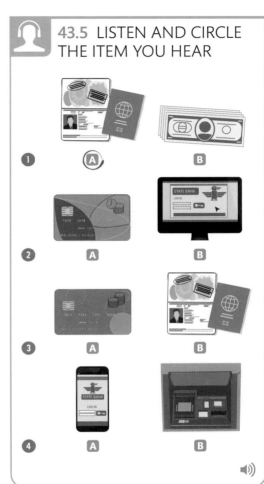

① Ⓐ    B
② A    B
③ A    B
④ A    B

## 43.6 USE THE CHART TO CREATE FIVE SENTENCES AND SAY THEM OUT LOUD

I'd like to open a bank account, please.

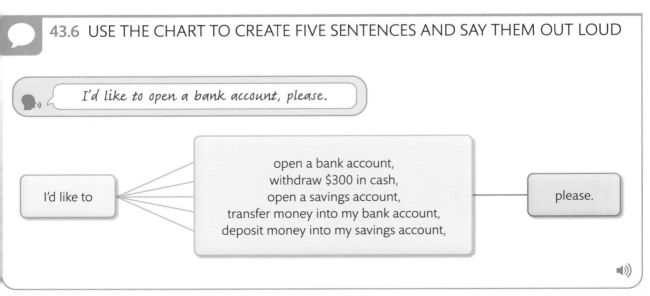

I'd like to

open a bank account,
withdraw $300 in cash,
open a savings account,
transfer money into my bank account,
deposit money into my savings account,

please.

## 43.7 ORDERING CURRENCY

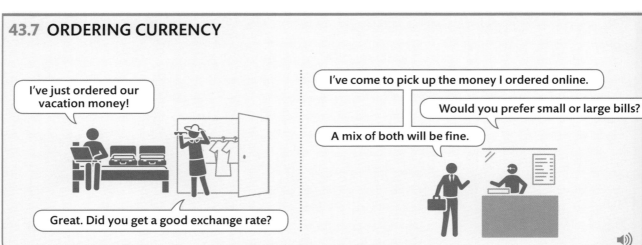

I've just ordered our vacation money!

Great. Did you get a good exchange rate?

I've come to pick up the money I ordered online.

Would you prefer small or large bills?

A mix of both will be fine.

## 43.8 CARD PROBLEMS

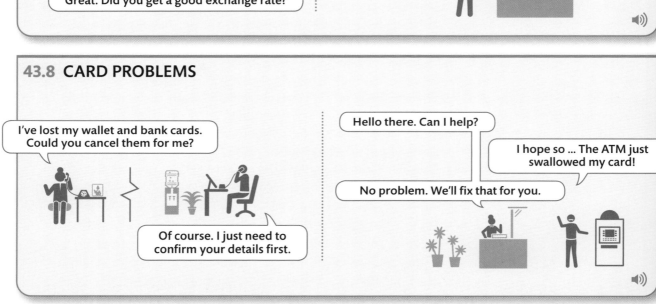

I've lost my wallet and bank cards. Could you cancel them for me?

Of course. I just need to confirm your details first.

Hello there. Can I help?

No problem. We'll fix that for you.

I hope so ... The ATM just swallowed my card!

## 43.9 WAYS TO PAY

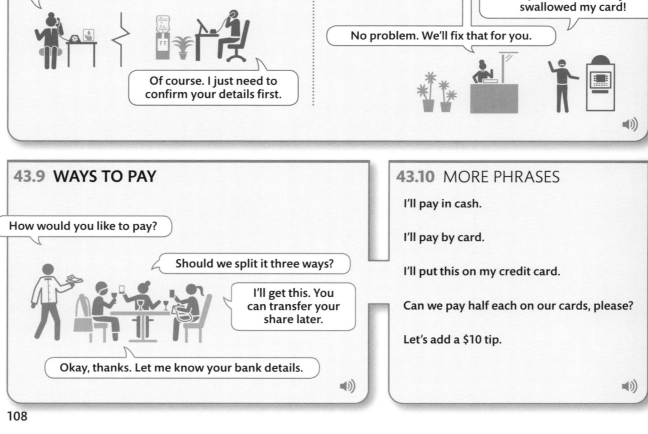

How would you like to pay?

Should we split it three ways?

I'll get this. You can transfer your share later.

Okay, thanks. Let me know your bank details.

## 43.10 MORE PHRASES

I'll pay in cash.

I'll pay by card.

I'll put this on my credit card.

Can we pay half each on our cards, please?

Let's add a $10 tip.

## 43.11 LISTEN TO PERSON A AND RESPOND AS PERSON B

| A | B |
|---|---|
| **1** Would you prefer small or large bills? | A mix of both will be fine. |
| **2** The ATM just swallowed my card! | No problem. We'll fix that for you. |
| **3** How would you like to pay? | Should we split it three ways? |
| **4** I've just ordered our vacation money! | Great. Did you get a good exchange rate? |
| **5** I've lost my wallet and bank cards. Could you cancel them for me? | Of course. I just need to confirm your details first. |

## 43.12 MATCH THE SENTENCES AND SAY THEM OUT LOUD

I've come to pick up → the money I ordered online.

**1** You can transfer — our vacation money!

**2** I've just ordered — swallowed my card!

**3** The ATM just — your share later.

**4** Should we split it — your bank details.

**5** Let me know — three ways?

# 44 At the library

## 44.1 JOINING THE LIBRARY

Hi there. How do I join the library?

I'll just need photo ID and proof of your address.

Do you run computer courses here?

Yes, here's a list of all our classes.

## 44.2 USING THE LIBRARY

I'd like to check these books out.

If you have your library card, you can use this scanner.

Do you have this as an audiobook?

Yes, we do. I'll show you how to download it.

Can we use a computer for our school project?

Of course. I'll book you one in the study area.

## 44.3 MORE PHRASES

I need to renew these books, please.

Where do I return these books?

Can you help me find a book, please?

Where is the children's section?

Could you recommend a good thriller?

Can I see your newspaper archive?

## 44.4 LISTEN TO PERSON A AND RESPOND AS PERSON B

**A** | **B**

1. Hi there. How do I join the library? | I'll just need photo ID and proof of your address.

2. Can we use a computer for our school project? | Of course. I'll book you one in the study area.

3. Do you have this as an audiobook? | Yes, we do. I'll show you how to download it.

4. Do you run computer courses here? | Yes, here's a list of all our classes.

5. I'd like to check these books out. | If you have your library card, you can use this scanner.

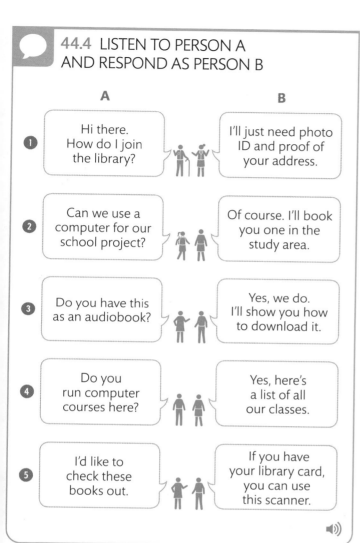

## 44.5 LISTEN AND NUMBER THE PICTURES IN THE ORDER THEY ARE DESCRIBED

A 1
B ☐
C ☐
D ☐
E ☐
F ☐

## 44.6 SAY THE SENTENCES OUT LOUD, FILLING IN THE BLANKS USING THE WORDS IN THE PANEL

audiobook    library    books    newspaper    section    courses

1. Do you run computer _____ here?

2. Do you have this as an _____ ?

3. I need to renew these _____ , please.

4. How do I join the _____ ?

5. Where is the children's _____ ?

6. Can I see your _____ archive?

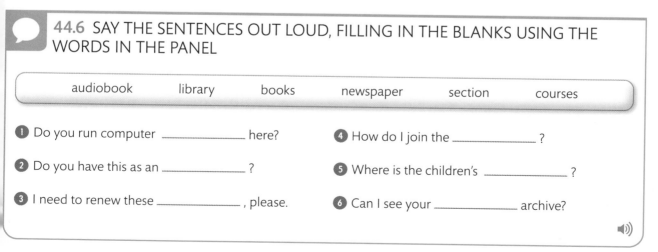

111

# 45 Work and study

## 45.1 JOBS / OCCUPATIONS

server

chef

teacher

cleaner

receptionist

lawyer

doctor

nurse

dentist

pharmacist

paramedic

childcare provider

courier

police officer

firefighter

security guard

pilot

flight attendant

mechanic

real estate agent

librarian

accountant

vet

sales assistant

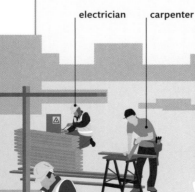

electrician   carpenter   engineer

architect

construction worker

app developer

farmer

hairdresser

plumber

artist

gardener

## 45.2 SCHOOL AND COLLEGE

school / college

classroom

lesson

students / pupils

homework

university

timetable

to take an exam / a test

to pass an exam / a test

to fail an exam / a test

lecture

dissertation

graduation

degree

diploma

## 45.3 WORLD OF WORK

employer

employee

freelancer

office worker

site worker

permanent job

temporary job

full-time job

part-time job

shift

overtime

flextime

to go on maternity leave

to resign

to retire

wages

salary

hourly rate

paycheck

benefits

raise

pay cut

bonus

vacation

sick leave

# 46 At school

## 46.1 VISITING A SCHOOL

We offer a wide range of subjects.

Is music part of the curriculum?

The children have math every day.

How often do they have science lessons?

## 46.2 MORE QUESTIONS

How many children are in each class?

How much homework is there?

What clubs do you offer?

Do you have a school uniform?

Is there an after-school club?

## 46.3 STARTING SCHOOL

You must be our new student. Welcome!

Yes, this is Tom. He's a bit nervous for his first day!

There's no need to worry, Tom. Let's go and meet your new class.

## 46.4 PARENTS' NIGHT

Zia is settling in very well.

Oh, good. How is she doing with English?

She's making really good progress.

## 46.5 VOCABULARY SCHOOL SUBJECTS

English

math

science

computing

history

geography

languages

physical education (PE)

art

music

theater

religious studies

## 46.6 LISTEN TO PERSON A AND RESPOND AS PERSON B

| A | B |
|---|---|
| **1** You must be our new student. Welcome! | Yes, this is Tom. He's a bit nervous for his first day! |
| **2** The children have math every day. | How often do they have science lessons? |
| **3** Zia is settling in very well. | Oh, good. How is she doing with English? |
| **4** We offer a wide range of subjects. | Is music part of the curriculum? |

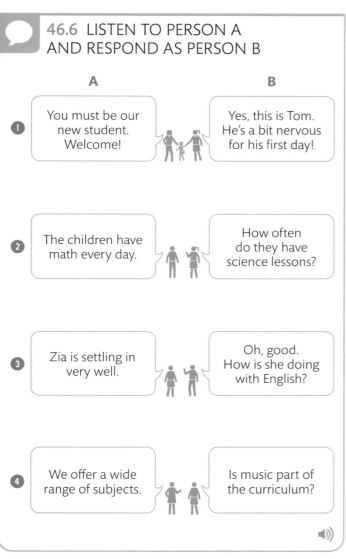

## 46.7 LISTEN AND CIRCLE THE ITEM YOU HEAR

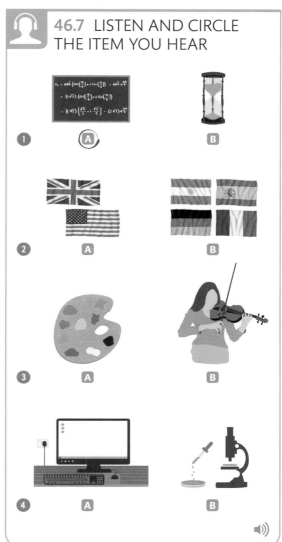

1. (A)  B
2. A  B
3. A  B
4. A  B

## 46.8 USE THE CHART TO CREATE FIVE SENTENCES AND SAY THEM OUT LOUD

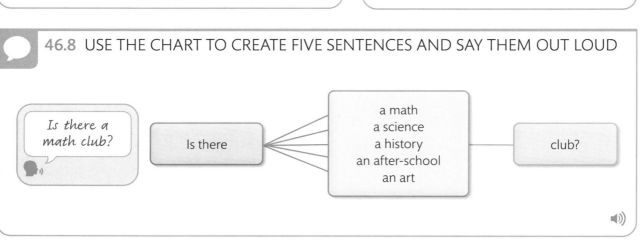

*Is there a math club?*

Is there → a math / a science / a history / an after-school / an art → club?

# 47 Continuing and higher education

## 47.1 CHOOSING A COURSE

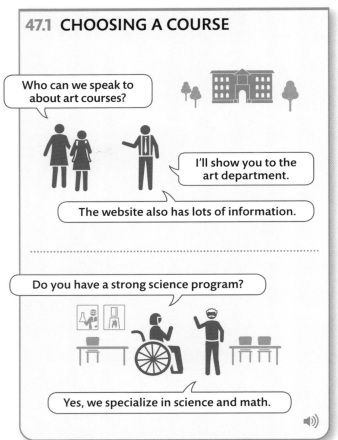

Who can we speak to about art courses?

I'll show you to the art department.

The website also has lots of information.

Do you have a strong science program?

Yes, we specialize in science and math.

## 47.2 VOCATIONAL COURSES

May I ask about your cooking course?

Sure. It's a two-year, full-time program.

Does the hairdressing course include work experience?

Yes. Students work once a week in a salon.

## 47.3 MORE QUESTIONS TO ASK

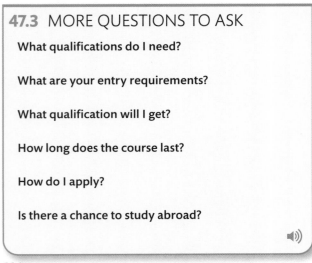

What qualifications do I need?

What are your entry requirements?

What qualification will I get?

How long does the course last?

How do I apply?

Is there a chance to study abroad?

## 47.4 EVENING CLASSES

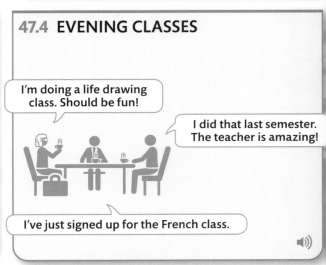

I'm doing a life drawing class. Should be fun!

I did that last semester. The teacher is amazing!

I've just signed up for the French class.

## 47.5 LISTEN TO PERSON A AND RESPOND AS PERSON B

**A**                                          **B**

❶ May I ask about your cooking course?    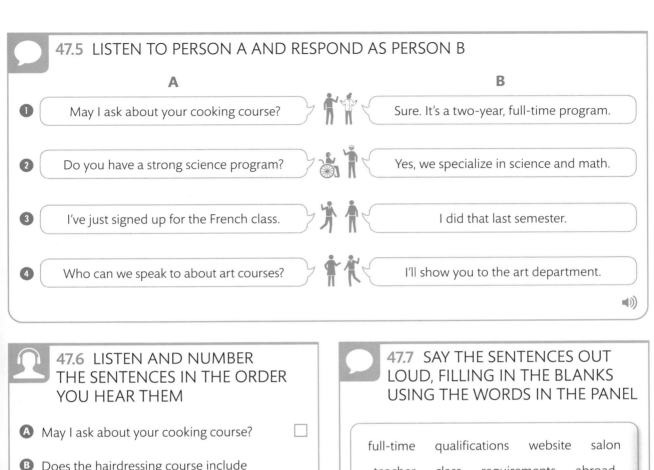  Sure. It's a two-year, full-time program.

❷ Do you have a strong science program?    Yes, we specialize in science and math.

❸ I've just signed up for the French class.    I did that last semester.

❹ Who can we speak to about art courses?    I'll show you to the art department.

---

## 47.6 LISTEN AND NUMBER THE SENTENCES IN THE ORDER YOU HEAR THEM

Ⓐ May I ask about your cooking course? ☐

Ⓑ Does the hairdressing course include work experience? ☐ 1

Ⓒ Who can we speak to about art courses? ☐

Ⓓ Yes. Students work once a week in a salon. ☐

Ⓔ I'll show you to the art department. ☐

Ⓕ I'm doing a life drawing class. Should be fun! ☐

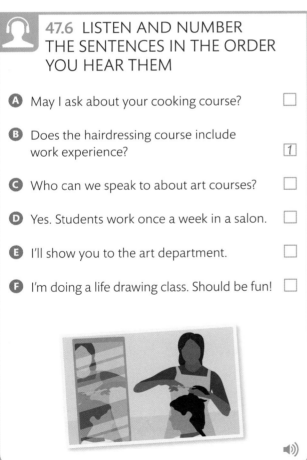

---

## 47.7 SAY THE SENTENCES OUT LOUD, FILLING IN THE BLANKS USING THE WORDS IN THE PANEL

> full-time    qualifications    website    salon
>
> teacher    class    requirements    abroad

❶ What are your entry _____ ?

❷ Sure. It's a two-year, _____ program.

❸ I've just signed up for the French _____ .

❹ The _____ is amazing!

❺ The _____ also has lots of information.

❻ What _____ do I need?

❼ Is there a chance to study _____ ?

❽ Students work once a week in a _____ .

117

## 47.8 VOCABULARY DEPARTMENTS AND SUBJECTS

humanities

social sciences

chemistry

physics

biology

medicine

law

engineering

art and design

business

economics

politics

## 47.9 FIRST DAY AT COLLEGE

Excuse me, I'm new here. Do you know where I can leave my bike?

Yes, the bike rack is around the corner. Enjoy your first day!

Hi, I'm Amy. I'm here for the business lecture.

Me, too. I'm Lucas.

Hello. I'm your lecturer, Professor Li. Take a seat.

## 47.10 FINDING YOUR WAY AROUND

Can you tell me where the biology department is?

I'm going there, too. I'll show you.

Any idea where the art school is?

It's right next to the coffee shop. I can show you the way.

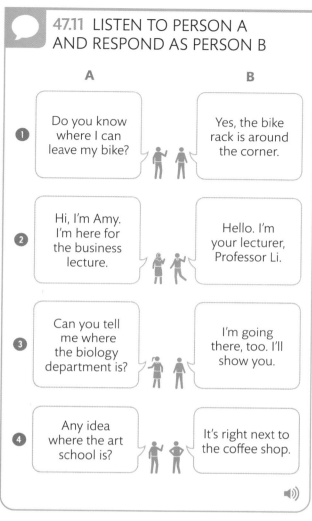

## 47.11 LISTEN TO PERSON A AND RESPOND AS PERSON B

**A** | **B**

1. Do you know where I can leave my bike? | Yes, the bike rack is around the corner.

2. Hi, I'm Amy. I'm here for the business lecture. | Hello. I'm your lecturer, Professor Li.

3. Can you tell me where the biology department is? | I'm going there, too. I'll show you.

4. Any idea where the art school is? | It's right next to the coffee shop.

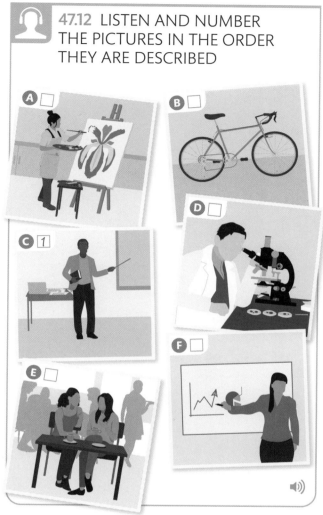

## 47.12 LISTEN AND NUMBER THE PICTURES IN THE ORDER THEY ARE DESCRIBED

A ☐   B ☐   C 1   D ☐   E ☐   F ☐

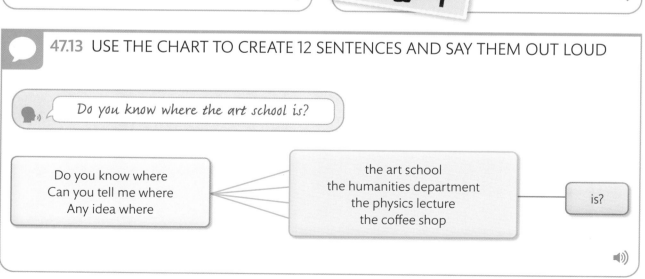

## 47.13 USE THE CHART TO CREATE 12 SENTENCES AND SAY THEM OUT LOUD

*Do you know where the art school is?*

| Do you know where
Can you tell me where
Any idea where | the art school
the humanities department
the physics lecture
the coffee shop | is? |

## 47.14 SETTLING IN

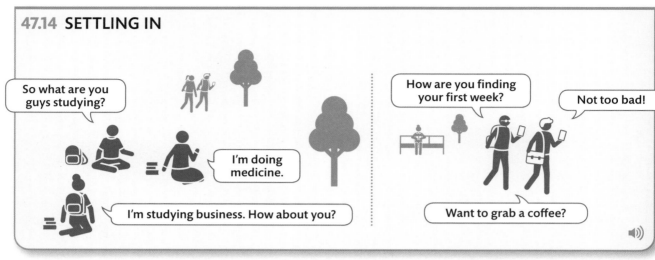

## 47.15 STUDENT SUPPORT

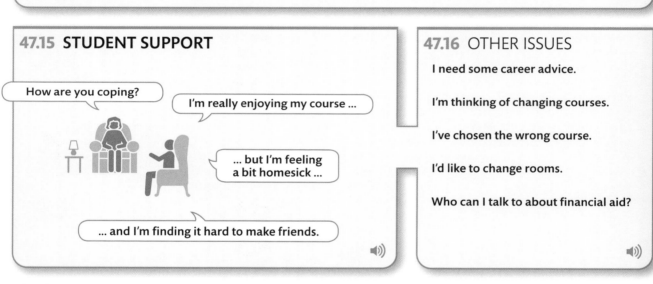

## 47.16 OTHER ISSUES

I need some career advice.

I'm thinking of changing courses.

I've chosen the wrong course.

I'd like to change rooms.

Who can I talk to about financial aid?

## 47.17 JOINING CLUBS

## 47.18 SAYING YES OR NO

Sounds like fun!

I'm in!

I'd be up for that!

I'd rather not, actually.

It's not for me, sorry.

I think I'll pass.

## 47.19 LISTEN AND CIRCLE THE ITEM YOU HEAR

1. Ⓐ  B
2. A  B
3. Ⓐ  B
4. A  B

## 47.20 RESPOND OUT LOUD TO THE AUDIO, FILLING IN THE BLANKS USING THE WORDS IN THE PANEL

up for that    too bad    rather not    make friends

1. How are you coping?
   I'm finding it hard to _____ .

2. Are you coming to the Activities Fair?
   I'd _____ , actually.

3. How are you finding your first week?
   Not _____ !

4. Wanna try out for the basketball team?
   I'd be _____ !

## 47.21 MATCH THE SENTENCES AND SAY THEM OUT LOUD

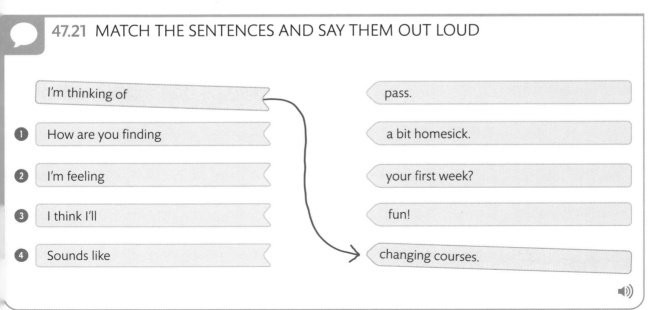

I'm thinking of — changing courses.

1. How are you finding — your first week?
2. I'm feeling — a bit homesick.
3. I think I'll — pass.
4. Sounds like — fun!

# 48 Looking for work

## 48.1 JOB SEARCHING

This job looks interesting ...

... flexible hours ...

... no experience needed ...

... sounds ideal!

Have you used this job search website?

Yes, I found my current job on there.

Is the job in the window still open?

BAR STAFF WANTED

Yes. Can you email us your resume?

## 48.2 AT THE EMPLOYMENT AGENCY

How can I help?

I'm looking for a part-time sales job.

Okay, let me get some details about you.

Have you worked in a restaurant before?

I worked as a server last summer.

## 48.3 QUESTIONS YOU MAY HEAR

What skills do you have?

What hours can you work?

What experience do you have?

What salary are you looking for?

Why did you leave your last job?

## 48.4 LISTEN TO PERSON A AND RESPOND AS PERSON B

| A | B |
|---|---|
| **1** How can I help? | I'm looking for a part-time sales job. |
| **2** Is the job in the window still open? | Yes. Can you email us your resume? |
| **3** Have you used this job search website? | Yes, I found my current job on there. |
| **4** Have you worked in a restaurant before? | I worked as a server last summer. |

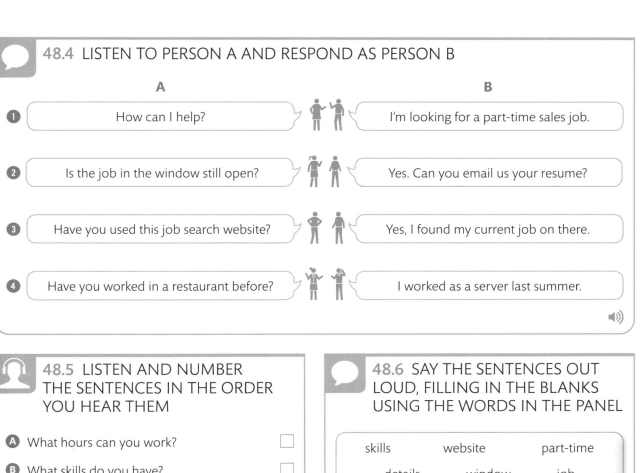

## 48.5 LISTEN AND NUMBER THE SENTENCES IN THE ORDER YOU HEAR THEM

**A** What hours can you work? ☐

**B** What skills do you have? ☐

**C** What salary are you looking for? ☐

**D** What experience do you have? ☐

**E** Have you worked in a restaurant before? ☐

**F** How can I help? 1

**G** Is the job in the window still open? ☐

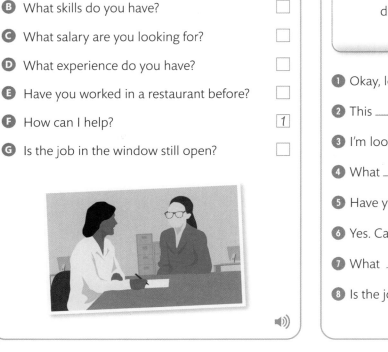

## 48.6 SAY THE SENTENCES OUT LOUD, FILLING IN THE BLANKS USING THE WORDS IN THE PANEL

| skills | website | part-time |
|---|---|---|
| details | window | job |
| hours | resume | |

**1** Okay, let me get some _____ about you.

**2** This _____ looks interesting ...

**3** I'm looking for a _____ sales job.

**4** What _____ can you work?

**5** Have you used this job search _____ ?

**6** Yes. Can you email us your _____ ?

**7** What _____ do you have?

**8** Is the job in the _____ still open?

# 49 Applying for a job

## 49.1 PREPARING A RESUME

I really want to apply for this job. I need to update my resume!

There are tons of examples online to help you.

It says the deadline for applications is tomorrow.

Really? I'd better email my resume tonight, then.

My resume is all checked and ready to go ...

Don't forget to send your cover letter, too!

## 49.2 APPLICATION FORMS

Have you finished your application yet?

I just need to fill in my personal details and it'll be ready.

This application form is taking ages!

Why don't you save it and take a break?

## 49.3 VOCABULARY
JOB APPLICATIONS

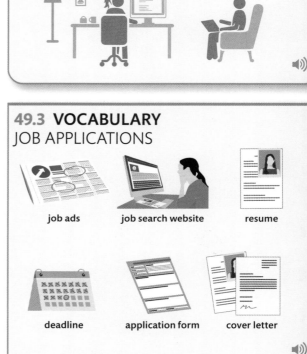

job ads

job search website

resume

deadline

application form

cover letter

## 49.4 LISTEN TO PERSON A AND RESPOND AS PERSON B

**A**

**B**

❶ I need to update my resume!

There are tons of examples online to help you.

❷ It says the deadline for applications is tomorrow.

Really? I'd better email my resume tonight, then.

❸ Have you finished your application yet?

I just need to fill in my personal details and it'll be ready.

❹ This application form is taking ages!

Why don't you save it and take a break?

## 49.5 LISTEN AND CIRCLE THE ITEM YOU HEAR

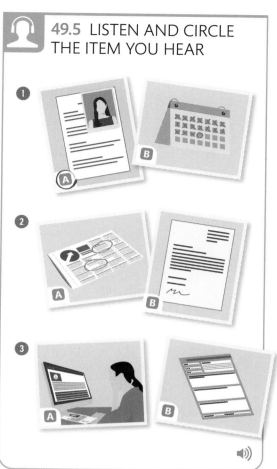

❶ A B

❷ A B

❸ A B

## 49.6 MATCH THE SENTENCES AND SAY THEM OUT LOUD

I need to update ──────→ my resume!

❶ I really want to apply for

your cover letter, too!

❷ I just need to fill in

your application yet?

❸ Don't forget to send

my personal details and it'll be ready.

❹ Have you finished

this job.

# 50 Job interviews

## 50.1 INTERVIEWERS' QUESTIONS

Why are you right for this position?

I have the qualifications and experience you're looking for.

What can you bring to our company?

Enthusiasm, energy, and lots of ideas.

Why did you apply for this job?

I'm really eager to use my planning skills.

## 50.2 MORE QUESTIONS YOU MAY HEAR

What experience do you have in ...?

What are your strengths?

What do you enjoy doing outside work?

What are your goals for the future?

Why do you want to leave your current job?

What salary are you expecting?

What's the notice period in your current job?

How soon could you start?

## 50.3 TALKING ABOUT YOURSELF

Tell me about yourself.

I'm reliable and organized.

I work well in a team.

I'm good with customers.

I'm used to working under pressure.

## 50.4 MORE PHRASES

I can adapt to new situations.

I'm a quick learner.

I'm self-motivated.

I have an excellent track record.

I enjoy solving problems.

## 50.5 LISTEN TO THE AUDIO AND MATCH THE CORRECT RESPONSE

What can you bring to our company?

I'm a quick learner.

1 Why are you right for this position?

I'm really eager to use my planning skills.

2 What are your strengths?

I'm used to working under pressure.

3 Tell me about yourself.

Enthusiasm, energy, and lots of ideas.

4 Why did you apply for this job?

I enjoy solving problems.

## 50.6 SAY THE SENTENCES OUT LOUD, FILLING IN THE BLANKS USING THE WORDS IN THE PANEL

working      notice      company      start      customers      salary

1 What can you bring to our _____ ?

2 What _____ are you expecting?

3 What's the _____ period in your current job?

4 How soon could you _____ ?

5 I'm used to _____ under pressure.

6 I'm good with _____ .

## 50.7 USE THE CHART TO CREATE FIVE SENTENCES AND SAY THEM OUT LOUD

*I have the experience you're looking for.*

I have

the experience
the skills
the qualifications
the enthusiasm
the strengths

you're looking for.

# 51 Starting a new job

## 51.1 SETTING UP

Hello, I'm Christina. It's my first day.

Welcome! Here's your pass. I'll let the manager know you're here.

I've set up your email account. Can you type in a password?

Okay. How long does it have to be?

## 51.2 MORE PHRASES

Your supervisor will show you where everything is.

Let's find you a locker.

Anything you need, just ask.

You'll need to clock out at the end of your shift.

Your first break is at 12:30.

## 51.3 MEETING COLLEAGUES

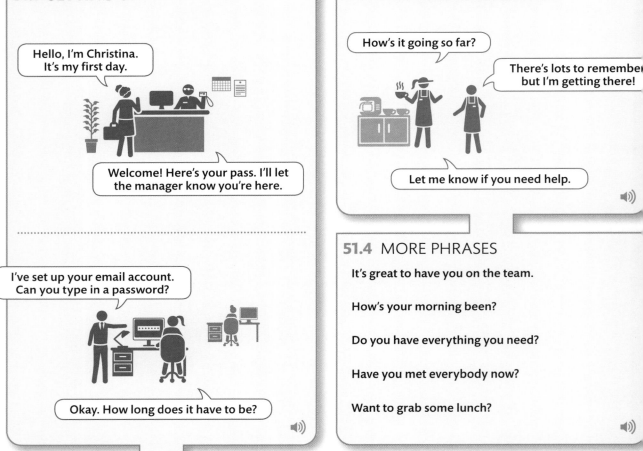

How's it going so far?

There's lots to remember but I'm getting there!

Let me know if you need help.

## 51.4 MORE PHRASES

It's great to have you on the team.

How's your morning been?

Do you have everything you need?

Have you met everybody now?

Want to grab some lunch?

## 51.5 HEALTH & SAFETY

You need to read these safety rules carefully.

And always wear your hard hat!

## 51.6 LISTEN TO PERSON A AND RESPOND AS PERSON B

**A**  **B**

1. Hello, I'm Christina. It's my first day. | Here's your pass. I'll let the manager know you're here.

2. How's it going so far? | There's lots to remember, but I'm getting there!

3. Can you type in a password? | Okay. How long does it have to be?

4. You need to read these safety rules carefully. | And always wear your hard hat!

## 51.7 LISTEN AND NUMBER THE SENTENCES IN THE ORDER YOU HEAR THEM

A. It's great to have you on the team. ☐

B. You'll need to clock out at the end of your shift. ☐1

C. How's it going so far? ☐

D. Have you met everybody now? ☐

E. Want to grab some lunch? ☐

F. Hello, I'm Christina. It's my first day. ☐

G. You need to read these safety rules carefully. ☐

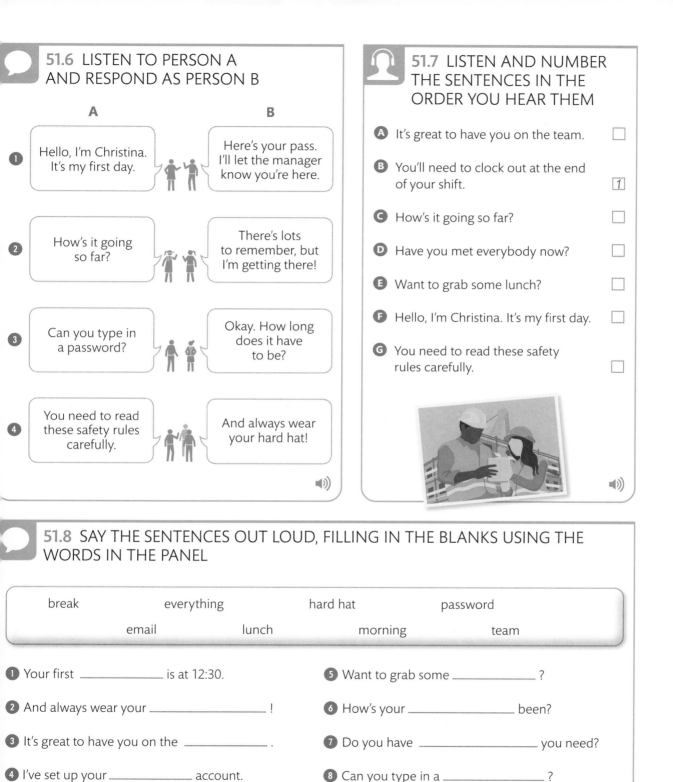

## 51.8 SAY THE SENTENCES OUT LOUD, FILLING IN THE BLANKS USING THE WORDS IN THE PANEL

| break | everything | hard hat | password |
| email | lunch | morning | team |

1. Your first _____ is at 12:30.

2. And always wear your _____ !

3. It's great to have you on the _____ .

4. I've set up your _____ account.

5. Want to grab some _____ ?

6. How's your _____ been?

7. Do you have _____ you need?

8. Can you type in a _____ ?

# 52 In the workplace

## 52.1 WORKPLACE ROUTINES

We have a team meeting at 4 p.m. on Tuesdays.

And a full staff meeting once a month.

Thanks. I'll put it in my calendar.

What time is your lunch break?

It's in half an hour. How about yours?

## 52.2 WORKPLACE ISSUES

Sorry, I have to change my shift on Monday.

Which one are you down for

I'm scheduled for the morning shift. Could I change to the afternoon?

This station is down again. It keeps crashing!

Not again! Okay, let's call the supervisor.

## 52.3 VOCABULARY AT WORK

meeting

lunch break

coffee break

morning shift

afternoon shift

evening shift

manager

supervisor

colleague

team

to clock in / out

locker

## 52.4 LISTEN TO PERSON A AND RESPOND AS PERSON B

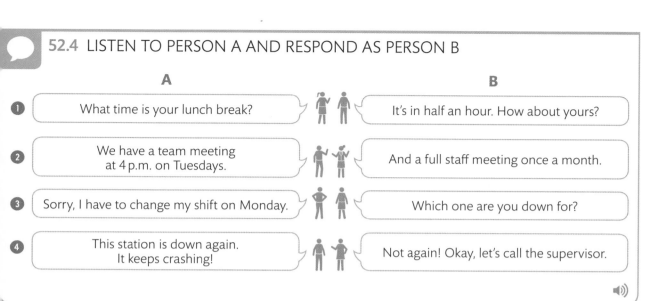

**A**

**B**

1. What time is your lunch break? — It's in half an hour. How about yours?

2. We have a team meeting at 4 p.m. on Tuesdays. — And a full staff meeting once a month.

3. Sorry, I have to change my shift on Monday. — Which one are you down for?

4. This station is down again. It keeps crashing! — Not again! Okay, let's call the supervisor.

## 52.5 LISTEN AND CIRCLE THE ITEM YOU HEAR

1. Ⓐ  Ⓑ
2. Ⓐ  Ⓑ
3. Ⓐ  Ⓑ
4. Ⓐ  Ⓑ

## 52.6 RESPOND OUT LOUD TO THE AUDIO, FILLING IN THE BLANKS USING THE WORDS IN THE PANEL

scheduled for   let's call   How about   put it in

1. What time is your lunch break?

   It's in half an hour. _____ yours?

2. This station is down again. It keeps crashing!

   Not again! Okay, _____ the supervisor.

3. Which one are you down for?

   I'm _____ the morning shift.

4. We have a team meeting at 4 p.m. on Tuesdays.

   Thanks. I'll _____ my calendar.

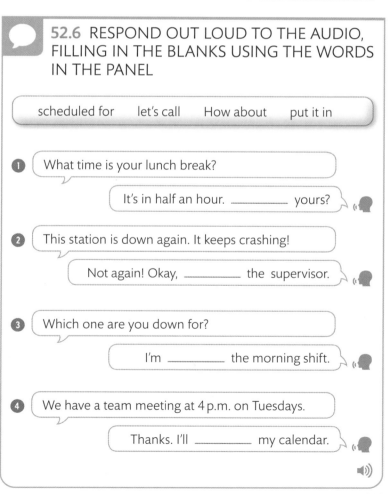

# 53 Giving a presentation

## 53.1 GETTING STARTED

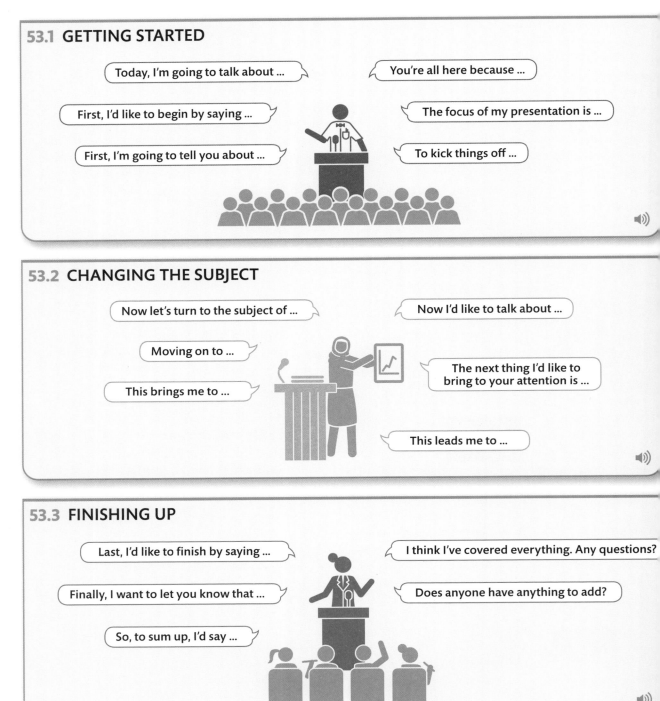

Today, I'm going to talk about ...

You're all here because ...

First, I'd like to begin by saying ...

The focus of my presentation is ...

First, I'm going to tell you about ...

To kick things off ...

## 53.2 CHANGING THE SUBJECT

Now let's turn to the subject of ...

Now I'd like to talk about ...

Moving on to ...

The next thing I'd like to bring to your attention is ...

This brings me to ...

This leads me to ...

## 53.3 FINISHING UP

Last, I'd like to finish by saying ...

I think I've covered everything. Any questions?

Finally, I want to let you know that ...

Does anyone have anything to add?

So, to sum up, I'd say ...

## 53.4 LISTEN AND NUMBER THE SENTENCES IN THE ORDER YOU HEAR THEM

**A** To kick things off ... ☐

**B** So, to sum up, I'd say ... 1

**C** Moving on to ... ☐

**D** First, I'm going to tell you about ... ☐

**E** Last, I'd like to finish by saying ... ☐

**F** This leads me to ... ☐

**G** First, I'd like to begin by saying ... ☐

**H** Does anyone have anything to add? ☐

## 53.5 MATCH THE SENTENCES AND SAY THEM OUT LOUD

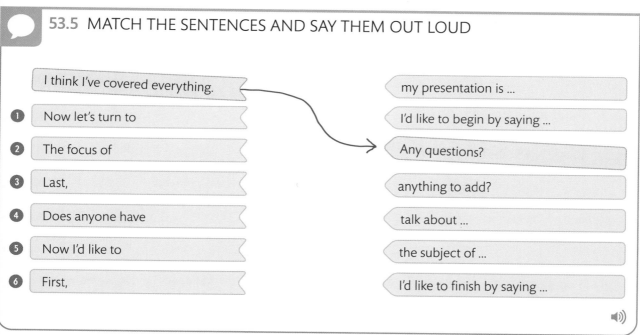

I think I've covered everything. → Any questions?

**1** Now let's turn to — my presentation is ...

**2** The focus of — I'd like to begin by saying ...

**3** Last, — anything to add?

**4** Does anyone have — talk about ...

**5** Now I'd like to — the subject of ...

**6** First, — I'd like to finish by saying ...

## 53.6 USE THE CHART TO CREATE 10 SENTENCES AND SAY THEM OUT LOUD

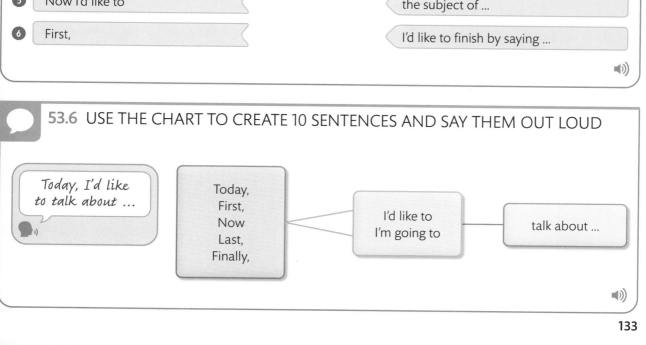

*Today, I'd like to talk about ...*

| Today, First, Now Last, Finally, | I'd like to / I'm going to | talk about ... |

133

# 54 Work meetings

## 54.1 SETTING THE AGENDA

I think we're all here, so let's get started.

What's on today's agenda?

We're starting with how to improve our customer service.

Listen up, everyone! There's a lot to get through.

First up is deciding next week's menus ...

... then we'll move on to the schedules.

## 54.2 TAKING TURNS TO TALK

So that's the situation. Let's hear your thoughts.

If I can just add ... It will be a slow process.

May I go first? For me, these changes are important.

Let's hear from James on this point.

Just to clarify ... Which changes exactly?

Can I jump in? I totally agree.

## 54.3 SHARING OPINIONS

Let's go around the table and see where we all stand.

I'm 100% on board with this.

If you ask me, it's a nonstarter.

## 54.4 MORE PHRASES

Why don't we try ...?

The way I see it is ...

How about if we ...?

I see where you're coming from, so ...

I'm wondering if we could ...?

## 54.5 LISTEN TO THE AUDIO AND MATCH THE SENTENCES

Listen up, everyone! ——→ There's a lot to get through.

Let's hear your thoughts.

1. Can I jump in?
2. If I can just add ...
3. So that's the situation.
4. Just to clarify ...
5. May I go first?

For me, these changes are important.

I totally agree.

Which changes exactly?

It will be a slow process.

## 54.6 LISTEN TO PERSON A AND RESPOND AS PERSON B

**A** | **B**

1. I think we're all here, so let's get started. | What's on today's agenda?
2. For me, these changes are important. | Just to clarify ... Which changes exactly?
3. If I can just add ... It will be a slow process. | Can I jump in? I totally agree.
4. I'm 100% on board with this. | If you ask me, it's a nonstarter.

## 54.7 SAY THE SENTENCES OUT LOUD, FILLING IN THE BLANKS USING THE WORDS IN THE PANEL

stand    jump    coming    started
point    clarify    ask

1. Let's hear from James on this _____ .
2. I think we're all here, so let's get _____ .
3. If you _____ me, it's a nonstarter.
4. I see where you're _____ from, so ...
5. Can I _____ in? I totally agree.
6. Just to _____ ... Which changes exactly?
7. Let's go around the table and see where we all _____ .

## 54.8 ENDING THE MEETING

"To sum up, we're going ahead with the new designs."

"Any questions before we wrap up?"

"To recap, we've agreed to change the timetable."

"I'll email the action points to you all later."

"Great. Thanks everyone for your input!"

## 54.9 NETWORKING

"I understand you work for AbiCo."

"That's right. Sorry, I didn't catch your name."

"It was great meeting you."

"You, too. Let's stay in touch. Here's my card."

"Thanks. I'll let you know if something suitable comes up."

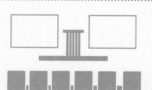

"Your project sounds really interesting."

"I'd love to keep the conversation going."

"I've enjoyed our discussion."

"Me, too. Let's follow up in the office."

x

## 54.10 LISTEN TO PERSON A AND RESPOND AS PERSON B

**A**

**B**

1. To sum up, we're going ahead with the new designs.

   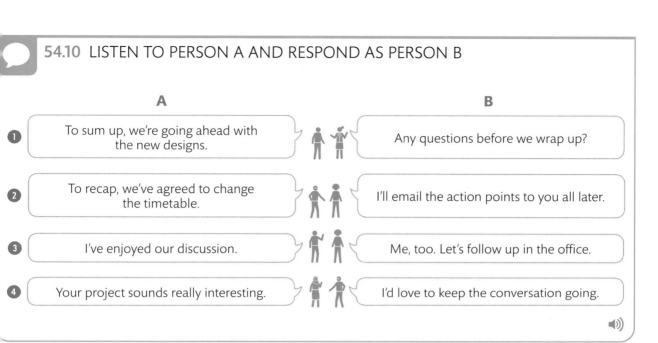

   Any questions before we wrap up?

2. To recap, we've agreed to change the timetable.

   I'll email the action points to you all later.

3. I've enjoyed our discussion.

   Me, too. Let's follow up in the office.

4. Your project sounds really interesting.

   I'd love to keep the conversation going.

## 54.11 LISTEN AND NUMBER THE SENTENCES IN THE ORDER YOU HEAR THEM

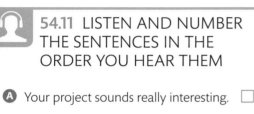

A. Your project sounds really interesting. ☐

B. Any questions before we wrap up? ☐

C. Sorry, I didn't catch your name. ☑ 1

D. Thanks everyone for your input! ☐

E. To sum up, we're going ahead with the new designs. ☐

F. Thanks. I'll let you know if something suitable comes up. ☐

G. You, too. Let's stay in touch. Here's my card. ☐

H. Me, too. Let's follow up in the office. ☐

## 54.12 RESPOND OUT LOUD TO THE AUDIO, FILLING IN THE BLANKS USING THE WORDS IN THE PANEL

| your name | in touch | follow up |

1. It was great meeting you.

   You, too. Let's stay _____ .

2. I understand you work for AbiCo.

   That's right. Sorry, I didn't catch _____ .

3. I've enjoyed our discussion.

   Me, too. Let's _____ in the office.

# 55 Online meetings

## 55.1 GETTING STARTED

Let's get started, shall we?

I'll share the presentation on my screen.

Can you hear me?

I think you're on mute.

That's everyone now.

Great! I'll run through the key points.

## 55.3 CONNECTION PROBLEMS

I think we've lost Sam.

My connection keeps dropping.

Sorry, everyo my Wi-Fi's sl

Sorry, my screen has frozen.

We can hear you, but we can't see you.

Try leaving the meeting and joining again.

## 55.2 MORE PHRASES

Would you like to speak first?

Could you repeat that, please?

Can you enlarge it on your screen?

Sorry for interrupting, please keep going.

## 55.4 THE NEXT MEETING

Should we schedule another meeting?

Good idea. I'll send you an invite.

## 55.5 LISTEN TO PERSON A AND RESPOND AS PERSON B

**A**

**B**

1. Let's get started, shall we?

I'll share the presentation on my screen.

2. Can you hear me?

I think you're on mute.

3. I think we've lost Sam.

My connection keeps dropping.

4. Sorry, my screen has frozen.

Try leaving the meeting and joining again.

## 55.6 LISTEN AND NUMBER THE SENTENCES IN THE ORDER THAT YOU HEAR THEM

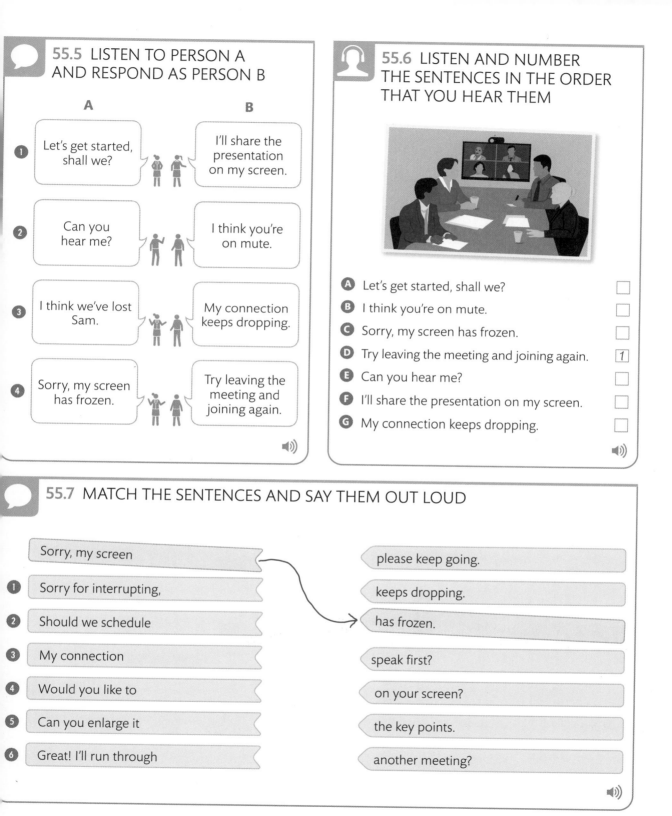

**A** Let's get started, shall we? ☐

**B** I think you're on mute. ☐

**C** Sorry, my screen has frozen. ☐

**D** Try leaving the meeting and joining again. `1`

**E** Can you hear me? ☐

**F** I'll share the presentation on my screen. ☐

**G** My connection keeps dropping. ☐

## 55.7 MATCH THE SENTENCES AND SAY THEM OUT LOUD

Sorry, my screen —— has frozen.

1. Sorry for interrupting, | please keep going.

2. Should we schedule | keeps dropping.

3. My connection | speak first?

4. Would you like to | on your screen?

5. Can you enlarge it | the key points.

6. Great! I'll run through | another meeting?

## 56.1 HOMES AND NEIGHBORHOODS

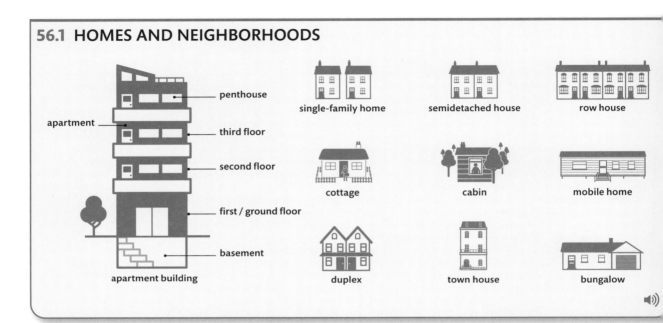

apartment building — penthouse, apartment, third floor, second floor, first / ground floor, basement

single-family home

semidetached house

row house

cottage

cabin

mobile home

duplex

town house

bungalow

## 56.2 ROOMS AND HOME AREAS

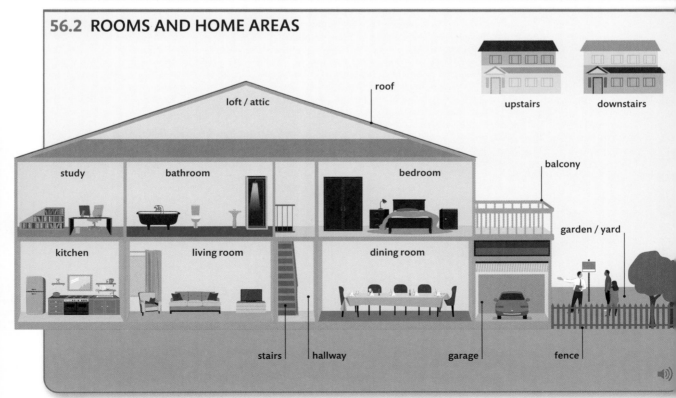

roof

loft / attic

upstairs

downstairs

balcony

garden / yard

study

bathroom

bedroom

kitchen

living room

dining room

stairs

hallway

garage

fence

## 56.3 HOME IMPROVEMENTS

to paint a door

to grout tiles

to strip the walls

to fill a crack

to rewire the house

to fix a fence

to hang shelves

to lay a carpet

to sew curtains

to build an extension

## 56.4 APPLIANCES AND FURNITURE

top-freezer fridge

oven

washing machine

dishwasher

kitchen sink

bathtub

shower

toilet

bathroom sink

mirror

bed

crib

closet

nightstand

chest of drawers

couch

armchair

coffee table

ottoman

toy box

shelf

bookcase

dining table

dining chair

television / TV

sideboard

# 57 Finding a new home

## 57.1 HOUSE HUNTING

"What sort of property are you looking for?"

"A one-bedroom place in the city center."

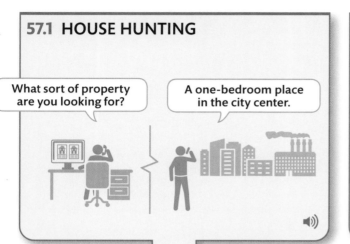

## 57.2 SAYING WHAT YOU WANT

I'm looking for an apartment on the ground floor.

We'd like a house with a yard.

I want a property close to the subway.

We'd prefer somewhere near a school.

We need at least two bedrooms.

## 57.3 VIEWING A PROPERTY

"Thanks for showing us around. I love the location!"

"What do you think of the inside?"

"It's a good size, but it needs a lot of work."

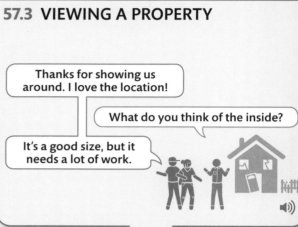

## 57.4 GIVING FEEDBACK

I think it's too small for us.

It's on a busy road.

I really like the layout.

We'd need to put in a new kitchen.

We like it, but the price is too high.

## 57.5 PUTTING IN AN OFFER

"How do you feel after seeing it again?"

"We love it even more!"

"Would you like to put in an offer?"

"Yes, for $5,000 under the asking price."

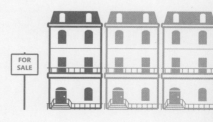

FOR SALE

## 57.6 LISTEN TO PERSON A AND RESPOND AS PERSON B

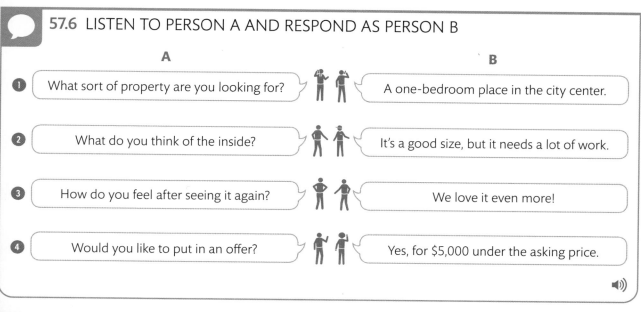

**A**

**B**

1. What sort of property are you looking for? — A one-bedroom place in the city center.

2. What do you think of the inside? — It's a good size, but it needs a lot of work.

3. How do you feel after seeing it again? — We love it even more!

4. Would you like to put in an offer? — Yes, for $5,000 under the asking price.

## 57.7 MATCH THE SENTENCES AND SAY THEM OUT LOUD

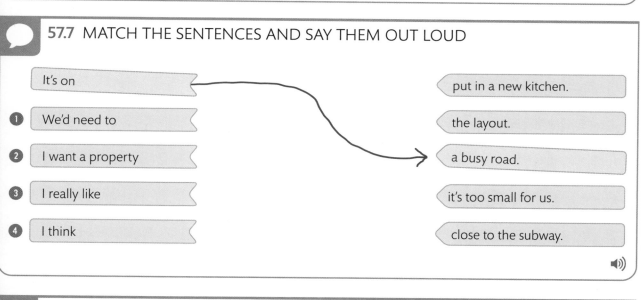

It's on — a busy road.

1. We'd need to — put in a new kitchen.

2. I want a property — the layout.

3. I really like — it's too small for us.

4. I think — close to the subway.

## 57.8 USE THE CHART TO CREATE NINE SENTENCES AND SAY THEM OUT LOUD

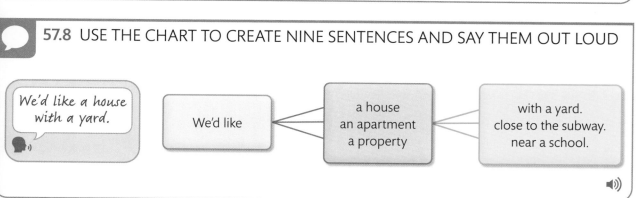

*We'd like a house with a yard.*

| We'd like | a house / an apartment / a property | with a yard. / close to the subway. / near a school. |

## 57.9 RENTING A HOME

How long is the lease?

One year, with an option to renew.

How soon could we move in?

As soon as you've signed the rental agreement!

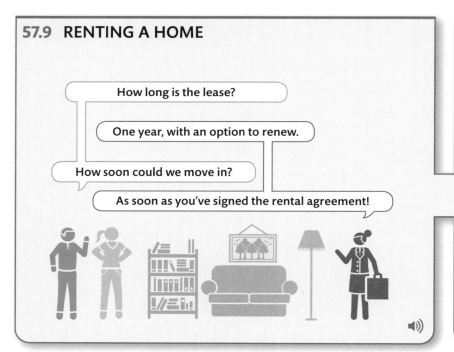

## 57.10 MORE QUESTIONS

How much is the rent?

Do I pay the rent monthly?

Does it have a washer and dryer?

Do you need a deposit?

Are utility bills included?

Are pets allowed?

Can I have a roommate?

What references do you need?

## 57.11 DURING THE RENTAL

Can I put this picture up?

Yes, as long as it doesn't leave marks on the wall.

The washing machine is leaking.

I'll get maintenance to come and look at it.

## 57.12 VOCABULARY RENTING PROPERTY

landlord / landlady

tenant

roommate

rent

deposit

rental agreement

furnished

unfurnished

utility bills

## 57.13 LISTEN AND NUMBER THE SENTENCES IN THE ORDER YOU HEAR THEM

**A** How soon could we move in? ☐

**B** One year, with an option to renew. ☐ 1

**C** Does it have a washer and dryer? ☐

**D** The washing machine is leaking. ☐

**E** Can I have a roommate? ☐

**F** How much is the rent? ☐

## 57.14 SAY THE SENTENCES OUT LOUD, REPLACING THE PICTURES WITH WORDS

**1** How much is the ____ ?

**2** Are ____ included?

**3** Can I put this ____ up?

**4** The ____ is leaking.

**5** Are ____ allowed?

**6** As soon as you've signed the ____ !

## 57.15 SAY THE SENTENCES OUT LOUD, FILLING IN THE BLANKS USING THE WORDS IN THE PANEL

| bills | roommate | pay | renew | deposit | references |

**1** Can I have a _____ ?

**2** One year, with an option to _____ .

**3** Are utility _____ included?

**4** Do you need a _____ ?

**5** Do I _____ the rent monthly?

**6** What _____ do you need?

# 58 Moving

## 58.1 PACKING UP

I'm moving! Do you have any spare boxes?

There are lots in the back. Help yourself!

Is everything packed and ready?

Yes, we're done. Let's load the van!

## 58.2 MOVING DAY

I'm here to pick up the keys to my house.

Here you are. Hope the move goes well!

Where do you want us to start?

Can you take the boxes in the kitchen first?

The unpacking is all done!

Nice work! Now, sit down and have some coffee.

## 58.3 VOCABULARY RELOCATION

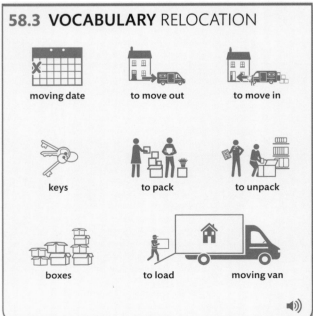

moving date

to move out

to move in

keys

to pack

to unpack

boxes

to load

moving van

## 58.4 MORE PHRASES

I've told everyone our moving date.

We have to move out by the weekend.

I've packed up the bedroom.

Let's load the moving van!

We can unpack in the morning.

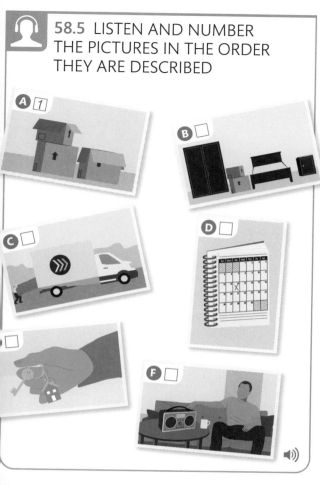

**58.5 LISTEN AND NUMBER THE PICTURES IN THE ORDER THEY ARE DESCRIBED**

A ☐ 1

B ☐

C ☐

D ☐

☐

F ☐

**58.6 SAY THE SENTENCES OUT LOUD, FILLING IN THE BLANKS USING THE WORDS IN THE PANEL**

| unpack | ready | the move | packed |
| weekend | load | boxes | moving |

1 Is everything packed and _____ ?

2 Hope _____ goes well!

3 Do you have any spare _____ ?

4 I've told everyone our _____ date.

5 We have to move out by the _____ .

6 I've _____ up the bedroom.

7 Let's _____ the moving van!

8 We can _____ in the morning.

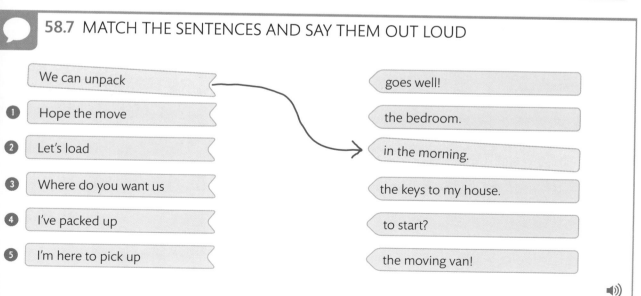

**58.7 MATCH THE SENTENCES AND SAY THEM OUT LOUD**

We can unpack — goes well!

1 Hope the move — the bedroom.

2 Let's load — in the morning.

3 Where do you want us — the keys to my house.

4 I've packed up — to start?

5 I'm here to pick up — the moving van!

# 59 Meeting the neighbors

## 59.1 INTRODUCING YOURSELF

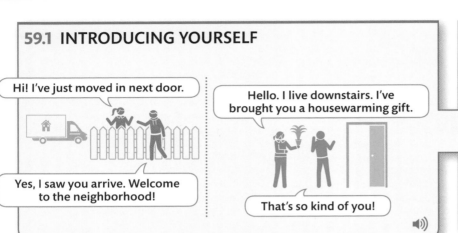

Hi! I've just moved in next door.

Yes, I saw you arrive. Welcome to the neighborhood!

Hello. I live downstairs. I've brought you a housewarming gift.

That's so kind of you!

## 59.2 MORE PHRASES

It's so nice to meet you.

We've moved here from Beijing.

I'm your new neighbor.

I wanted to introduce myself.

I just came over to say hello.

## 59.3 SOCIALIZING

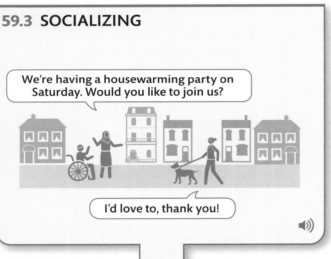

We're having a housewarming party on Saturday. Would you like to join us?

I'd love to, thank you!

## 59.5 SHARING INFORMATION

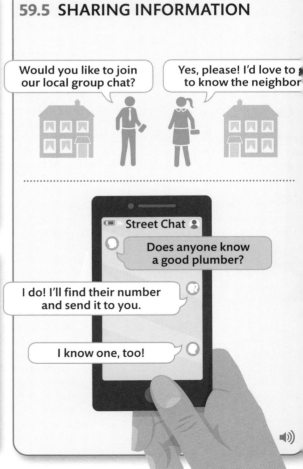

Would you like to join our local group chat?

Yes, please! I'd love to get to know the neighbor

**Street Chat**

Does anyone know a good plumber?

I do! I'll find their number and send it to you.

I know one, too!

## 59.4 MORE PHRASES

Would you like to stop by for drinks later?

Are you free for lunch on Sunday?

Can you come over for coffee tomorrow?

I'm having a cookout next week, if you'd like to come?

## 59.6 LISTEN TO PERSON A AND RESPOND AS PERSON B

**A**

**B**

① Hi! I've just moved in next door.

Yes, I saw you arrive. Welcome to the neighborhood!

② Hello. I live downstairs. I've brought you a housewarming gift.

That's so kind of you!

③ We're having a housewarming party on Saturday. Would you like to join us?

I'd love to, thank you!

④ Would you like to join our local group chat?

Yes, please! I'd love to get to know the neighbors.

⑤ Does anyone know a good plumber?

I do! I'll find their number and send it to you.

## 59.7 LISTEN AND NUMBER THE SENTENCES IN THE ORDER YOU HEAR THEM

🅐 It's so nice to meet you. ☐

🅑 Can you come over for coffee tomorrow? ☐

🅒 I'm your new neighbor. ☐

🅓 I wanted to introduce myself. ☐

🅔 I just came over to say hello. ☐

🅕 Are you free for lunch on Sunday? ☐

🅖 We've moved here from Beijing. ☐ 1

🅗 Would you like to stop by for drinks later? ☐

## 59.8 USE THE CHART TO CREATE NINE SENTENCES AND SAY THEM OUT LOUD

*Are you free for drinks later?*

Are you free for

drinks
lunch
coffee

later?
tomorrow?
on Sunday?

# 60 Household chores

## 60.1 SHARING TASKS

Hey, what are you up to?

I'm making a chore list.

Your turn to wash the dishes, then!

Whose turn is it to empty the dishwasher?

I did it last time, so it's yours!

Have you finished doing laundry yet?

Almost! Can you help me put it away?

🌐 GOOD TO KNOW

In English, it's easy to confuse the verbs **to make** and **to do**! **To do** is associated with work and often used for chores. The main exception is **to make the bed**.

## 60.2 SPRING-CLEANING

There we go. The house looks much tidier now!

Phew! That was a major spring-clean!

I've cleaned the counters and the oven.

Great job! The kitchen was in a bad state.

## 60.3 VOCABULARY HOUSEWORK

to do laundry

to wash dishes

to do the vacuuming

to empty the dishwasher

to clean the bathtub

to sweep the floor

to put the trash out

to tidy up

to make the bed

## 60.4 LISTEN TO PERSON A AND RESPOND AS PERSON B

**A**

**B**

① Hey, what are you up to?

I'm making a chore list.

② Have you finished doing laundry yet?

Almost! Can you help me put it away?

③ I've cleaned the counters and the oven.

Great job! The kitchen was in a bad state.

④ There we go. The house looks much tidier now!

Phew! That was a major spring-clean!

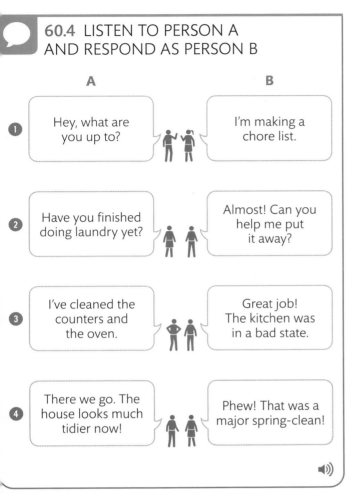

## 60.5 LISTEN AND CIRCLE THE ITEM YOU HEAR

① (A) B

② A B

③ A B

④ A B

## 60.6 MATCH THE SENTENCES AND SAY THEM OUT LOUD

Have you finished doing → laundry yet?

① Whose turn is it to empty — the dishwasher?

② I've cleaned the counters — and the oven.

③ Great job! The kitchen — was in a bad state.

④ Phew! That was — a major spring-clean!

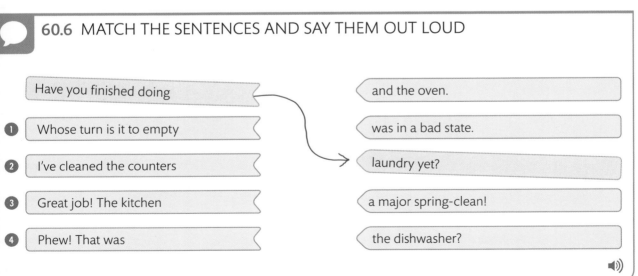

### 61.1 DIY DECORATING

How are you coming along?

The tiles are all up. Just the grouting to go and I'm done!

I've finished stripping the walls.

Great! Let's hang this new wallpaper, then.

It's looking good!

Thank you. One more coat of paint should do it, I think.

### 61.2 HIRING A PROFESSIONAL

ABC Decorators, how can I help?

Hi, we need someone to hang some shelves

Sure, we can do that for you.

Are you able to come over and give us a quot

I could come over on Thursday.

### 61.3 MORE PHRASES

Could you put together this chest of drawers?

Can you give us a quote for fixing our fence?

We need someone to paint our kitchen walls.

I'd like a quote for laying a carpet.

Is that your best quote?

Will you supply the materials?

## 61.4 LISTEN TO PERSON A AND RESPOND AS PERSON B

**A**

**B**

**1** How are you coming along?

The tiles are all up. Just the grouting to go and I'm done!

**2** I've finished stripping the walls.

Great! Let's hang this new wallpaper, then.

**3** ABC Decorators, how can I help?

Hi, we need someone to hang some shelves.

**4** Are you able to come over and give us a quote?

I could come over on Thursday.

**5** Hi, we need someone to put up some shelves.

Sure, we can do that for you.

## 61.5 LISTEN AND NUMBER THE SENTENCES IN THE ORDER YOU HEAR THEM

**A** Thank you. One more coat of paint should do it, I think. ☐

**B** Can you give us a quote for fixing our fence? ☐

**C** We need someone to paint our kitchen walls. [1]

**D** Is that your best quote? ☐

**E** Are you able to come over and give us a quote? ☐

**F** I'd like a quote for laying a carpet. ☐

**G** ABC Decorators, how can I help? ☐

**H** The tiles are all up. Just the grouting to go and I'm done! ☐

**I** How are you coming along? ☐

## 61.6 USE THE CHART TO CREATE EIGHT SENTENCES AND SAY THEM OUT LOUD

*Could you give us a quote for fixing our fence?*

| Could you Are you able to | give us a quote for | fixing our fence? hanging some shelves? laying a carpet? painting our kitchen walls? |

# 62 Pets

## 62.1 ADOPTING A RESCUE ANIMAL

Hi, I'd like to adopt a cat.

I'm looking to adopt one of your dogs.

Are you looking for a particular breed?

Does she like other cats?

Is she good with children?

Is anyone home during the day?

Yes, I work from home.

## 62.2 SEEING THE VET

What seems to be the problem?

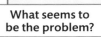

She's lost weight and stopped eating.

I think he has a broken leg.

Yes, we'll need to do an X-ray.

## 62.3 MORE PROBLEMS

My dog has hurt his paw.

My cat keeps getting sick.

My rabbit is losing her fur.

My puppy is very quiet.

She's always thirsty.

## 62.4 VOCABULARY PET CARE

vaccination

flea treatment

eye drops

grooming

microchip

pet passport

## 62.5 LOOKING AFTER YOUR PET

So we have to get him microchipped ...

... give him his flea treatment ...

... get him a passport ...

... and book his vaccinations!

## 62.6 LISTEN TO PERSON A AND RESPOND AS PERSON B

A | B

1 I'm looking to adopt one of your dogs. | Are you looking for a particular breed?

2 Is anyone home during the day? | Yes, I work from home.

3 What seems to be the problem? | She's lost weight and stopped eating.

4 I think he has a broken leg. | Yes, we'll need to do an X-ray.

## 62.7 LISTEN AND NUMBER THE PICTURES IN THE ORDER THEY ARE DESCRIBED

A 1    B ☐

C ☐    D ☐

E ☐    F ☐

## 62.8 MATCH THE SENTENCES AND SAY THEM OUT LOUD

My cat keeps — getting sick.

1 Is she good — with children?

2 I think he has — a broken leg.

3 She's lost weight — and stopped eating.

4 Hi, I'd like to — adopt a cat.

5 We have to get him microchipped — and book his vaccinations!

# 63 Home emergencies

## 63.1 POWER PROBLEMS

"What's happening?"

"The power has gone out. I'll check the fuse box."

"A breaker has tripped. Let's see if I can get it working …"

"Try turning the lights on now …"

"The power is back on!"

## 63.2 PROFESSIONAL HELP

"My dishwasher's leaking …"

"I can be there in an hour. My callout fee is $80."

"Okay, so what seems to be the problem?"

"The faucet has been dripping for days."

"My shower keeps turning cold!"

"When was the furnace last serviced?"

## 63.3 MORE PHRASES

I have a leaking roof.

My toilet is overflowing.

There's no hot water.

The heat won't come on.

The window is broken.

## 63.4 VOCABULARY HOUSEHOLD PROBLEMS

broken window

burst pipe

broken-down furnace

overflowing toilet

leaking roof

clogged sink

dripping faucet

power outage

## 63.5 LISTEN TO PERSON A AND RESPOND AS PERSON B

| A | B |
|---|---|
| **1** What's happening? | The power has gone out. |
| **2** Try turning the lights on now ... | The power is back on! |
| **3** Okay, so what seems to be the problem? | The faucet has been dripping for days. |
| **4** My shower keeps turning cold! | When was the furnace last serviced? |

## 63.6 LISTEN AND NUMBER THE SENTENCES IN THE ORDER YOU HEAR THEM

**A** My toilet is overflowing. ☐

**B** When was the furnace last serviced? ☐

**C** Try turning the lights on now ... ☐

**D** The window is broken. ☐ 1

**E** The power is back on! ☐

**F** I have a leaking roof. ☐

**G** There's no hot water. ☐

**H** A breaker has tripped. ☐

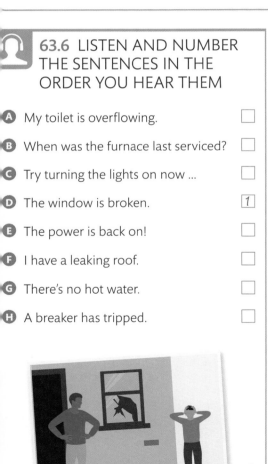

## 63.7 RESPOND OUT LOUD TO THE AUDIO, FILLING IN THE BLANKS USING THE WORDS IN THE PANEL

back on     serviced     dripping     gone out

**1** What's happening?

The power has _____ .

**2** Try turning the lights on now ...

The power is _____ !

**3** Okay, so what seems to be the problem?

The faucet has been _____ for days.

**4** My shower keeps turning cold!

When was the furnace last _____ ?

# Home entertainment

## 64.1 WATCHING TV

What should we watch tonight?

We could try this new detective series.

That was great—want to check out the next episode?

It's not streaming yet. How about some sports?

Do you have the remote? I can't hear anything.

Yes, here it is. I'll turn it up

## 64.2 GAMING

I'm so gonna win this!

Oh no! You got me again!

Your screen time's up now.

But I really want to finish this game! Just five more minutes ...

Should we play the next level?

I'm just grabbing a bite to eat—be right back!

## 64.3 MORE PHRASES

Can you turn on the subtitles?

Do you have another controller?

My tablet has frozen!

Is the console plugged in?

## 64.4 **VOCABULARY** HOME ENTERTAINMENT

smart TV

remote

subtitles

headphones

console

smart speakers

controller

tablet

## 64.5 LISTEN TO PERSON A AND RESPOND AS PERSON B

**A**

**B**

1. **A:** What should we watch tonight?
   **B:** We could try this new detective series.

2. **A:** Do you have the remote? I can't hear anything.
   **B:** Yes, here it is. I'll turn it up.

3. **A:** I'm so gonna win this!
   **B:** Oh no! You got me again!

4. **A:** Should we play the next level?
   **B:** I'm just grabbing a bite to eat—be right back!

## 64.6 LISTEN AND NUMBER THE PICTURES IN THE ORDER THEY ARE DESCRIBED

A ☐    B [1]

C ☐    D ☐

E ☐    F ☐

G ☐    H ☐

## 64.7 MATCH THE SENTENCES AND SAY THEM OUT LOUD

Do you have — another controller?

1. Should we play — the next level?

2. Can you turn on — the subtitles?

3. Is the console — plugged in?

4. What should we — watch tonight?

159

# 65 Getting around

## 65.1 TRANSPORTATION

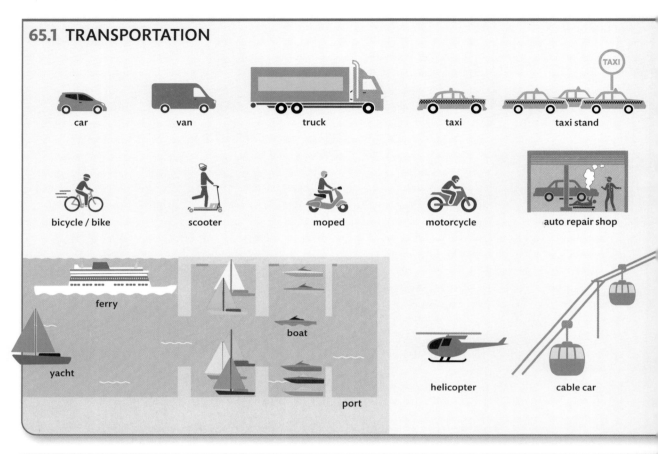

car · van · truck · taxi · taxi stand

bicycle / bike · scooter · moped · motorcycle · auto repair shop

ferry · boat · yacht · port · helicopter · cable car

## 65.2 VERBS

to board a plane · to take off · to land · to tap in · to tap out

to wait for a bus · to get on a bus · to drive a car · to give someone a ride · to book a taxi / cab

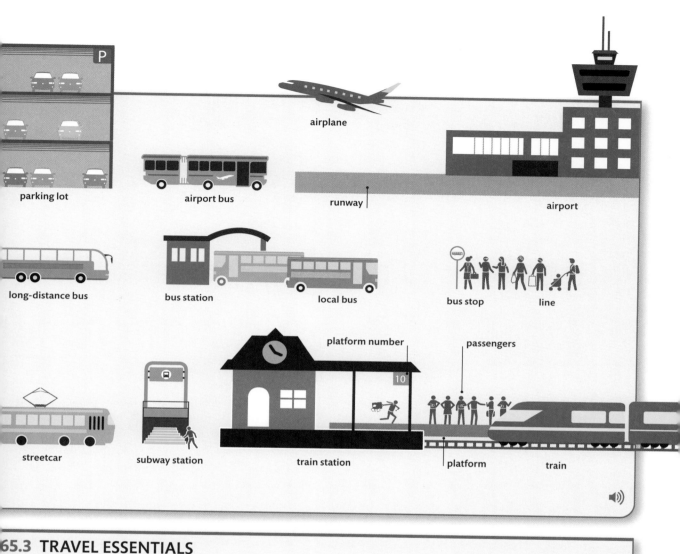

parking lot

airport bus

airplane

runway

airport

long-distance bus

bus station

local bus

bus stop

line

platform number

passengers

streetcar

subway station

train station

platform

train

## 65.3 TRAVEL ESSENTIALS

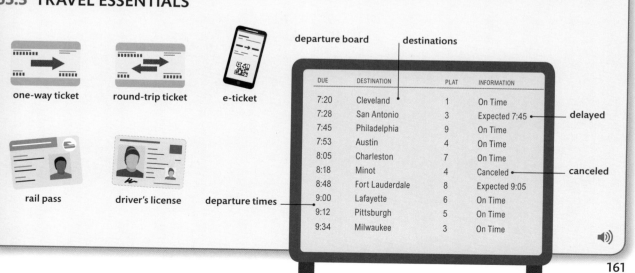

one-way ticket

round-trip ticket

e-ticket

rail pass

driver's license

departure board

destinations

departure times

| DUE | DESTINATION | PLAT | INFORMATION | |
|-----|-------------|------|-------------|---|
| 7:20 | Cleveland | 1 | On Time | |
| 7:28 | San Antonio | 3 | Expected 7:45 | delayed |
| 7:45 | Philadelphia | 9 | On Time | |
| 7:53 | Austin | 4 | On Time | |
| 8:05 | Charleston | 7 | On Time | |
| 8:18 | Minot | 4 | Canceled | canceled |
| 8:48 | Fort Lauderdale | 8 | Expected 9:05 | |
| 9:00 | Lafayette | 6 | On Time | |
| 9:12 | Pittsburgh | 5 | On Time | |
| 9:34 | Milwaukee | 3 | On Time | |

# 66 Local and long-distance buses

## 66.1 GETTING THE BUS

Does this bus go to the town center?

Yes, via the railway station.

Can I have a one-way ticket to the museum, please?

That's $3, please.

Thanks. I'll pay by contactless.

Are we nearly at the library?

We're almost there—it's the next stop.

## 66.2 MORE QUESTIONS

Where is the nearest bus stop?

Is this the right stop for the airport bus?

How much is the fare?

Are you stopping at the shopping center?

What time is the next bus?

What time is the last bus from this stop?

## 66.3 LONG-DISTANCE BUS JOURNEYS

Could I see your ticket, please?

Here you go.

Great. We arrive in Atlanta at 4:45.

Hello. Are there bathrooms on the bus?

And is there Wi-Fi on board?

Yes, they're right at the bac[k]

Yup, just log on to our netwo[rk]

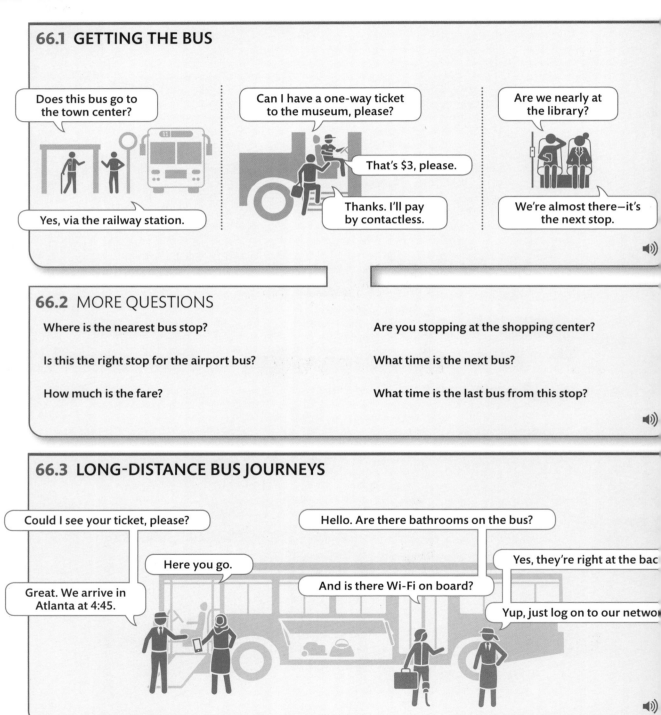

## 66.4 LISTEN TO PERSON A AND RESPOND AS PERSON B

| | A | | B |
|---|---|---|---|
| 1 | Could I see your ticket, please? | | Here you go. |
| 2 | Does this bus go to the town center? | | Yes, via the railway station. |
| 3 | That's $3, please. | | Thanks. I'll pay by contactless. |
| 4 | Are we nearly at the library? | | We're almost there—it's the next stop. |

## 66.5 LISTEN TO THE AUDIO AND MATCH THE CORRECT RESPONSE

That's $3, please.

Yup, just log on to our network.

1. Are we nearly at the library?

Yes, via the railway station.

2. Does this bus go to the town center?

We're almost there—it's the next stop.

3. Hello. Are there bathrooms on the bus?

Thanks. I'll pay by contactless.

4. Is there Wi-Fi on board?

Yes, they're right at the back.

## 66.6 USE THE CHART TO CREATE NINE SENTENCES AND SAY THEM OUT LOUD

*Excuse me, does this bus go to the library?*

| Excuse me, | does this bus go to<br>are we nearly at<br>is this the right stop for | the library?<br>the town center?<br>the shopping center? |
|---|---|---|

163

# 67 Train and subway travel

## 67.1 BUYING TICKETS

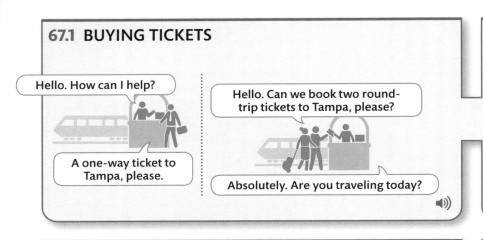

Hello. How can I help?

A one-way ticket to Tampa, please.

Hello. Can we book two round-trip tickets to Tampa, please?

Absolutely. Are you traveling today?

## 67.2 MORE PHRASES

How much is a one-way ticket to Houston?

Can I reserve a seat?

Let's wait in the waiting area.

Do I tap in at the turnstile?

## 67.3 ASKING FOR INFORMATION

Which platform for the Seattle train?

Platform 6. It leaves in 15 minutes.

There's a really long line for tickets!

Let's try the ticket machines.

## 67.4 MORE QUESTIONS

Has the Atlanta train left yet?

When is the Newark train due?

Does this train stop at Birmingham?

What time is the next Nashville service?

## 67.5 VOCABULARY TRAIN TRAVEL

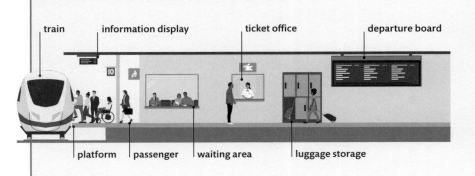

train

information display

ticket office

departure board

platform    passenger    waiting area    luggage storage

seat

ticket machine

ticket inspector

turnstile

## 67.6 LISTEN TO PERSON A AND RESPOND AS PERSON B

**A**

**B**

1. Hello. How can I help?

   A one-way ticket to Tampa, please.

2. Hello. Can we book two round-trip tickets to Tampa, please?

   Absolutely. Are you traveling today?

3. There's a really long line for tickets!

   Let's try the ticket machines.

4. Which platform for the Seattle train?

   Platform 6. It leaves in 15 minutes.

## 67.7 LISTEN AND NUMBER THE PICTURES IN THE ORDER THEY ARE DESCRIBED

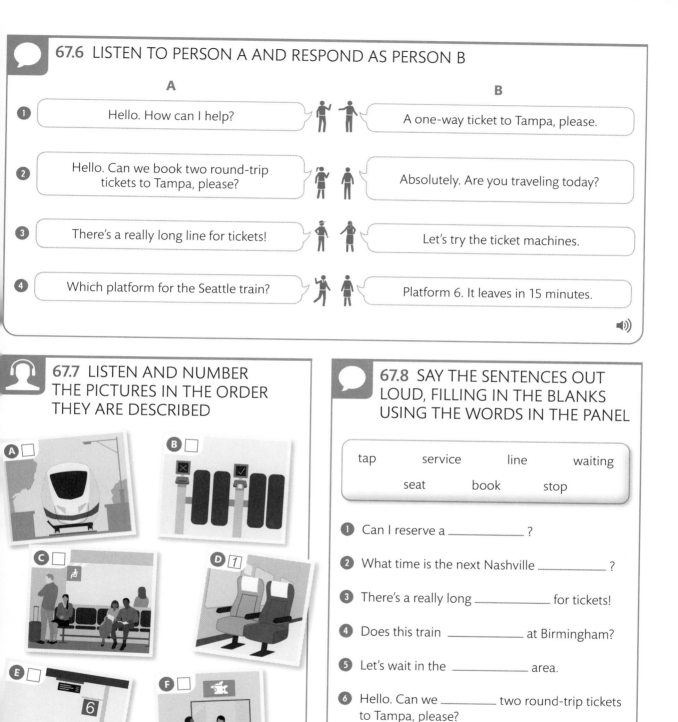

A ☐

B ☐

C ☐

D 1

E 6

F ☐

## 67.8 SAY THE SENTENCES OUT LOUD, FILLING IN THE BLANKS USING THE WORDS IN THE PANEL

| tap | service | line | waiting |
|-----|---------|------|---------|
| | seat | book | stop |

1. Can I reserve a _____ ?

2. What time is the next Nashville _____ ?

3. There's a really long _____ for tickets!

4. Does this train _____ at Birmingham?

5. Let's wait in the _____ area.

6. Hello. Can we _____ two round-trip tickets to Tampa, please?

7. Do I _____ in at the turnstile?

## 67.9 PROBLEMS AND WARNINGS

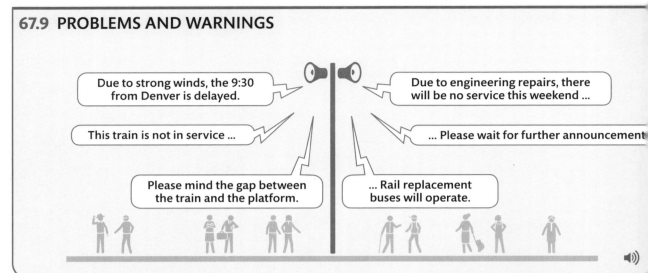

## 67.10 ON THE TRAIN

## 67.11 ON THE SUBWAY

## 67.12 LISTEN TO PERSON A AND RESPOND AS PERSON B

**A**

**B**

**1** Which way is the dining car, please? — That way, next carriage!

**2** Do you mind if I plug my laptop in here? — Sure, no problem.

**3** Excuse me, how many stops is it to Broadway? — Let's see … it's five stops from here.

**4** How do I get to Central Park? — Take the A train to Columbus Circle.

## 67.13 LISTEN AND NUMBER THE SENTENCES IN THE ORDER YOU HEAR THEM

**A** Please mind the gap between the train and the platform. ☐

**B** Please wait for further announcements. ☑1

**C** Rail replacement buses will operate. ☐

**D** Due to strong winds, the 9:30 from Denver is delayed. ☐

**E** Thanks. Can I see your rail pass, too, please? ☐

## 67.14 USE THE CHART TO CREATE EIGHT SENTENCES AND SAY THEM OUT LOUD

*Excuse me, how do I get to Tampa?*

Excuse me,

how do I get
how many stops is it
how much is a round-trip ticket
how much is a one-way ticket

to Tampa?
to Atlanta?

# 68 At the airport

## 68.1 DEPARTURES

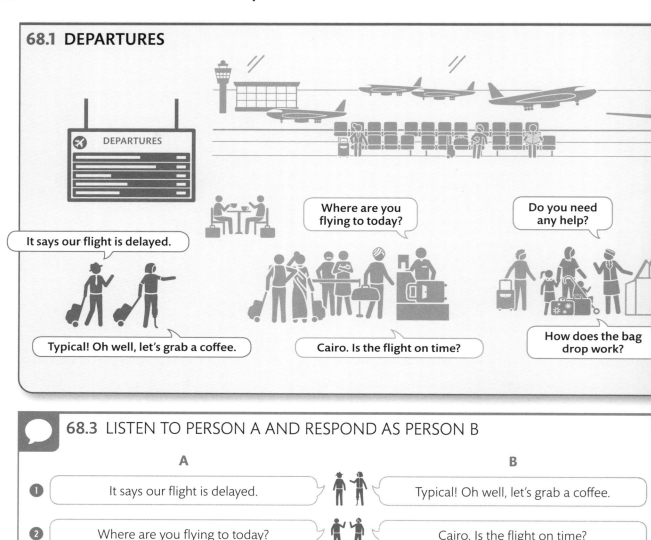

It says our flight is delayed.

Typical! Oh well, let's grab a coffee.

Where are you flying to today?

Cairo. Is the flight on time?

Do you need any help?

How does the bag drop work?

## 68.3 LISTEN TO PERSON A AND RESPOND AS PERSON B

| A | B |
|---|---|
| ❶ It says our flight is delayed. | Typical! Oh well, let's grab a coffee. |
| ❷ Where are you flying to today? | Cairo. Is the flight on time? |
| ❸ Do you need any help? | How does the bag drop work? |
| ❹ Place your bag in the bin, please! | Then come through the scanner. |
| ❺ Which gate is it for Athens? | Gate 14. Hurry—it's closing in 10 minutes! |

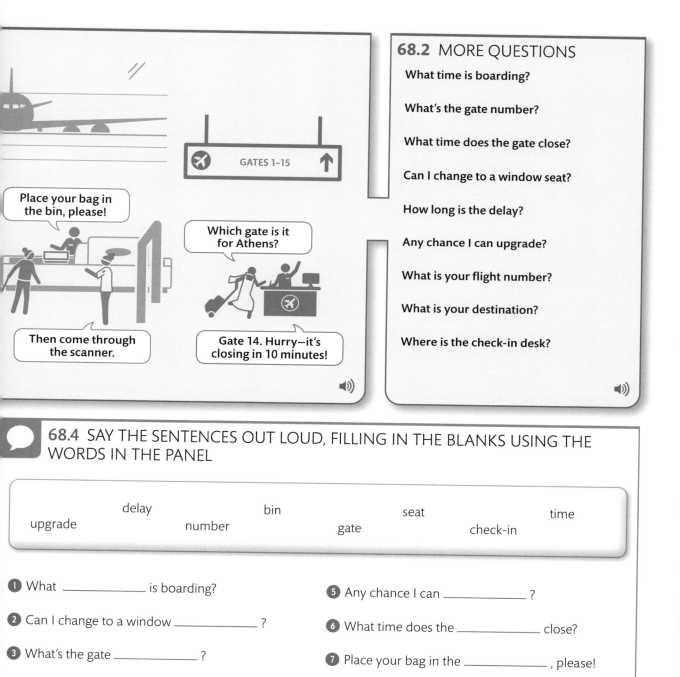

**Place your bag in the bin, please!**

**GATES 1–15**

**Then come through the scanner.**

**Which gate is it for Athens?**

**Gate 14. Hurry—it's closing in 10 minutes!**

## 68.2 MORE QUESTIONS

**What time is boarding?**

**What's the gate number?**

**What time does the gate close?**

**Can I change to a window seat?**

**How long is the delay?**

**Any chance I can upgrade?**

**What is your flight number?**

**What is your destination?**

**Where is the check-in desk?**

## 68.4 SAY THE SENTENCES OUT LOUD, FILLING IN THE BLANKS USING THE WORDS IN THE PANEL

| | | | | | |
|---|---|---|---|---|---|
| upgrade | delay | number | bin | seat | time |
| | | | gate | check-in | |

➊ What _____ is boarding?

➋ Can I change to a window _____ ?

➌ What's the gate _____ ?

➍ How long is the _____ ?

➎ Any chance I can _____ ?

➏ What time does the _____ close?

➐ Place your bag in the _____ , please!

➑ Where is the _____ desk?

## 68.5 BOARDING AND TAKING OFF

Welcome! Can I see your boarding pass?

Hello! Here you go.

I'll put our stuff in the overhead bin.

Thanks. I'll keep my bag under the seat.

Ladies and gentlemen, welcome to Flight 86A for Beijing.

We are ready for departure.

## 68.6 DURING THE FLIGHT

We'll shortly be passing through the cabin with snacks and drinks.

This is your captain speaking. We are experiencing some turbulence.

Please return to your seat and fasten your seat belt.

## 68.7 LANDING

Your tray tables should be securely fastened.

Make sure your seat is in the upright position.

Please switch your digital devices to "airplane" mode.

We will arrive in Beijing at 9:20 local time.

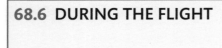

## 68.8 VOCABULARY IN THE CABIN

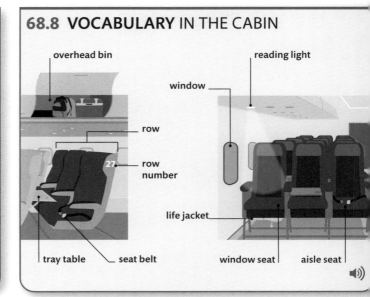

overhead bin

reading light

window

row

row number

life jacket

tray table

seat belt

window seat

aisle seat

## 68.9 LISTEN AND NUMBER THE PICTURES IN THE ORDER THEY ARE DESCRIBED

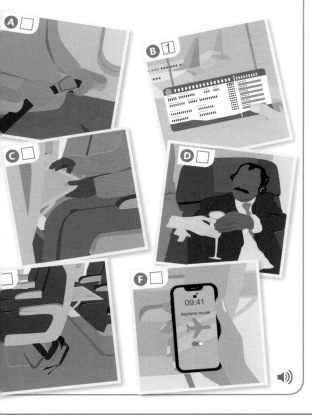

A ☐

B ☐ 1

C ☐

D ☐

☐

F ☐

09:41
Airplane mode

🔊

## 68.10 LISTEN AND NUMBER THE SENTENCES IN THE ORDER YOU HEAR THEM

Ⓐ I'll put our stuff in the overhead bin. ☐

Ⓑ We are experiencing some turbulence. ☐

Ⓒ Ladies and gentlemen, welcome to Flight 86A for Beijing. ☐

Ⓓ Make sure your seat is in the upright position. ☐ 1

Ⓔ We will arrive in Beijing at 9:20 local time. ☐

Ⓕ We are ready for departure. ☐

🔊

## 68.11 MATCH THE SENTENCES AND SAY THEM OUT LOUD

Welcome! Can I see → your boarding pass?

to "airplane" mode.

should be securely fastened.

1. I'll put our stuff — in the overhead bin.

2. Please switch your digital devices

3. We'll shortly be passing through — the cabin with snacks and drinks.

4. Your tray tables

5. Make sure your seat — is in the upright position.

🔊

## 68.12 ARRIVALS

What is the purpose of your trip?

I'm visiting friends.

Which baggage-claim carousel do we need to go to?

It's carousel 3. I'll grab a cart.

I can't see our suitcases anywhere!

Let's go check at the baggage desk.

## 68.13 RENTING A CAR

Hi! I'm here to pick up a rental car. Here's my booking confirmation.

Great! Can I see your driver's license, please?

Is the car ready for us?

Yes, it's in section 6. Enjoy your trip!

## 68.14 LISTEN AND CIRCLE THE ITEM YOU HEAR

1  A  B

2  A  B

3  A  B

4  A  B

**Can I see your customs declaration form?**

CUSTOMS

**Here it is!**

**Hi, can I help?**

**Yes, I need to exchange some Euros. What's your rate?**

**Where do we meet our taxi?**

**The driver should be waiting for us.**

68.15 LISTEN TO PERSON A AND RESPOND AS PERSON B

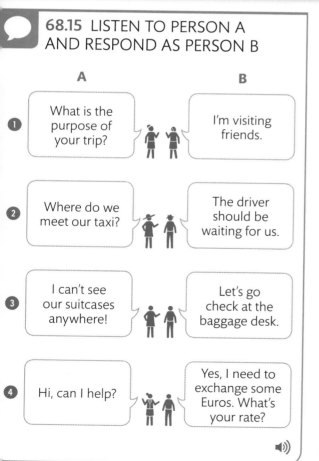

| A | B |
|---|---|
| ❶ What is the purpose of your trip? | I'm visiting friends. |
| ❷ Where do we meet our taxi? | The driver should be waiting for us. |
| ❸ I can't see our suitcases anywhere! | Let's go check at the baggage desk. |
| ❹ Hi, can I help? | Yes, I need to exchange some Euros. What's your rate? |

68.16 SAY THE SENTENCES OUT LOUD, REPLACING THE PICTURES WITH WORDS

❶ Where do we meet our ⬚ ?

❷ I can't see our ⬚ anywhere!

❸ It's carousel 3. I'll grab a ⬚ .

❹ Yes, I need to exchange some ⬚ .

❺ I'm here to pick up a rental ⬚ .

# 69 Cycling

## 69.1 BUYING A BIKE

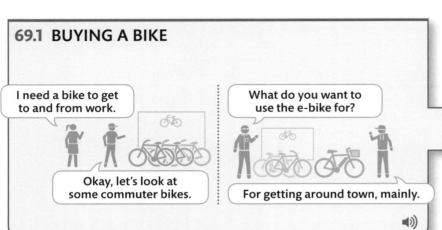

I need a bike to get to and from work.

Okay, let's look at some commuter bikes.

What do you want to use the e-bike for?

For getting around town, mainly.

## 69.2 QUESTIONS YOU MAY HEAR

What type of bike do you want?

What's your budget?

Would you like a test ride?

Will you be taking it on public transportation?

## 69.3 RENTING A BIKE

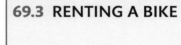

How do I rent this city bike?

You just need to download the app!

Where can we park after our ride?

There are bike docks all over town.

## 69.4 BIKE PROBLEMS

What's up with the bike?

The chain is broken.

The front tire is flat.

The brakes are loose.

The battery needs charging.

## 69.5 VOCABULARY PARTS OF A BICYCLE

saddle

frame

brake

handlebars

light

tire

pedal

gears

wheel

spokes

chain

helmet

to repair

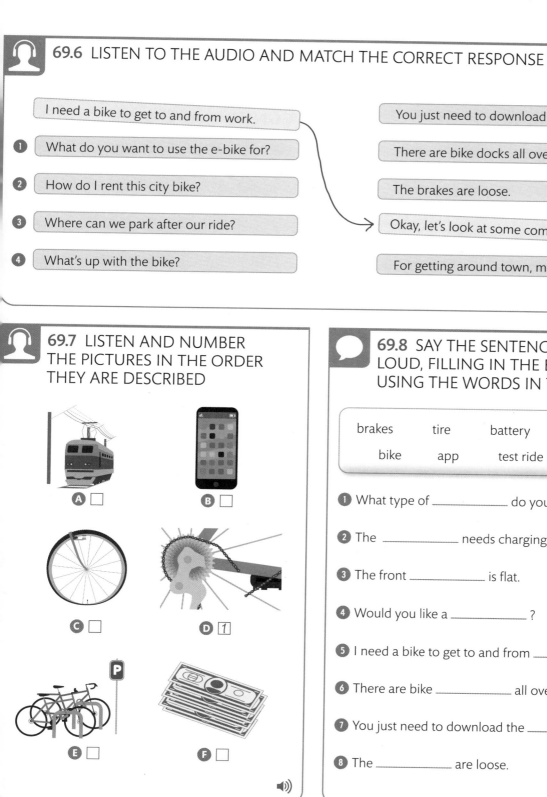

## 69.6 LISTEN TO THE AUDIO AND MATCH THE CORRECT RESPONSE

I need a bike to get to and from work.

You just need to download the app!

1 What do you want to use the e-bike for?

There are bike docks all over town.

2 How do I rent this city bike?

The brakes are loose.

3 Where can we park after our ride?

Okay, let's look at some commuter bikes.

4 What's up with the bike?

For getting around town, mainly.

## 69.7 LISTEN AND NUMBER THE PICTURES IN THE ORDER THEY ARE DESCRIBED

A ☐

B ☐

C ☐

D 1

E ☐

F ☐

## 69.8 SAY THE SENTENCES OUT LOUD, FILLING IN THE BLANKS USING THE WORDS IN THE PANEL

| brakes | tire | battery | work |
| bike | app | test ride | docks |

1 What type of _____ do you want?

2 The _____ needs charging.

3 The front _____ is flat.

4 Would you like a _____ ?

5 I need a bike to get to and from _____ .

6 There are bike _____ all over town.

7 You just need to download the _____ !

8 The _____ are loose.

175

# 70 Taxis

## 70.1 TAKING A TAXI

Where's the nearest taxi stand?

The cabs wait over there, across the street.

Can you take me to this address?

No problem. Let me put your suitcase in the trunk.

Can you drop me here, please?

Sure. That will be $19.10.

## 70.2 BOOKING IN ADVANCE

Hello. Can I book a taxi from the airport?

For how many people and when do you need it?

Tomorrow at 11 a.m. There are four of us.

Where are you traveling to?

To Monroe Township.

How many pieces of luggage do you have?

One small suitcase and one large one.

Okay. That's all booked for you.

## 70.3 MORE PHRASES

How long will it take to get there?

Can we make an extra stop?

Keep the change.

Can I pay with contactless?

How soon will the cab be here?

I'll book a ride-share via the app.

I left my laptop in one of your taxis.

I'm traveling with my service dog.

## 70.4 LISTEN TO PERSON A AND RESPOND AS PERSON B

| A | | B |
|---|---|---|
| ① Where's the nearest taxi stand? | | The cabs wait over there, across the street. |
| ② For how many people and when do you need it? | | Tomorrow at 11 a.m. There are four of us. |
| ③ How many pieces of luggage do you have? | | One small suitcase and one large one. |
| ④ Can you drop me here, please? | | Sure. That will be $19.10. |

## 70.5 LISTEN AND NUMBER THE SENTENCES IN THE ORDER YOU HEAR THEM

Ⓐ Keep the change. ☐

Ⓑ One small suitcase and one large one. ☐

Ⓒ Where's the nearest taxi stand? 1

Ⓓ Can you drop me here, please? ☐

Ⓔ How soon will the cab be here? ☐

Ⓕ Can you take me to this address? ☐

Ⓖ Let me put your suitcase in the trunk. ☐

Ⓗ I'll book a ride-share via the app. ☐

## 70.6 SAY THE SENTENCES OUT LOUD, FILLING IN THE BLANKS USING THE WORDS IN THE PANEL

| long | pay | address | cab | drop | taxis | book | dog |
|---|---|---|---|---|---|---|---|

① Hello. Can I _____ a taxi from the airport?

② How soon will the _____ be here?

③ Can you _____ me here, please?

④ I'm traveling with my service _____ .

⑤ I left my laptop in one of your _____ .

⑥ Can you take me to this _____ ?

⑦ How _____ will it take to get there?

⑧ Can I _____ with contactless?

# At the auto repair shop

## 71.1 BOOKING AN APPOINTMENT

ABC Autos, how can I help?

Could I book an appointment for my car, please?

When will my car be ready?

It should be ready to pick up at 5:30.

## 71.2 FAULTS AND REPAIRS

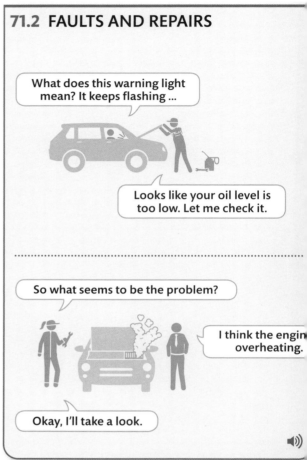

What does this warning light mean? It keeps flashing ...

Looks like your oil level is too low. Let me check it.

So what seems to be the problem?

I think the engine overheating.

Okay, I'll take a look.

## 71.3 MORE PROBLEMS

The headlight isn't working.

The oil needs to be changed.

The steering wheel is jammed.

The windshield is cracked.

The tire keeps going flat.

## 71.4 VOCABULARY CAR PARTS

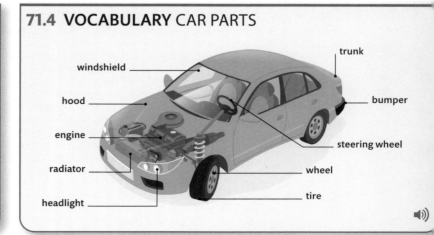

windshield

trunk

hood

bumper

engine

steering wheel

radiator

wheel

headlight

tire

## 71.5 LISTEN TO PERSON A AND RESPOND AS PERSON B

A

B

**①** ABC Autos, how can I help?

Could I book an appointment for my car, please?

**②** When will my car be ready?

It should be ready to pick up at 5:30.

**③** What does this warning light mean? It keeps flashing ...

Looks like your oil level is too low. Let me check it.

**④** So what seems to be the problem?

I think the engine's overheating.

## 71.6 LISTEN AND CIRCLE THE ITEM YOU HEAR

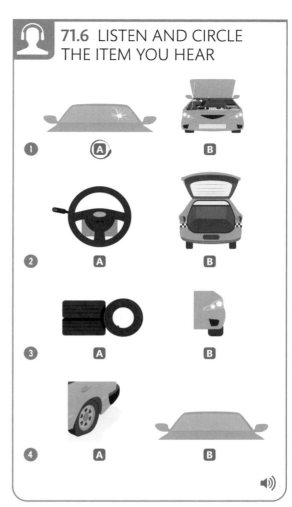

**①** A    B

**②** A    B

**③** A    B

**④** A    B

## 71.7 MATCH THE SENTENCES AND SAY THEM OUT LOUD

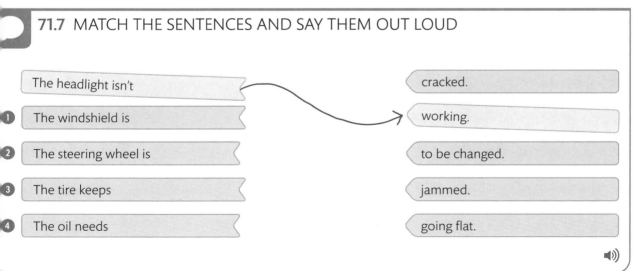

The headlight isn't — working.

**①** The windshield is — cracked.

**②** The steering wheel is — to be changed.

**③** The tire keeps — jammed.

**④** The oil needs — going flat.

179

# 72 On vacation

## 72.1 ACCOMMODATIONS

hotel • motel • bed and breakfast • hostel

chalet • cabin • campground • camper

accessible • pet-friendly • Wi-Fi • swimming pool

balcony • crib • room service • buffet

## 72.2 TRAVEL ESSENTIALS

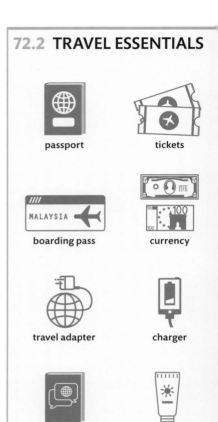

passport • tickets

boarding pass • currency

travel adapter • charger

phrase book • sunscreen

## 72.3 VERBS

 to book a flight
to make a reservation
to go on vacation
to rent a cottage
to stay in a hotel
to book a campsite

to pack (a suitcase)
to exchange money
to go abroad
to rent a car
to check in
to check out

## 72.4 VACATION ACTIVITIES

surfing

waterskiing

kayaking

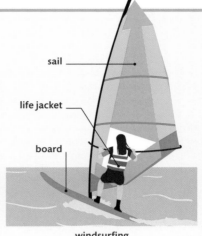

sail

life jacket

board

swimming

snorkeling

scuba diving

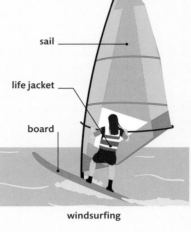
windsurfing

paragliding

hiking

playing golf

rock climbing

snowboarding

skiing

## 72.5 SIGHTSEEING AND ATTRACTIONS

tourism map

INFORMATION
tourism office

guided tour

museum

art gallery

flea market

castle

palace

church

gardens

water park

boat trip

wildlife park

mountains

island

beach

lighthouse

pier

# 73 Booking a vacation

## 73.1 TALKING TO THE TRAVEL AGENT

So what kind of trip are you looking for?

I was thinking about a safari. What do you offer?

I saw a cruise on your website. Is it all-inclusive?

Yes, it covers all meals, entertainment, and activities.

This spa day looks amazing ...

... It has five-star reviews ...

... Adults only ...

... 20% discount ...

Sounds perfect. Let's book it!

## 73.2 MORE QUESTIONS

What amenities are there?

What's your cancelation policy?

Do I need a visa?

Is it suitable for young children?

Can I bring my guide dog?

## 73.3 VOCABULARY
### TYPES OF VACATIONS

beach vacation

city break

spa day

winter sports

camper

camping trip

hiking tour

cruise

safari

all-inclusive

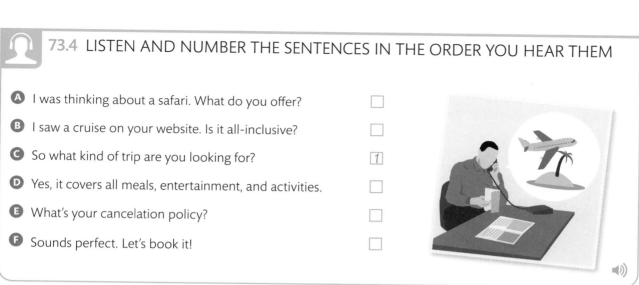

**A** I was thinking about a safari. What do you offer? ☐

**B** I saw a cruise on your website. Is it all-inclusive? ☐

**C** So what kind of trip are you looking for? ☐ 1

**D** Yes, it covers all meals, entertainment, and activities. ☐

**E** What's your cancelation policy? ☐

**F** Sounds perfect. Let's book it! ☐

## 73.5 MATCH THE SENTENCES AND SAY THEM OUT LOUD

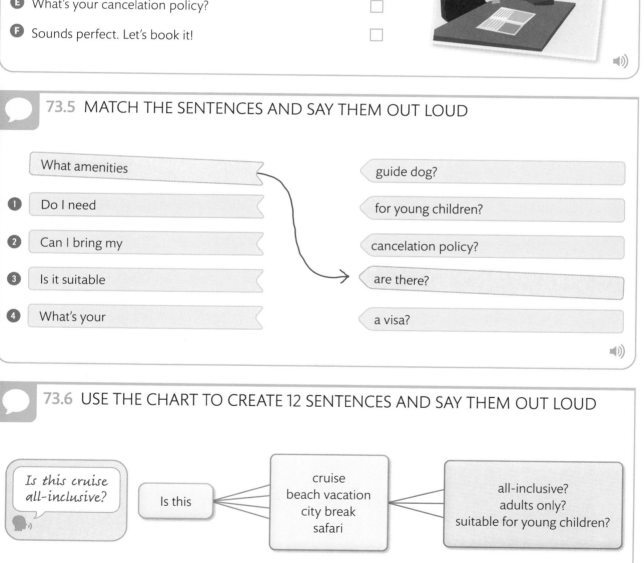

What amenities — are there?

1 Do I need — guide dog?

2 Can I bring my — for young children?

3 Is it suitable — cancelation policy?

4 What's your — a visa?

## 73.6 USE THE CHART TO CREATE 12 SENTENCES AND SAY THEM OUT LOUD

*Is this cruise all-inclusive?*

Is this → cruise / beach vacation / city break / safari → all-inclusive? / adults only? / suitable for young children?

## 74.1 ARRIVAL AND CHECK-IN

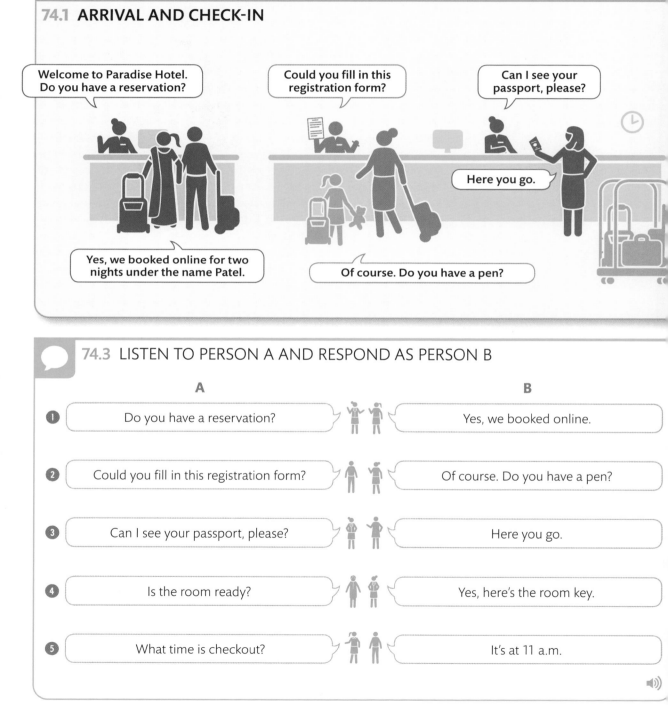

Welcome to Paradise Hotel. Do you have a reservation?

Could you fill in this registration form?

Can I see your passport, please?

Here you go.

Yes, we booked online for two nights under the name Patel.

Of course. Do you have a pen?

## 74.3 LISTEN TO PERSON A AND RESPOND AS PERSON B

| A | B |
|---|---|
| ❶ Do you have a reservation? | Yes, we booked online. |
| ❷ Could you fill in this registration form? | Of course. Do you have a pen? |
| ❸ Can I see your passport, please? | Here you go. |
| ❹ Is the room ready? | Yes, here's the room key. |
| ❺ What time is checkout? | It's at 11 a.m. |

Is the room ready?

Yes, here's the room key.

What time is checkout?

It's at 11 a.m.

## 74.2 MORE PHRASES

I paid in advance on the booking site.

Do you have a king bed available?

We'd like a room with queen beds, please.

The restaurant serves dinner until 10 p.m.

The swimming pool opens again at 6 a.m.

Your room is on the second floor.

Breakfast is from 7:30 a.m. to 10 a.m.

## 74.4 LISTEN AND CIRCLE THE ITEM YOU HEAR

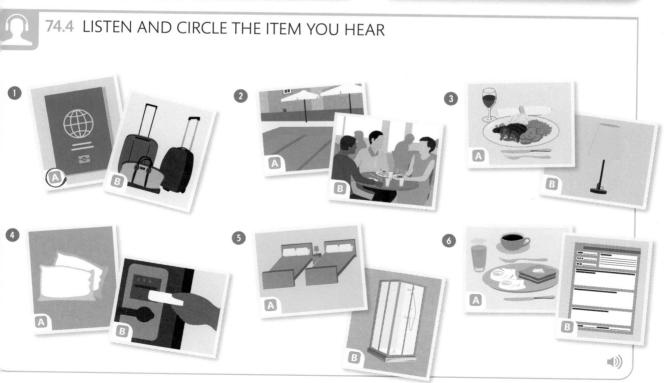

## 74.5 ASKING FOR THINGS

Could I have some fresh towels, please?

Yes, I'll have some sent up right away.

## 74.6 MORE PHRASES

I'd like ...

... a hair dryer brought to my room.

... a club sandwich sent up, please.

... two extra pillows.

... a 7 a.m. wake-up call.

## 74.7 DESCRIBING PROBLEMS

The TV won't turn on.

Okay, let me take a look.

## 74.8 MORE PROBLEMS

The Wi-Fi password is wrong.

The lamp is broken.

The room is too hot.

My window doesn't close properly.

The shower is leaking.

My room key isn't working.

## 74.9 VOCABULARY AT THE HOTEL

passport

registration form

king bed

queen beds

club sandwich

shower

room key

luggage

pillows

lamp

towels

hair dryer

## 74.10 LISTEN AND NUMBER THE PICTURES IN THE ORDER THEY ARE DESCRIBED

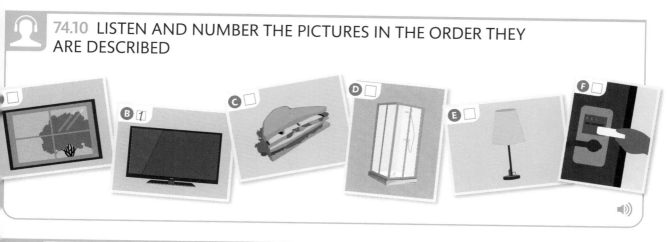

## 74.11 MATCH THE SENTENCES AND SAY THEM OUT LOUD

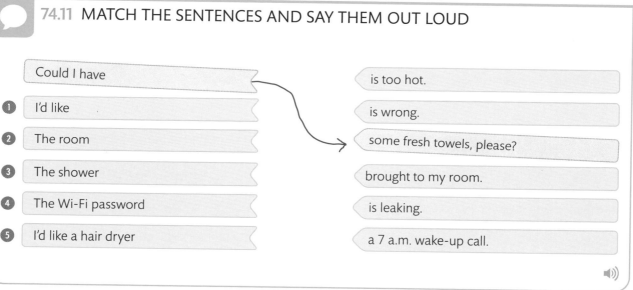

| | | |
|---|---|---|
| | Could I have | is too hot. |
| 1 | I'd like | is wrong. |
| 2 | The room | some fresh towels, please? |
| 3 | The shower | brought to my room. |
| 4 | The Wi-Fi password | is leaking. |
| 5 | I'd like a hair dryer | a 7 a.m. wake-up call. |

## 74.12 USE THE CHART TO CREATE EIGHT SENTENCES AND SAY THEM OUT LOUD

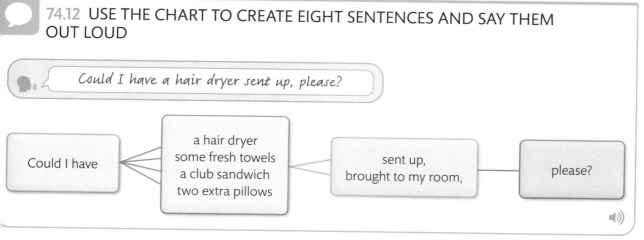

Could I have a hair dryer sent up, please?

| Could I have | a hair dryer<br>some fresh towels<br>a club sandwich<br>two extra pillows | sent up,<br>brought to my room, | please? |

## 74.13 AT BREAKFAST

Am I too late for breakfast?

No, you're just in time.

Can I get your room number?

Can we sit anywhere we like?

Yes, and help yourselves to the buffet.

Could I have some more coffee?

Sure, I'll bring it to your table.

### GOOD TO KNOW

In spoken English, we often use **a bit** or **a little**—instead of the more formal **quite** or **rather**—when we want to describe something negative. For example, we wouldn't say our breakfast was **a bit** delicious, but we might say it was **a bit** bland or **a little** cold.

## 74.14 CHECKING OUT

Did you enjoy your stay?

It was great, thanks

The room was a bit noisy.

Here's your bill if you'd like to check it.

That all looks fine.

Are you paying by card?

## 74.15 MORE PHRASES

Dinner was delicious.

Our breakfast was a bit cold.

The bed was a little hard.

Is it possible to stay an extra night?

Can I leave my luggage here?

Could you call me a cab, please?

## 74.16 MATCH THE SENTENCES AND SAY THEM OUT LOUD

Am I too late — for breakfast?

1. Did you enjoy — your stay?
2. Yes, and help yourselves — to the buffet.
3. Here's your bill — if you'd like to check it.
4. Is it possible to — stay an extra night?
5. Can I get — your room number?

Right column options:
- if you'd like to check it.
- your room number?
- for breakfast?
- stay an extra night?
- to the buffet.
- your stay?

## 74.17 SAY THE SENTENCES OUT LOUD, REPLACING THE PICTURES WITH WORDS

1. Could I have some more ☕ ?
2. Are you paying by 💳 ?
3. Could you call me a 🚕 , please?
4. The 🛏 was a little hard.
5. Can I leave my 🧳 here?

## 74.18 SAY THE SENTENCES OUT LOUD, FILLING IN THE BLANKS USING THE WORDS IN THE PANEL

room    checkout    floor

delicious    restaurant    queen beds

passport    king

1. Can I see your _____ , please?
2. What time is _____ ?
3. We'd like a room with _____ , please.
4. The _____ was a bit noisy.
5. Dinner was _____ .
6. Do you have a _____ bed available?
7. The _____ serves dinner until 10 p.m.
8. Your room is on the second _____ .

# 75 City sightseeing

## 75.1 VISITING THE SIGHTS

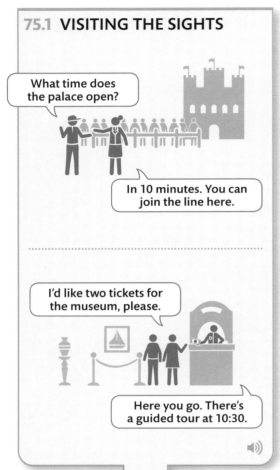

What time does the palace open?

In 10 minutes. You can join the line here.

I'd like two tickets for the museum, please.

Here you go. There's a guided tour at 10:30.

## 75.2 MORE PHRASES

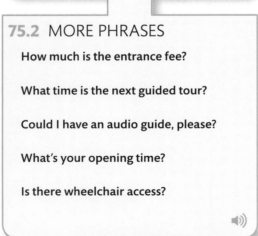

How much is the entrance fee?

What time is the next guided tour?

Could I have an audio guide, please?

What's your opening time?

Is there wheelchair access?

## 75.3 ON A TOUR BUS

On your right, you'll see the oldest building in the city.

Look—we're here on the map, and there's our hotel

Wow! Check that out!

Quick! Take a picture!

Want to get off at the next stop?

## 75.4 VOCABULARY TOURIST ESSENTIALS

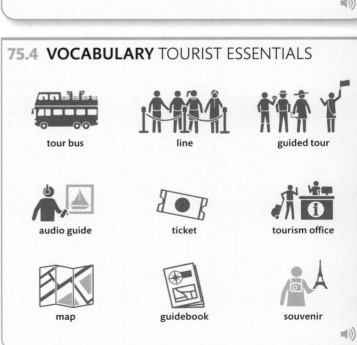

tour bus

line

guided tour

audio guide

ticket

tourism office

map

guidebook

souvenir

## 75.5 LISTEN AND CIRCLE THE ITEM YOU HEAR

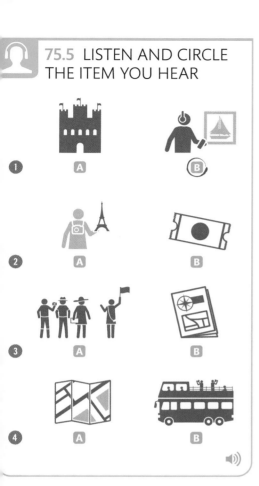

## 75.6 LISTEN TO PERSON A AND RESPOND AS PERSON B

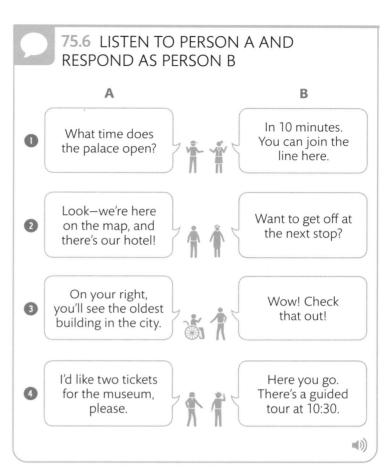

| A | B |
| --- | --- |
| ① What time does the palace open? | In 10 minutes. You can join the line here. |
| ② Look—we're here on the map, and there's our hotel! | Want to get off at the next stop? |
| ③ On your right, you'll see the oldest building in the city. | Wow! Check that out! |
| ④ I'd like two tickets for the museum, please. | Here you go. There's a guided tour at 10:30. |

## 75.7 MATCH THE SENTENCES AND SAY THEM OUT LOUD

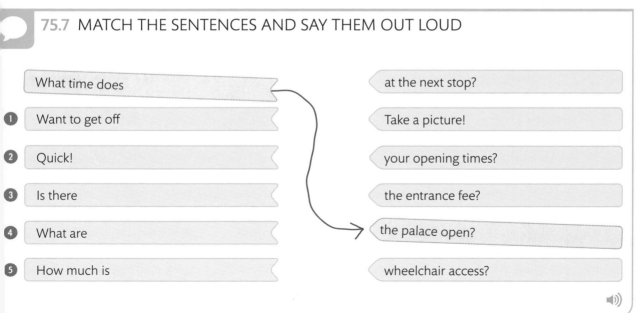

What time does → the palace open?

① Want to get off → at the next stop?

② Quick! → Take a picture!

③ Is there → wheelchair access?

④ What are → your opening times?

⑤ How much is → the entrance fee?

# 76 Going camping

## 76.1 ARRIVING AT THE CAMPGROUND

Hello, how can I help you?

Hi, we've booked a campsite for two nights.

Where can we pitch our tent?

Over in that field, across from the trailers.

Can we park our camper near the general store?

Yes, of course.

There's lots to do here! The beach is just over there ...

Great! We'll set up camp, then head out to explore.

## 76.2 AT THE GENERAL STORE

Can we light a campfire?

Yes, you can. Do you need firewood?

We forgot to bring camping gas! Do you have any?

Sure, on that shelf over there. Anything else?

Yes. I'll take a box of matches, too.

## 76.3 VOCABULARY CAMPING

tent

campfire

shower block

trailer

camper

general store

matches

camping stove

camping gas

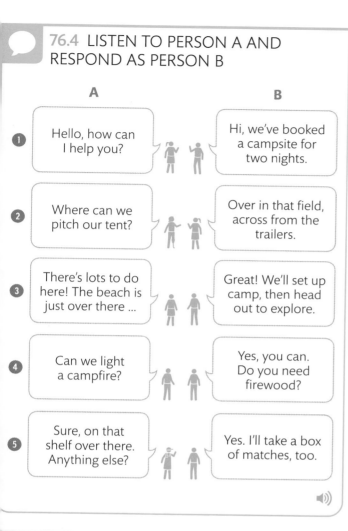

## 76.4 LISTEN TO PERSON A AND RESPOND AS PERSON B

**A**

**B**

1. A: Hello, how can I help you?
   B: Hi, we've booked a campsite for two nights.

2. A: Where can we pitch our tent?
   B: Over in that field, across from the trailers.

3. A: There's lots to do here! The beach is just over there ...
   B: Great! We'll set up camp, then head out to explore.

4. A: Can we light a campfire?
   B: Yes, you can. Do you need firewood?

5. A: Sure, on that shelf over there. Anything else?
   B: Yes. I'll take a box of matches, too.

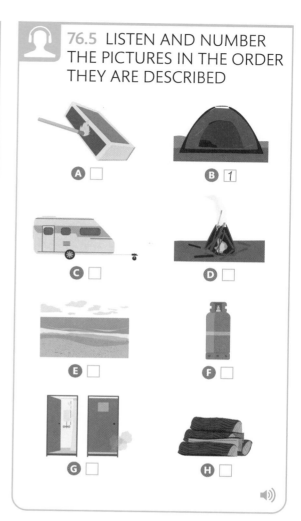

## 76.5 LISTEN AND NUMBER THE PICTURES IN THE ORDER THEY ARE DESCRIBED

A ☐

B 1

C ☐

D ☐

E ☐

F ☐

G ☐

H ☐

## 76.6 USE THE CHART TO CREATE NINE SENTENCES AND SAY THEM OUT LOUD

*Can we pitch our tent over in that field?*

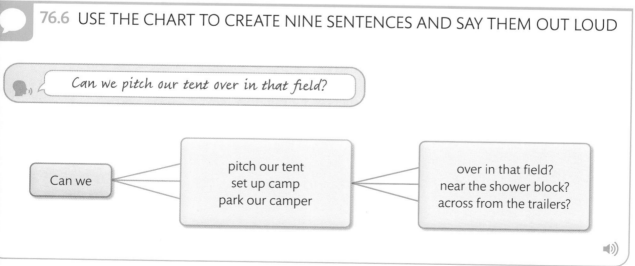

Can we

pitch our tent
set up camp
park our camper

over in that field?
near the shower block?
across from the trailers?

# At the beach

## 77.1 ARRIVING AT THE BEACH

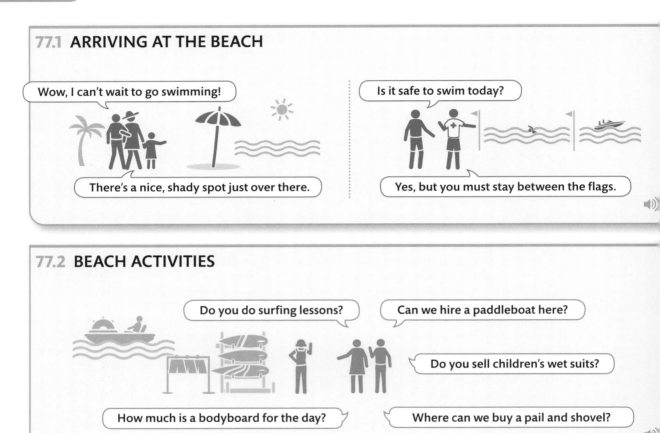

Wow, I can't wait to go swimming!

There's a nice, shady spot just over there.

Is it safe to swim today?

Yes, but you must stay between the flags.

## 77.2 BEACH ACTIVITIES

Do you do surfing lessons?

Can we hire a paddleboat here?

Do you sell children's wet suits?

How much is a bodyboard for the day?

Where can we buy a pail and shovel?

## 77.3 VOCABULARY AT THE BEACH

wet suit

bodyboard

paddleboard

paddleboat

flag

lifeguard

surfboard

beach chair

beach ball

sun lounger

shovel

pail

## 77.4 LISTEN AND NUMBER THE SENTENCES IN THE ORDER YOU HEAR THEM

**A** Can we hire a paddleboat here? ☐

**B** Wow, I can't wait to go swimming! ☐

**C** There's a nice, shady spot just over there. ☐

**D** Is it safe to swim today? ☐

**E** How much is a bodyboard for the day? 1

**F** Yes, but you must stay between the flags. ☐

**G** Do you do surfing lessons? ☐

**H** Where can we buy a pail and shovel? ☐

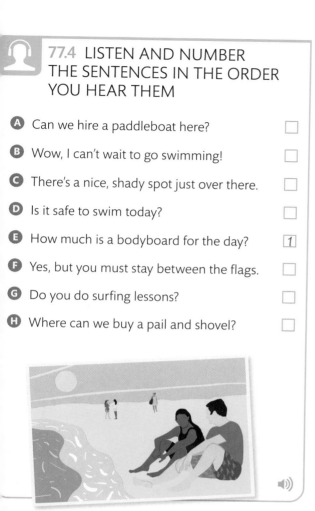

## 77.5 SAY THE SENTENCES OUT LOUD, REPLACING THE PICTURES WITH WORDS

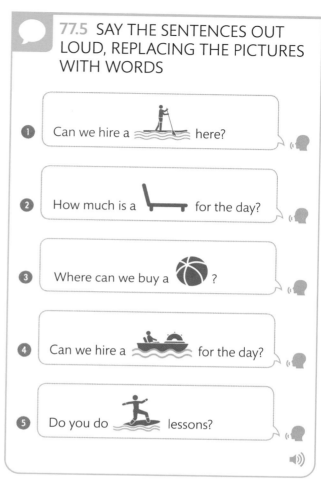

**1** Can we hire a [picture] here?

**2** How much is a [picture] for the day?

**3** Where can we buy a [picture]?

**4** Can we hire a [picture] for the day?

**5** Do you do [picture] lessons?

## 77.6 MATCH THE SENTENCES AND SAY THEM OUT LOUD

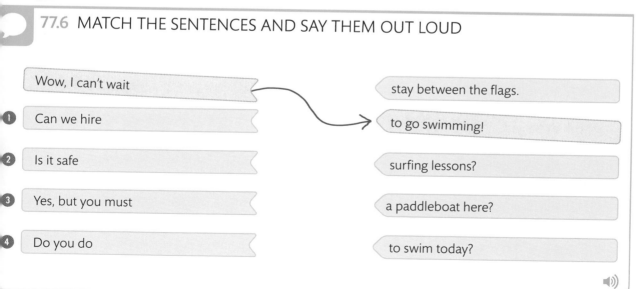

Wow, I can't wait → to go swimming!

**1** Can we hire — a paddleboat here?

**2** Is it safe — to swim today?

**3** Yes, but you must — stay between the flags.

**4** Do you do — surfing lessons?

195

## 78.1 ASKING FOR DIRECTIONS

Excuse me, do you know the way to the bus station?

Yes, go straight ahead and it's on your left.

Can you tell me how to get to the museum?

Let me think ... Take the first right after the library.

## 78.2 FOLLOWING DIRECTIONS

Hi there, is the bank this way?

No, you need to go past the church ...

... and take the first left ...

... then cross the road ...

... and turn right at the traffic lights.

It's just next to the hospital.

Thanks for your help!

## 78.3 VOCABULARY DIRECTIONS

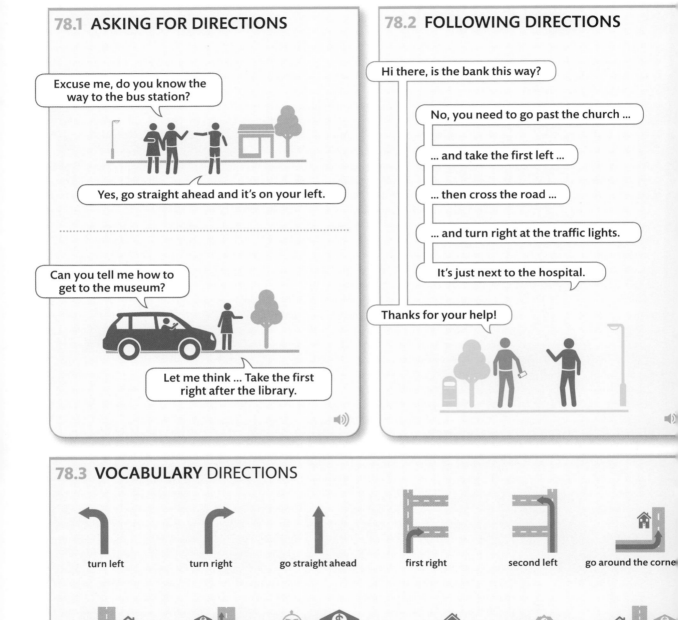

turn left

turn right

go straight ahead

first right

second left

go around the corner

cross the road

go past

next to

behind

in front of

across from

## 78.4 LISTEN AND NUMBER THE PICTURES IN THE ORDER THEY ARE DESCRIBED

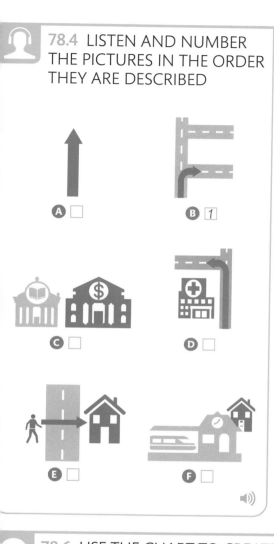

A ☐    B 1

C ☐    D ☐

E ☐    F ☐

## 78.5 SAY THE SENTENCES OUT LOUD, FILLING IN THE BLANKS USING THE WORDS IN THE PANEL

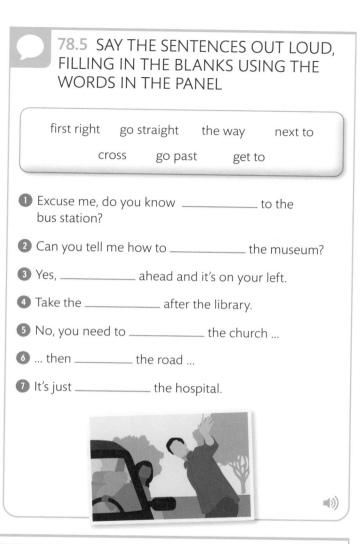

first right    go straight    the way    next to

cross    go past    get to

1 Excuse me, do you know _____ to the bus station?

2 Can you tell me how to _____ the museum?

3 Yes, _____ ahead and it's on your left.

4 Take the _____ after the library.

5 No, you need to _____ the church ...

6 ... then _____ the road ...

7 It's just _____ the hospital.

## 78.6 USE THE CHART TO CREATE EIGHT SENTENCES AND SAY THEM OUT LOUD

Excuse me, do you know the way to the church?

| Excuse me, | do you know the way to / can you tell me how to get to | the church? / the museum? / the bus station? / the bank? |

# 79 Vacation problems

## 79.1 LOST BELONGINGS

My bag's been stolen with my passport inside!

Okay, let me take down some details.

Excuse me, my suitcase hasn't shown up.

The airline desk can help you.

Hello, you left your phone behi

Oh gosh, thank you so much

## 79.2 DELAYS AND CANCELLATIONS

I'm sorry, your flight is delayed.

We'll let you know more as soon as we can.

I can't see our platform number anywhere ...

Look at the board. Our train has been canceled!

## 79.3 MORE PHRASES

Your luggage has an extra charge.

Your gate has just closed.

The baggage handlers are on strike.

The train is canceled due to lack of available train crew.

## 79.4 ILLNESS AND INJURY

Wanna come hiking tomorrow?

I can't—I've thrown my back out!

You look awful!

Yeah, I won't make it to the beach. I have a stomach bug!

Hello, I've had an accident on vacation and I can't fly home!

Your insurance should cov you if you get a doctor's no

## 79.5 LISTEN TO PERSON A AND RESPOND AS PERSON B

**A**

**B**

1. My bag's been stolen with my passport inside!
   Okay, let me take down some details.

2. Excuse me, my suitcase hasn't shown up.
   The airline desk can help you.

3. Hello, you left your phone behind!
   Oh gosh, thank you so much!

4. Wanna come hiking tomorrow?
   I can't—I've thrown my back out!

## 79.6 LISTEN AND NUMBER THE SENTENCES IN THE ORDER YOU HEAR THEM

**A** We'll let you know more as soon as we can. ☐

**B** Your luggage has an extra charge. ☐

**C** Your gate has just closed. ☐1

**D** I'm sorry, your flight is delayed. ☐

**E** My bag's been stolen with my passport inside! ☐

**F** Your insurance should cover you if you get a doctor's note. ☐

**G** Okay, let me take down some details. ☐

**H** Hello, I've had an accident on vacation and I can't fly home! ☐

**I** The baggage handlers are on strike. ☐

## 79.7 MATCH THE SENTENCES AND SAY THEM OUT LOUD

The baggage handlers — are on strike.

1. The train is canceled

2. Yeah, I won't make it to the beach.

3. Look at the board.

4. Your insurance should cover you

I have a stomach bug!

if you get a doctor's note.

due to lack of available train crew.

Our train has been canceled!

# 80 Health and medicine

## 80.1 THE HUMAN BODY

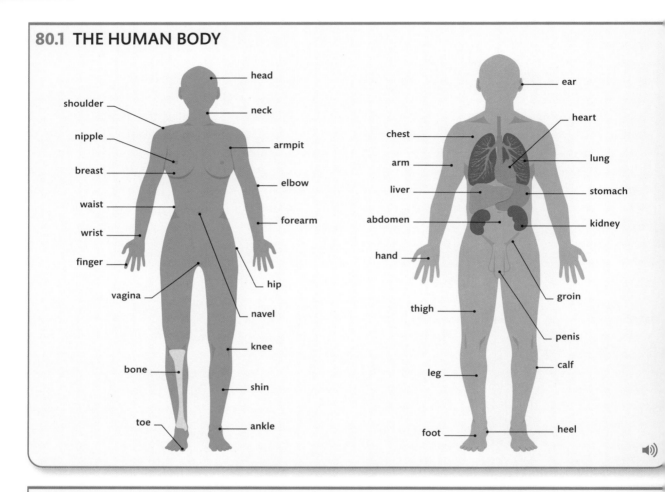

shoulder · head · neck · nipple · armpit · breast · elbow · waist · forearm · wrist · finger · vagina · hip · navel · knee · bone · shin · toe · ankle

ear · chest · heart · arm · lung · liver · stomach · abdomen · kidney · hand · groin · thigh · penis · leg · calf · foot · heel

## 80.2 MEDICAL PROFESSIONALS

doctor

nurse

surgeon

anesthesiologist

paramedic

pharmacist

midwife

pediatrician

optician

physical therapist

dentist

therapist

## 80.3 ILLNESSES AND INJURIES

 cough

 cold

 runny nose

 virus

 fever

 sore throat

 infection

 allergy

 headache

 earache

 nausea

 diarrhea

 food poisoning

 upset stomach

 rash

 scrape

 bruise

 swelling

 cut

 burn

 bite

 cramp

 sprain

 broken bone

## 80.4 EMERGENCIES, DIAGNOSES, AND TREATMENT

 ambulance

 hospital

 ER (emergency room)

 emergency

 accident

 hospital porter

 temperature

 blood pressure

 blood work

 heart rate

 X-ray

 scan

 checkup

 dressing

 stitches

 injection / shot

 medication

 antibiotics

# 81 At the pharmacy

## 81.1 DESCRIBING YOUR SYMPTOMS

I have a really sore eye.

It could be an infection.

I have an itchy rash on my arm.

Hmm ... it looks like an allergy.

Really? What do you recommend?

This ointment should help.

## 81.2 MORE PHRASES

My knee really hurts.

I have a really bad headache.

My back is killing me.

### 🌐 GOOD TO KNOW

In spoken English, we frequently use **really** to emphasize something: I have a **really** sore eye; My eye **really** hurts. **Really** has a similar function to **very**, but it's a little more informal. We also use it to express interest or surprise: **Really? What do you recommend?**

## 81.3 QUESTIONS YOU MAY HEAR

Do you have any other symptoms?

Yes, I also have a runny nose.

Do you have any allergies?

Yes, I'm allergic to aspirin.

Are you taking any other medication?

Yes, I'm taking antibiotics.

How long have you had symptoms?

For about a week

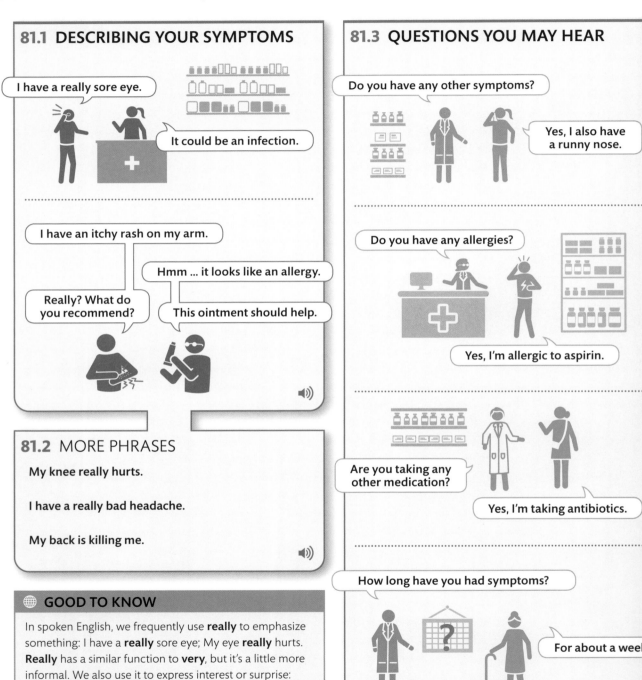

## 81.4 LISTEN AND NUMBER THE PICTURES IN THE ORDER THEY ARE DESCRIBED

A ☐
B ☐
C 1
D ☐
E ☐
F ☐

## 81.5 LISTEN TO PERSON A AND RESPOND AS PERSON B

**A** — **B**

1. Do you have any other symptoms? — Yes, I also have a runny nose.

2. Do you have any allergies? — Yes, I'm allergic to aspirin.

3. Are you taking any other medication? — Yes, I'm taking antibiotics.

4. How long have you had symptoms? — For about a week.

5. Hmm ... it looks like an allergy. — Really? What do you recommend?

## 81.6 USE THE CHART TO CREATE FIVE SENTENCES AND SAY THEM OUT LOUD

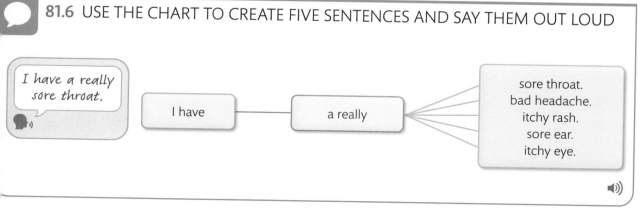

I have a really sore throat.

| I have | a really | sore throat. |
| | | bad headache. |
| | | itchy rash. |
| | | sore ear. |
| | | itchy eye. |

## 81.7 TREATMENT AND DOSAGE

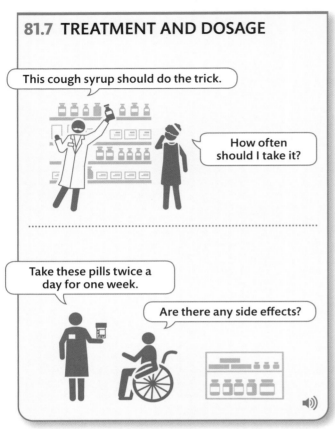

This cough syrup should do the trick.

How often should I take it?

Take these pills twice a day for one week.

Are there any side effects?

## 81.8 PRESCRIPTIONS

I've come to pick up a prescription.

Please take a seat and we'll let you know when it's ready

I'm here to pick up my refill.

Here you go. Any question for the pharmacist?

## 81.9 **VOCABULARY** IN A PHARMACY

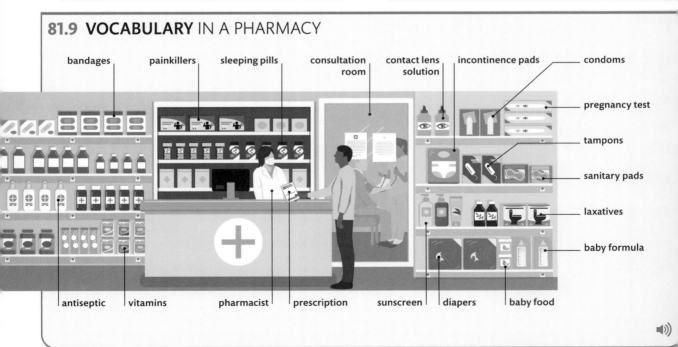

bandages

painkillers

sleeping pills

consultation room

contact lens solution

incontinence pads

condoms

pregnancy test

tampons

sanitary pads

laxatives

baby formula

antiseptic

vitamins

pharmacist

prescription

sunscreen

diapers

baby food

204

## 81.10 LISTEN TO THE AUDIO AND MATCH THE CORRECT RESPONSE

Do you have any allergies?

**1** Are you taking any other medication?

**2** This cough syrup should do the trick.

**3** How long have you had symptoms?

**4** Do you have any other symptoms?

**5** I have an itchy rash on my arm.

For about a week.

How often should I take it?

Yes, I'm taking antibiotics.

Yes, I'm allergic to aspirin.

Hmm ... it looks like an allergy.

Yes, I also have a runny nose.

## 81.11 LISTEN AND NUMBER THE SENTENCES IN THE ORDER YOU HEAR THEM

**A** Are there any side effects? ☐

**B** This cough syrup should do the trick. ☐

**C** I've come to pick up a prescription. ☐ 1

**D** Any questions for the pharmacist? ☐

**E** Take these pills twice a day for one week. ☐

**F** I'm here to pick up my refill. ☐

**G** Please take a seat and we'll let you know when it's ready. ☐

**H** How often should I take it? ☐

**I** How long have you had symptoms? ☐

## 81.12 SAY THE SENTENCES OUT LOUD, REPLACING THE PICTURES WITH WORDS

**1** I have a really sore  .

**2** I also have a runny [nose] .

**3** My [hand] really hurts.

**4** I have an itchy rash on my [foot] .

**5** My [ear] is killing me.

205

# 82 Booking an appointment

## 82.1 AT THE DOCTOR'S OFFICE

Hi there, I'd like to book an appointment with Doctor Cole.

Can I ask what it's concerning?

I think I might have an eye infection.

We could squeeze you in later at 4:30?

That's great, thanks.

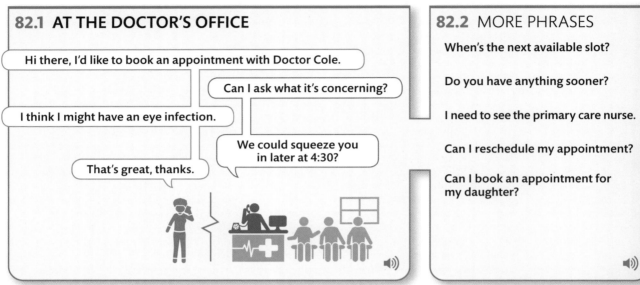

## 82.2 MORE PHRASES

When's the next available slot?

Do you have anything sooner?

I need to see the primary care nurse.

Can I reschedule my appointment?

Can I book an appointment for my daughter?

## 82.3 AT THE DENTIST

I'd like to book a checkup, please.

Have you been with us before?

No, I haven't.

I'm sorry, we're not taking new patients.

I have an appointment next week, but I need to cancel it.

No problem. Can I take your name?

SMILE Dental

## 82.4 EMERGENCY APPOINTMENTS

I need an emergency appointment. I have a really bad toothache.

We have a slot in half hour if that's any goo

If you need an urgent appointment, we'll place you on the triage list …

… and the doctor will call you back as soon as possible.

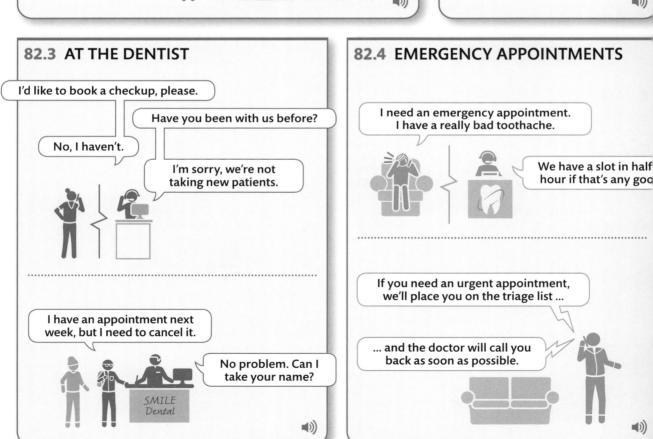

## 82.5 LISTEN TO PERSON A AND RESPOND AS PERSON B

**A** **B**

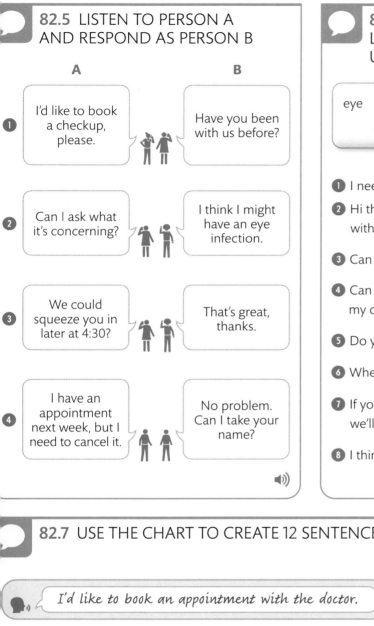

1. I'd like to book a checkup, please.
   Have you been with us before?

2. Can I ask what it's concerning?
   I think I might have an eye infection.

3. We could squeeze you in later at 4:30?
   That's great, thanks.

4. I have an appointment next week, but I need to cancel it.
   No problem. Can I take your name?

## 82.6 SAY THE SENTENCES OUT LOUD, FILLING IN THE BLANKS USING THE WORDS IN THE PANEL

> eye   anything   reschedule   available
>
> nurse   triage   appointment   Doctor

1. I need to see the primary care _____ .

2. Hi there, I'd like to book an appointment with _____ Cole.

3. Can I _____ my appointment?

4. Can I book an _____ for my daughter?

5. Do you have _____ sooner?

6. When's the next _____ slot?

7. If you need an urgent appointment, we'll place you on the _____ list ...

8. I think I might have an _____ infection.

## 82.7 USE THE CHART TO CREATE 12 SENTENCES AND SAY THEM OUT LOUD

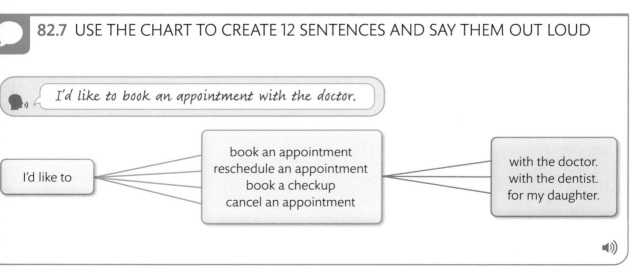

*I'd like to book an appointment with the doctor.*

| I'd like to | book an appointment reschedule an appointment book a checkup cancel an appointment | with the doctor. with the dentist. for my daughter. |

# 83 Seeing the doctor

## 83.1 DESCRIBING SYMPTOMS

What seems to be the problem?

I keep getting splitting headaches.

I've had a bad cough for a week and it's getting worse.

Okay, let me listen to your chest.

## 83.2 MORE PHRASES

I've been vomiting all night.

My shoulder has been hurting.

My son has a fever.

I've been under the weather.

I've found a lump in my breast.

## 83.3 GENERAL CARE

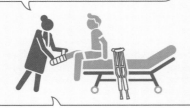

It seems to be healing up nicely ...

... I'll just change your bandage.

Which arm would you like the injection in?

Right, please! I'm left-handed.

## 83.4 MORE PHRASES

I'll refer you for some tests.

Can I book a flu shot?

Let's take your temperature.

I'd like a prescription refilled.

I'm due for a checkup.

## 83.5 ADVICE AND DIAGNOSIS

What do you advise?

You need to rest and drink plenty of fluids.

It looks like a mild infection.

Will I need antibiotics?

Come back in two weeks and we'll see how it's looking.

## 83.6 LISTEN TO PERSON A AND RESPOND AS PERSON B

**A** | **B**

**1** Which arm would you like the injection in? — Right, please! I'm left-handed.

**2** What seems to be the problem? — I keep getting splitting headaches.

**3** I've had a bad cough for a week and it's getting worse. — Okay, let me listen to your chest.

**4** What do you advise? — You need to rest and drink plenty of fluids.

## 83.7 LISTEN AND NUMBER THE SENTENCES IN THE ORDER YOU HEAR THEM

**A** I've found a lump in my breast. ☐

**B** I'm due for a checkup. ☐ *1*

**C** ... I'll just change your bandage. ☐

**D** I've been under the weather. ☐

**E** Come back in two weeks and we'll see how it's looking. ☐

**F** I've been vomiting all night. ☐

**G** It seems to be healing up nicely ... ☐

**H** I'd like a prescription refilled. ☐

## 83.8 MATCH THE SENTENCES AND SAY THEM OUT LOUD

My shoulder → has been hurting.

**1** I've had a bad cough for a week — vomiting all night.

**2** I've been — a checkup.

**3** I'm due for — the weather.

**4** I've been under — and it's getting worse.

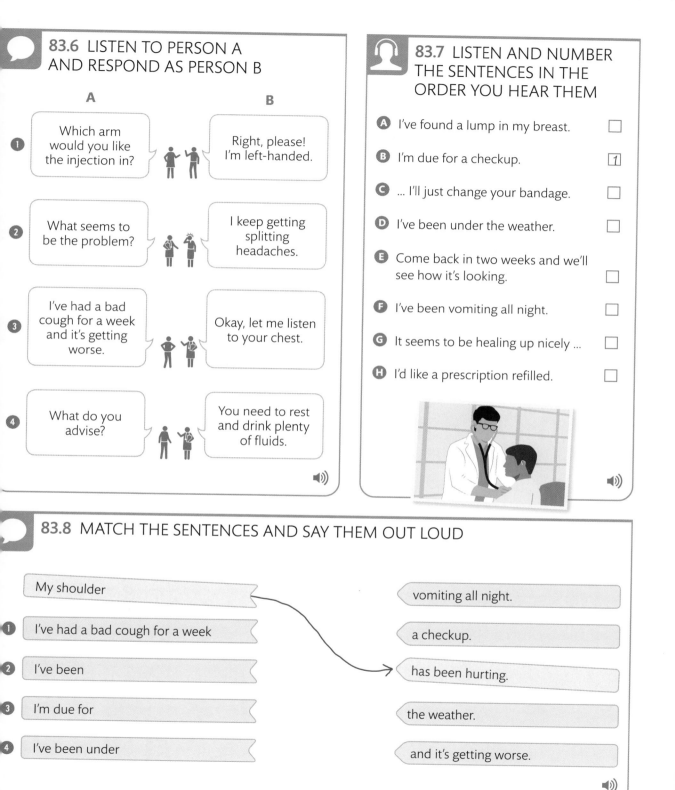

209

# 84 Injuries and emergencies

## 84.1 IN AN EMERGENCY

Which service do you require?

I need an ambulance.

What's the emergency?

My husband has severe chest pains.

I'll send an ambulance for you right away.

## 84.2 MORE PHRASES

I've had an accident.

Please come quickly!

She had a fall.

I need a doctor immediately.

He's having a seizure.

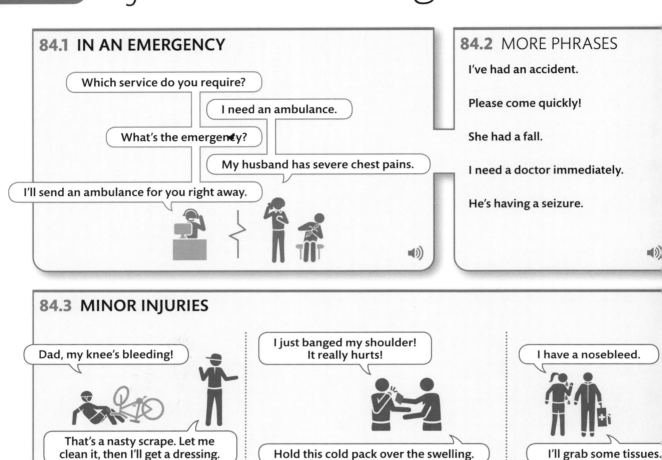

## 84.3 MINOR INJURIES

Dad, my knee's bleeding!

That's a nasty scrape. Let me clean it, then I'll get a dressing.

I just banged my shoulder! It really hurts!

Hold this cold pack over the swelling.

I have a nosebleed.

I'll grab some tissues.

## 84.4 MORE SERIOUS INJURIES

Is my ankle broken or just sprained?

Not sure … I'm sending you for an X-ray.

My daughter gashed her arm.

It looks like she may need stitches.

I burned my hand on the stove. It's really painful.

Let me take a l[

## 84.5 MATCH THE SENTENCES AND SAY THEM OUT LOUD

I've had   →   some tissues.

1. I need a     stove. It's really painful.

2. I burned my hand on the     an accident.

3. I'll grab     severe chest pains.

4. My husband has     a seizure.

5. He's having     doctor immediately.

## 84.6 LISTEN AND CIRCLE THE ITEM YOU HEAR

1. A    B (circled)
2. A    B
3. A    B
4. A    B

## 84.7 RESPOND OUT LOUD TO THE AUDIO, FILLING IN THE BLANKS USING THE WORDS IN THE PANEL

scrape    swelling    stitches    pains

1. My daughter gashed her arm.
   It looks like she may need _____.

2. I just banged my shoulder! It really hurts!
   Hold this cold pack over the _____.

3. What's the emergency?
   My husband has severe chest _____.

4. Dad, my knee's bleeding!
   That's a nasty _____.

# 85 The hospital

## 85.1 AT THE HOSPITAL

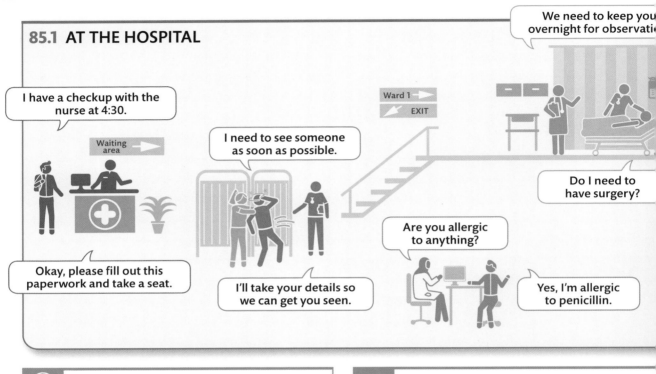

We need to keep you overnight for observation

I have a checkup with the nurse at 4:30.

I need to see someone as soon as possible.

Ward 1 →
↙ EXIT

Do I need to have surgery?

Waiting area →

Are you allergic to anything?

Okay, please fill out this paperwork and take a seat.

I'll take your details so we can get you seen.

Yes, I'm allergic to penicillin.

## 85.3 LISTEN AND NUMBER THE PICTURES IN THE ORDER THEY ARE DESCRIBED

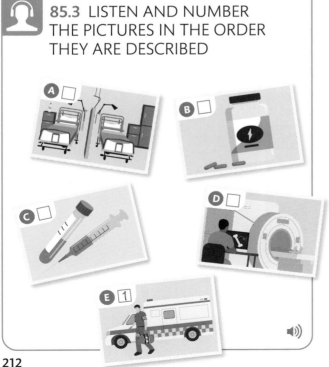

A ☐
B ☐
C ☐
D ☐
E ☐ 1

## 85.4 SAY THE SENTENCES OUT LOUD, FILLING IN THE BLANKS USING THE WORDS IN THE PANEL

checkup     possible     examine

doctor     surgery     medical

❶ I need to see someone as soon as _____ .

❷ We have a _____ emergency.

❸ How soon will I be seen by a _____ ?

❹ I have a _____ with the nurse at 4:30.

❺ Do I need to have _____ ?

❻ I'm going to need to _____ you.

How long have you been feeling like this?

The pain started about two hours ago.

Okay, I'm going to do some blood work.

Good news! I got the all clear!

X-ray ➡

That's such a relief!

## 85.2 MORE PHRASES

We have a medical emergency.

Do you have health insurance?

Are you taking any regular medications?

Do you have someone you'd like to call?

I'm going to need to examine you.

I'm here for my scan.

How soon will I be seen by a doctor?

We'll move you to another ward for observation.

## 85.5 LISTEN TO PERSON A AND RESPOND AS PERSON B

| A | B |
| --- | --- |
| ❶ I need to see someone as soon as possible. | I'll take your details so we can get you seen. |
| ❷ Are you allergic to anything? | Yes, I'm allergic to penicillin. |
| ❸ How long have you been feeling like this? | The pain started about two hours ago. |
| ❹ Good news! I got the all clear! | That's such a relief! |
| ❺ I have a checkup with the nurse at 4:30. | Okay, please fill out this paperwork and take a seat. |
| ❻ The pain started about two hours ago. | Okay, I'm going to do some blood work. |

## 85.6 HAVING SURGERY

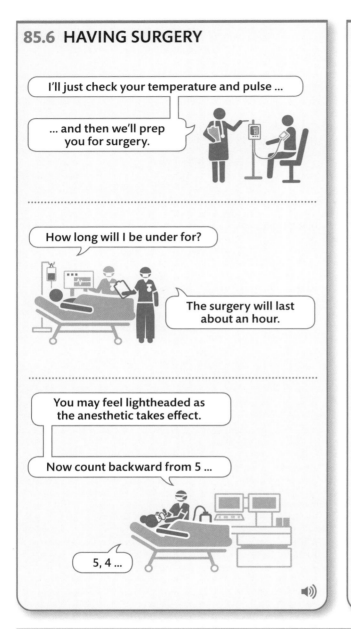

I'll just check your temperature and pulse ...

... and then we'll prep you for surgery.

How long will I be under for?

The surgery will last about an hour.

You may feel lightheaded as the anesthetic takes effect.

Now count backward from 5 ...

5, 4 ...

## 85.7 RECOVERING FROM TREATMENT

The surgery went well.

There were no complications.

Can you give me something for the pain?

Yes, of course. I'll just take your blood pressure first.

How are you feeling?

Still a bit groggy.

Don't worry. We'll have you up and about in no time.

## 85.8 **VOCABULARY** HOSPITAL TREATMENT

surgery

operating theater

anesthetic

ward

intensive care unit

visiting hours

## 85.9 LISTEN TO PERSON A AND RESPOND AS PERSON B

| | A | | B |
|---|---|---|---|
| 1 | Now count backward from 5 ... | | 5, 4 ... |
| 2 | How long will I be under for? | | The surgery will last about an hour. |
| 3 | How are you feeling? | | Still a bit groggy. |
| 4 | Can you give me something for the pain? | | Yes, of course. I'll just take your blood pressure first. |

## 85.10 LISTEN AND NUMBER THE SENTENCES IN THE ORDER YOU HEAR THEM

**A** How long will I be under for? ☐

**B** Now count backward from 5 ... ☐

**C** There were no complications. ☐

**D** ... and then we'll prep you for surgery. ☐

**E** Still a bit groggy. ☐

**F** I'll just check your temperature and pulse ... ☐

**G** How are you feeling? ☑ 1

**H** The surgery went well. ☐

## 85.11 SAY THE SENTENCES OUT LOUD, FILLING IN THE BLANKS USING THE WORDS IN THE PANEL

| complications | pressure | groggy | about |
|---|---|---|---|
| under | backward | anesthetic | temperature |

1 I'll just take your blood _____ first.

2 Still a bit _____ .

3 Don't worry. We'll have you up and _____ in no time.

4 I'll just check your _____ and pulse ...

5 You may feel lightheaded as the _____ takes effect.

6 How long will I be _____ for?

7 Now count _____ from 5 ...

8 There were no _____ .

215

# 86 Dental care

## 86.1 TALKING TO THE DENTIST

I have a bad toothache.

Do I need braces?

I think my crown has come loose.

My filling has come out.

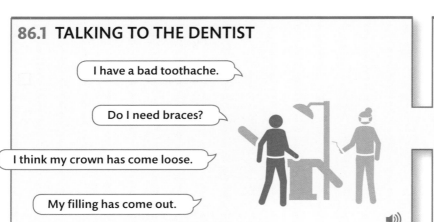

## 86.2 MORE PHRASES

Can I have my teeth whitened?

I brush my teeth twice a day.

I need to see the hygienist.

My son's first teeth are coming through.

## 86.3 ADVICE AND DIAGNOSIS

Remember to floss regularly.

It looks like you need a small filling.

Would you like to rinse your mouth out?

Make sure you don't brush too hard.

## 86.4 MORE PHRASES

Open a bit wider for me, please.

You have a buildup of plaque.

You'll need this tooth pulled.

Let me know if you feel any pain.

You have a small cavity.

## 86.5 VOCABULARY AT THE DENTIST

dentist

whitening

toothache

to floss

to brush

to rinse

cavity

filling

plaque

crown

toothbrush

braces

## 86.6 LISTEN AND NUMBER THE PICTURES IN THE ORDER THEY ARE DESCRIBED

**A** 1      **B** ☐      **C** ☐      **D** ☐      **E** ☐      **F** ☐

🔊

## 86.7 LISTEN AND NUMBER THE SENTENCES IN THE ORDER YOU HEAR THEM

**A** I have a bad toothache. ☐

**B** You have a small cavity. ☐

**C** Remember to floss regularly. 1

**D** You have a buildup of plaque. ☐

**E** Open a bit wider for me, please. ☐

**F** I need to see the hygienist. ☐

**G** Let me know if you feel any pain. ☐

**H** Make sure you don't brush too hard. ☐

**I** You'll need this tooth pulled. ☐

**J** It looks like you need a small filling. ☐

🔊

## 86.8 MATCH THE SENTENCES AND SAY THEM OUT LOUD

It looks like you need → a small filling.

**1** I brush my teeth — my teeth whitened?

**2** I need to see — the hygienist.

**3** I think my crown — are coming through.

**4** Can I have — twice a day.

**5** My son's first teeth — has come loose.

🔊

217

## 87.1 ASKING FOR THERAPY

I'm having a really tough time. Can I talk to you?

I'm finding it hard to cope.

Can I see someone face-to-face?

I'm feeling very low.

We have a walk-in clinic near you.

You don't have to go through this alone.

## 87.2 THERAPY QUESTIONS

How did that make you feel?

How is this affecting you?

So what you're saying is …

Can we explore this more?

## 87.3 GROUP THERAPY

Let's go around the group and say how we're feeling.

I've been a bit up and down.

I'm doing better this week.

These sessions are really helping me.

I'm anxious all the time.

## 87.4 MORE PHRASES

How are you feeling today?

That's a real trigger for me.

Your feelings are valid.

Talking about it really helps.

## 87.5 VOCABULARY EMOTIONS

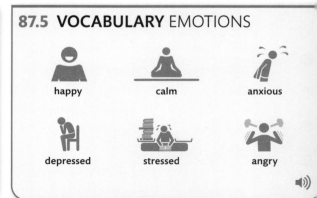

happy

calm

anxious

depressed

stressed

angry

## 87.6 LISTEN TO PERSON A AND RESPOND AS PERSON B

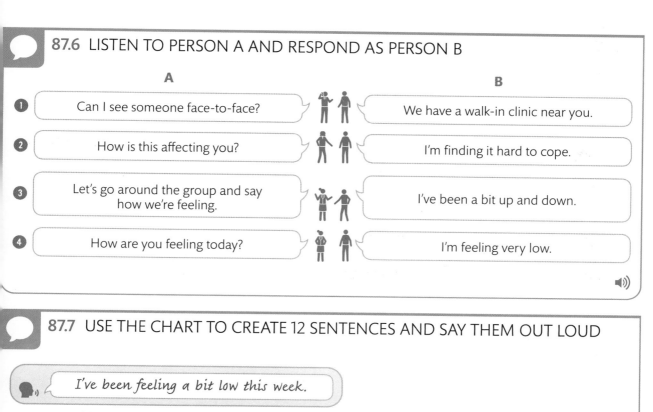

**A**

1. Can I see someone face-to-face?

2. How is this affecting you?

3. Let's go around the group and say how we're feeling.

4. How are you feeling today?

**B**

We have a walk-in clinic near you.

I'm finding it hard to cope.

I've been a bit up and down.

I'm feeling very low.

## 87.7 USE THE CHART TO CREATE 12 SENTENCES AND SAY THEM OUT LOUD

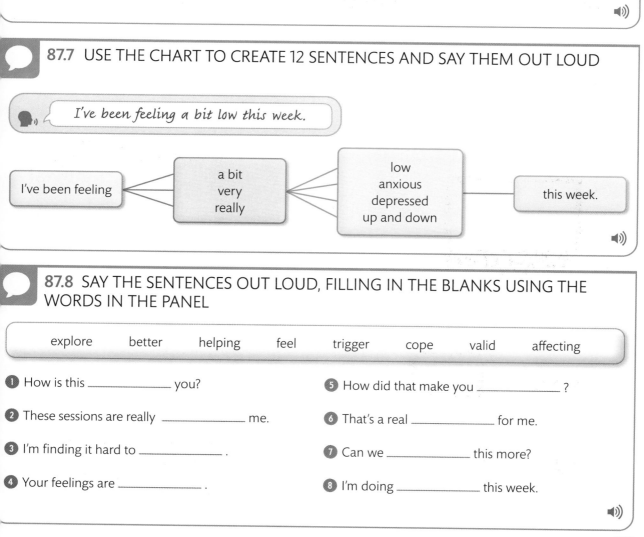

I've been feeling a bit low this week.

| I've been feeling | a bit / very / really | low / anxious / depressed / up and down | this week. |

## 87.8 SAY THE SENTENCES OUT LOUD, FILLING IN THE BLANKS USING THE WORDS IN THE PANEL

explore    better    helping    feel    trigger    cope    valid    affecting

1. How is this _____ you?

2. These sessions are really _____ me.

3. I'm finding it hard to _____ .

4. Your feelings are _____ .

5. How did that make you _____ ?

6. That's a real _____ for me.

7. Can we _____ this more?

8. I'm doing _____ this week.

## 88.1 PHONE CALLS, TEXTS, AND EMAILS

| to call | to leave a voicemail | to take a message | to put on hold | to transfer a call | to put on speaker |

| text / message | video call | email | email address | to click | to tap |

## 88.2 DEVICES

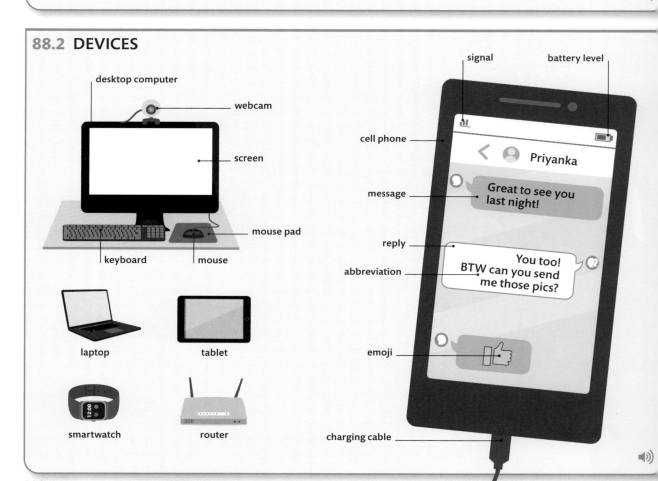

desktop computer
webcam
screen
mouse pad
keyboard
mouse

laptop
tablet
smartwatch
router

signal
battery level
cell phone
message
Priyanka
Great to see you last night!
reply
You too!
abbreviation
BTW can you send me those pics?
emoji
charging cable

## 88.3 THE INTERNET

website

Wi-Fi

broadband

Internet provider

data

account

settings

network

signal

hot spot

virus

password

menu

app

cookies

link

to browse

to stream

## 88.4 SOCIAL MEDIA

to follow

to like

to go viral

to trend

to DM someone

to live stream

to troll

to scroll

to share

to block

podcast

post

influencer

follower

hashtag

selfie

## 88.5 READING

book

e-reader

magazine

subscription

headline

article

**GIRL RAISES MONEY FOR CHARITY**

newspaper

# 89 Formal phone calls

## 89.1 MAKING A CALL

Hi, could I speak to ...?

Hello, I wonder if you can help me ...

I'm calling about ...

I'm calling you regarding ...

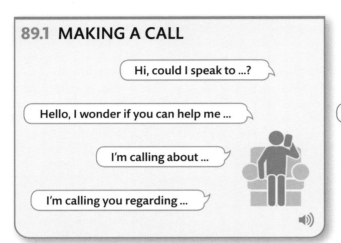

## 89.2 CALLING CUSTOMER SERVICE

Hello, customer service, how can I help?

I'll just put you on hold while I transfer you.

Thank you for waiting.

Thanks for calling.

## 89.3 LEAVING MESSAGES AND CALLING BACK

Janos isn't available right now. Can I take a message?

Yes. Please ask him to call Ash at ABC Tech as soon as possible.

## 89.4 MORE PHRASES

Can I leave a message?

He knows where to reach me.

She'll call you back shortly.

We'll need to check our system and get back to you.

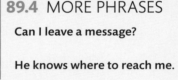

## 89.5 ENDING A CALL

Is there anything else I can help you with?

No, that's all. Thanks for your help. Goodbye.

I appreciate the call, thank you.

My pleasure.

## 89.6 MORE PHRASES

Thanks for your call.

Thank you so much for calling.

Let's speak again soon.

You've been a great help.

Have a nice evening.

## 89.7 LISTEN TO PERSON A AND RESPOND AS PERSON B

**A**

**B**

1. Janos isn't available right now. Can I take a message?

Yes. Please ask him to call Ash at ABC Tech as soon as possible.

2. I appreciate the call, thank you.

My pleasure.

3. Thank you so much for calling.

Let's speak again soon.

4. Is there anything else I can help you with?

No, that's all. Thanks for your help. Goodbye.

## 89.8 LISTEN AND NUMBER THE SENTENCES IN THE ORDER YOU HEAR THEM

A. I appreciate the call, thank you. ☐

B. Hi, could I speak to ...? ☐ 1

C. I'm calling you regarding ... ☐

D. Have a nice evening. ☐

E. Let's speak again soon. ☐

F. She'll call you back shortly. ☐

G. You've been a great help. ☐

H. Thanks for your call. ☐

## 89.9 MATCH THE SENTENCES AND SAY THEM OUT LOUD

Hello, customer service,　→　how can I help?

1. We'll need to check our system

to reach me.

2. Is there anything else

if you can help me ...

3. He knows where

I can help you with?

4. Hello, I wonder

and get back to you.

5. Thank you so much

for calling.

# 90 Informal phone calls

## 90.1 MAKING AND RECEIVING CALLS

Hi, Mom. How's it going?

Good, thank you. I'm just checking in about tonight.

Hey bud, whereabouts are you?

Hey, I'm right here!

## 90.2 MORE PHRASES

You okay?

Lovely to hear from you!

Sorry, I can't talk now.

I'll message you back.

I'll put you on speaker.

## 90.3 PHONE PROBLEMS

Dad? Can you hear me?

Hello? You're breaking up—the signal is terrible.

I dropped my phone and the screen is cracked.

Okay. We can fix it for you.

## 90.4 MORE PHRASES

I'm out of data. I'll text.

My phone has died.

My screen has frozen.

I can't remember my PIN.

I've been locked out.

## 90.5 ENDING A CALL

I need to go now. My bus is here.

Okay, see you later!

Do you have time for a chat?

Afraid not, sorry. I'm only on 5 percent battery.

So I'll see you at 8:30?

Sounds perfect. See you then!

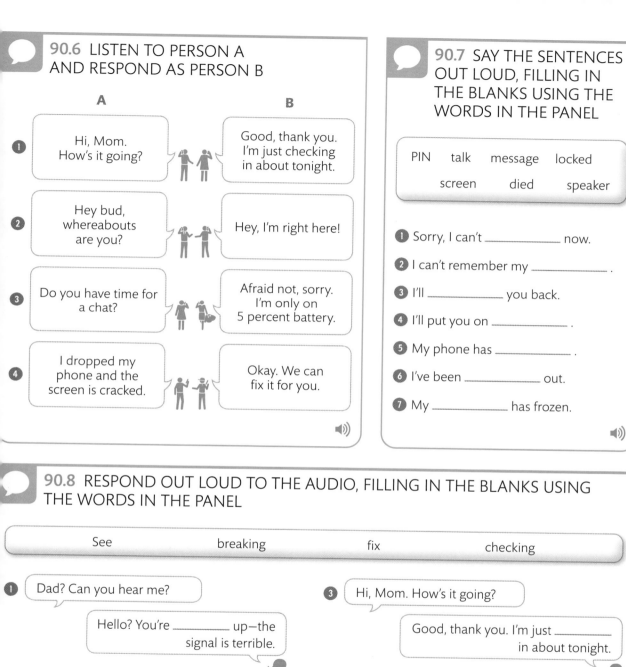

## 90.6 LISTEN TO PERSON A AND RESPOND AS PERSON B

**A** **B**

1. Hi, Mom. How's it going? — Good, thank you. I'm just checking in about tonight.

2. Hey bud, whereabouts are you? — Hey, I'm right here!

3. Do you have time for a chat? — Afraid not, sorry. I'm only on 5 percent battery.

4. I dropped my phone and the screen is cracked. — Okay. We can fix it for you.

## 90.7 SAY THE SENTENCES OUT LOUD, FILLING IN THE BLANKS USING THE WORDS IN THE PANEL

PIN    talk    message    locked

screen    died    speaker

1. Sorry, I can't _____ now.
2. I can't remember my _____ .
3. I'll _____ you back.
4. I'll put you on _____ .
5. My phone has _____ .
6. I've been _____ out.
7. My _____ has frozen.

## 90.8 RESPOND OUT LOUD TO THE AUDIO, FILLING IN THE BLANKS USING THE WORDS IN THE PANEL

See          breaking          fix          checking

1. Dad? Can you hear me?

   Hello? You're _____ up—the signal is terrible.

2. So I'll see you at 8:30?

   Sounds perfect. _____ you then!

3. Hi, Mom. How's it going?

   Good, thank you. I'm just _____ in about tonight.

4. I dropped my phone and the screen is cracked.

   Okay. We can _____ it for you.

225

# Using the Internet

## 91.1 ACCESSING WI-FI

Is it okay if I use your Wi-Fi?

Sure, the code's on the router.

How do I connect to the Internet?

Choose "free Wi-Fi" from the menu, then you can register.

I can't get a signal!

You can join my hot spot if you like.

Thanks!

## 91.2 STAYING SAFE

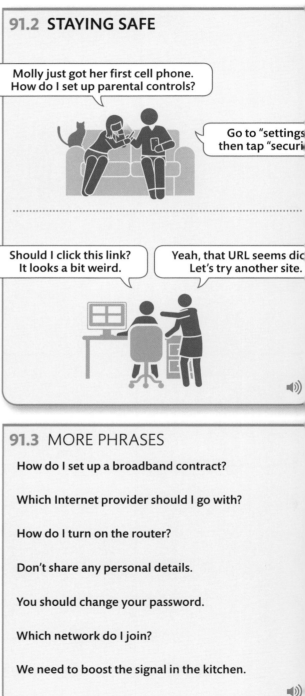

Molly just got her first cell phone. How do I set up parental controls?

Go to "settings" then tap "securi...

Should I click this link? It looks a bit weird.

Yeah, that URL seems did... Let's try another site.

## 91.3 MORE PHRASES

How do I set up a broadband contract?

Which Internet provider should I go with?

How do I turn on the router?

Don't share any personal details.

You should change your password.

Which network do I join?

We need to boost the signal in the kitchen.

## 91.4 LISTEN TO PERSON A AND RESPOND AS PERSON B

**A**                                          **B**

1. Is it okay if I use your Wi-Fi?     Sure, the code's on the router.

2. How do I connect to the Internet?     Choose "free Wi-Fi" from the menu, then you can register.

3. I can't get a signal!     You can join my hot spot if you like.

4. Should I click this link? It looks a bit weird.     Yeah, that URL seems dicey. Let's try another site.

## 91.5 LISTEN AND NUMBER THE SENTENCES IN THE ORDER YOU HEAR THEM

Ⓐ How do I set up a broadband contract? ☐

Ⓑ Which Internet provider should I go with? ☐

Ⓒ How do I turn on the router? ☐

Ⓓ Which network do I join? ☐ 1

Ⓔ Don't share any personal details. ☐

Ⓕ You should change your password. ☐

## 91.6 RESPOND OUT LOUD TO THE AUDIO, FILLING IN THE BLANKS USING THE WORDS IN THE PANEL

| site | hot spot | menu | security |

1. How do I connect to the Internet?

   Choose "free Wi-Fi" from the _____ , then you can register.

2. Molly just got her first cell phone. How do I set up parental controls?

   Go to "settings," then tap "_____ ."

3. I can't get a signal!

   You can join my _____ if you like.

4. Should I click this link? It looks a bit weird.

   Yeah, that URL seems dicey. Let's try another_____ .

## 91.7 EVERYDAY TASKS

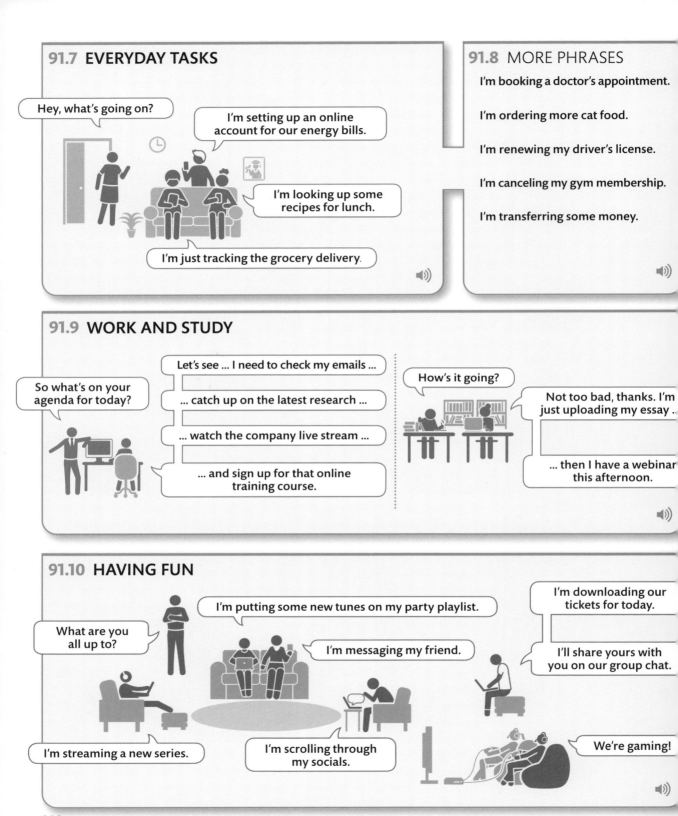

Hey, what's going on?

I'm setting up an online account for our energy bills.

I'm looking up some recipes for lunch.

I'm just tracking the grocery delivery.

## 91.8 MORE PHRASES

I'm booking a doctor's appointment.

I'm ordering more cat food.

I'm renewing my driver's license.

I'm canceling my gym membership.

I'm transferring some money.

## 91.9 WORK AND STUDY

So what's on your agenda for today?

Let's see ... I need to check my emails ...

... catch up on the latest research ...

... watch the company live stream ...

... and sign up for that online training course.

How's it going?

Not too bad, thanks. I'm just uploading my essay ...

... then I have a webinar this afternoon.

## 91.10 HAVING FUN

What are you all up to?

I'm putting some new tunes on my party playlist.

I'm messaging my friend.

I'm downloading our tickets for today.

I'll share yours with you on our group chat.

I'm streaming a new series.

I'm scrolling through my socials.

We're gaming!

## 91.11 LISTEN AND NUMBER THE PICTURES IN THE ORDER THEY ARE DESCRIBED

A ☐

B ⬚1

C ☐

D ☐

E ☐

F ☐

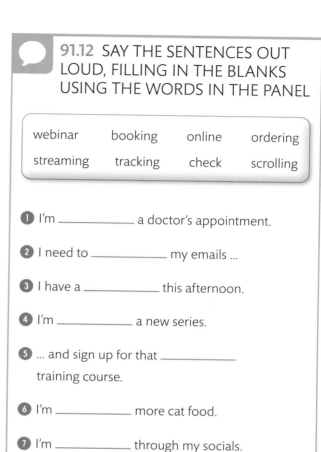

## 91.12 SAY THE SENTENCES OUT LOUD, FILLING IN THE BLANKS USING THE WORDS IN THE PANEL

| webinar | booking | online | ordering |
| streaming | tracking | check | scrolling |

1 I'm _____ a doctor's appointment.

2 I need to _____ my emails ...

3 I have a _____ this afternoon.

4 I'm _____ a new series.

5 ... and sign up for that _____ training course.

6 I'm _____ more cat food.

7 I'm _____ through my socials.

8 I'm just _____ the grocery delivery.

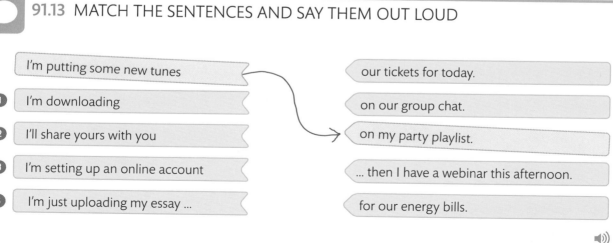

## 91.13 MATCH THE SENTENCES AND SAY THEM OUT LOUD

I'm putting some new tunes → on my party playlist.

our tickets for today.

1 I'm downloading

on our group chat.

2 I'll share yours with you

3 I'm setting up an online account

... then I have a webinar this afternoon.

4 I'm just uploading my essay ...

for our energy bills.

# 92 Digital problems

## 92.1 CONNECTION ISSUES

We can't hear you— you're breaking up!

Yeah, my Internet is really laggy today.

It says the TV's not connected to the Internet!

I think the network is down again.

I'm trying to get tickets, but the website keeps crashing.

There's too much traffic.

Oh no! I hope we don't miss out ...

## 92.2 TROUBLESHOOTING

My screen has completely frozen.

You could try restarting the computer ...

... or you could connect from a different device.

The Internet is really acting up.

Turning it off and on again might help ...

... or just move closer to the router.

## 92.3 DIGITAL SECURITY

It's asking me to set up authentication on my account.

Do you have your phone? I can show you how to do it.

I got scammed! Someone stole my bank details online.

No way! Have you canceled everything?

Yes, the bank helped me. It's all sorted.

## 92.4 LISTEN TO PERSON A AND RESPOND AS PERSON B

**A**

**B**

① It says the TV's not connected to the Internet!    I think the network is down again.

② We can't hear you—you're breaking up!    Yeah, my Internet is really laggy today.

③ It's asking me to set up authentication on my account.    Do you have your phone? I can show you how to do it.

④ The Internet is really acting up.    Turning it off and on again might help ...

## 92.5 LISTEN AND NUMBER THE SENTENCES IN THE ORDER YOU HEAR THEM

Ⓐ Turning it off and on again might help ... ☐

Ⓑ My screen has completely frozen. ☐

Ⓒ It's asking me to set up authentication on my account. ☐

Ⓓ ... or just move closer to the router. ☐

Ⓔ No way! Have you canceled everything? ☐

Ⓕ There's too much traffic. [1]

## 92.6 MATCH THE SENTENCES AND SAY THEM OUT LOUD

Someone stole    restarting the computer ...

① It's asking me to set up    completely frozen.

② I'm trying to get tickets,    my bank details online.

③ My screen has    from a different device.

④ You could try    authentication on my account.

⑤ ... or you could connect    but the website keeps crashing.

# 93 Emails

## 93.1 SENDING AND RECEIVING

Did you get my email?

I did, thanks. Sorry I haven't gotten back to you.

Has Anna sent you the trip details?

Yeah, I'll forward you her message.

## 93.2 MORE PHRASES

Your email went to my junk folder.

I've sent the file as an attachment.

Can you check this draft email?

I'm just updating my email signature.

How do I unsubscribe from updates?

## 93.3 EMAIL ISSUES

Does this attachment look okay to you?

It looks suspicious— I wouldn't download it.

I'm getting so much junk mail!

Okay, let's have a look at your filters.

I think I deleted the email with the concert tickets!

Check your trash. Maybe it's still there.

## 93.4 VOCABULARY SENDING EMAILS

inbox

outbox

junk / spam mail

trash

contact

draft

to send

to forward

to delete

to reply

to reply all

to download

to upload

attachment

## 93.5 LISTEN TO PERSON A AND RESPOND AS PERSON B

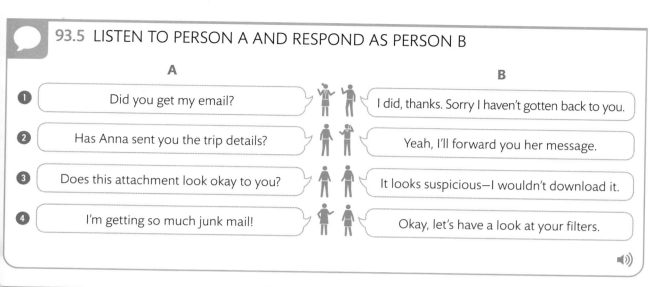

**A**

**B**

1. Did you get my email? — I did, thanks. Sorry I haven't gotten back to you.

2. Has Anna sent you the trip details? — Yeah, I'll forward you her message.

3. Does this attachment look okay to you? — It looks suspicious—I wouldn't download it.

4. I'm getting so much junk mail! — Okay, let's have a look at your filters.

## 93.6 LISTEN AND CIRCLE THE ITEM YOU HEAR

1. A B
2. A B
3. A B
4. A B
5. A B
6. A B

## 93.7 RESPOND OUT LOUD TO THE AUDIO, FILLING IN THE BLANKS USING THE WORDS IN THE PANEL

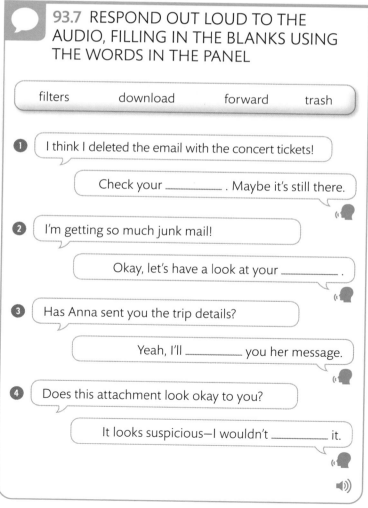

filters     download     forward     trash

1. I think I deleted the email with the concert tickets!

   Check your _____ . Maybe it's still there.

2. I'm getting so much junk mail!

   Okay, let's have a look at your _____ .

3. Has Anna sent you the trip details?

   Yeah, I'll _____ you her message.

4. Does this attachment look okay to you?

   It looks suspicious—I wouldn't _____ it.

## 94.1 TEXTING AND MESSAGING

This traffic is awful. We're going to be late for lunch!

Okay, I'll text and tell them to start without us.

I found a great campsite. I messaged you the link.

I'm just clicking on it now.

This is Magda, she just joined the choir.

Hi Magda, I'll add you to the group chat

## 94.2 TEXT SPEAK

OMG, that video is hilarious! 😄

I know, right? LOL

BTW, RU coming out with us tonight?

IDK, will have to see how I feel TBH

## 94.3 ABBREVIATIONS

| | |
|---|---|
| OMG | oh my god |
| LOL | laughing out loud |
| BTW | by the way |
| RU | are you |
| IDK | I don't know |
| TBH | to be honest |

## 94.4 VIDEO CALLS

Hey, Mom. Can you see me okay?

I can, sweetheart! Can you see me?

I can only see the top of your head! Try moving your tablet.

## 🌐 GOOD TO KNOW

In informal written English that people use for texting and messaging, it is common to omit punctuation, particularly periods at the end of messages. You may also see text-speak abbreviations in lowercase letters, such as **idk**, instead of in block capital letters, such as **IDK**.

## 94.5 LISTEN TO PERSON A AND RESPOND AS PERSON B

**A**

**B**

❶ This traffic is awful. We're going to be late for lunch!

Okay, I'll text and tell them to start without us.

❷ I found a great campsite. I messaged you the link.

I'm just clicking on it now.

❸ This is Magda, she just joined the choir.

Hi Magda, I'll add you to the group chat!

❹ Hey, Mom. Can you see me okay?

I can, sweetheart! Can you see me?

## 94.6 LISTEN AND NUMBER THE SENTENCES IN THE ORDER YOU HEAR THEM

Ⓐ I'm just clicking on it now. ☐

Ⓑ BTW, RU coming out with us tonight? ☐ 1

Ⓒ Okay, I'll text and tell them to start without us. ☐

Ⓓ OMG, that video is hilarious! ☐

Ⓔ Hi Magda, I'll add you to the group chat! ☐

Ⓕ I know, right? LOL ☐

Ⓖ IDK, will have to see how I feel TBH ☐

Ⓗ Hey, Mom. Can you see me okay? ☐

Ⓘ I messaged you the link. ☐

## 94.7 RESPOND OUT LOUD TO THE AUDIO, FILLING IN THE BLANKS USING THE WORDS IN THE PANEL

| IDK | see | LOL | clicking |

❶ I messaged you the link.

I'm just _____ on it now.

❷ BTW, RU coming out with us tonight?

_____ , will have to see how I feel TBH

❸ Hey, Mom. Can you see me okay?

I can, sweetheart! Can you _____ me?

❹ OMG, that video is hilarious!

I know, right? _____

235

# 95 Social media

## 95.1 USING SOCIAL MEDIA

Did you get any good photos on your trip?

They're all up on my profile.

Check out this selfie I took at the Taj Mahal!

I've just followed you so we can stay in touch.

Cool, I can see you in my notifications.

Oh no! That guy I met just DM'd me.

Not him! Just block him.

## 95.2 GOING VIRAL

My dog-grooming videos have gone viral!

I saw! I think you've broken the Internet.

You have tons of followers!

Yeah, a few big accounts have been sharing my posts.

Did you see that reel of Ush making a massive cake?

It's adorable, right? It has hundreds of "likes"!

## 95.3 BUILDING A BUSINESS

So we need to grow our social reach.

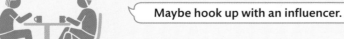

More video content would help.

Or how about a monthly podcast?

Maybe hook up with an influencer.

We could live stream the launch party.

## 95.4 MORE PHRASES

There are tons of comments on my post!

That's just a troll. I'm blocking them.

Click the follow button to get all our updates!

## 95.5 LISTEN TO PERSON A AND RESPOND AS PERSON B

**A**

**B**

❶ I've just followed you so we can stay in touch.

Cool, I can see you in my notifications.

❷ Oh no! That guy I met just DM'd me.

Not him! Just block him.

❸ Did you see that reel of Usha making a massive cake?

It's adorable, right? It has hundreds of "likes"!

❹ You have tons of followers!

Yeah, a few big accounts have been sharing my posts.

## 95.6 LISTEN TO THE AUDIO AND MATCH THE CORRECT RESPONSE

Did you get any good photos on your trip?

Or how about a monthly podcast?

❶ My dog-grooming videos have gone viral!

Not him! Just block him.

❷ We could live stream the launch party.

I saw! I think you've broken the Internet.

❸ Oh no! That guy I met just DM'd me.

They're all up on my profile.

## 95.7 SAY THE SENTENCES OUT LOUD, FILLING IN THE BLANKS USING THE WORDS IN THE PANEL

| Internet | podcast | troll | profile | comments | content |

❶ Or how about a monthly _____ ?

❷ That's just a _____ . I'm blocking them.

❸ I saw! I think you've broken the _____ .

❹ There are tons of _____ on my post!

❺ They're all up on my _____ .

❻ More video _____ would help.

# 96 Reading

## 96.1 DISCUSSING BOOKS

It's the best book I've read in ages.

I agree. I couldn't put it down!

Yeah, it had me on the edge of my seat!

The ending was a bit of a letdown.

I found it pretty rough going, actually.

## 96.2 AT THE BOOKSTORE

Can you recommend a good vacation read?

Yes, this one is a real page-turner.

Can I help at all?

No, thanks. I'm just browsing.

I'm afraid that book's out of stock.

Okay, could you or it for me, please

## 96.3 MAGAZINES AND NEWSPAPERS

Want a flip through *Fashion Monthly*?

Yes, please, if you've finished with it.

Have you seen today's headlines?

No, what's been going on?

Did you renew our subscription to *World Weekly*?

Sorry, not yet—I'll do it now!

## 96.4 LISTEN TO PERSON A AND RESPOND AS PERSON B

**A**            **B**

**1** Have you seen today's headlines?    No, what's been going on?

**2** Want a flip through *Fashion Monthly*?    Yes, please, if you've finished with it.

**3** Can you recommend a good vacation read?    Yes, this one is a real page-turner.

**4** It's the best book I've read in ages.    I agree. I couldn't put it down!

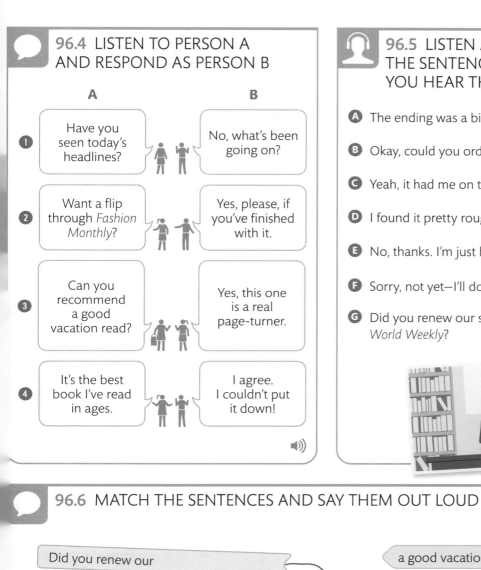

## 96.5 LISTEN AND NUMBER THE SENTENCES IN THE ORDER YOU HEAR THEM

**A** The ending was a bit of a letdown. ☐

**B** Okay, could you order it for me, please? ☐

**C** Yeah, it had me on the edge of my seat! ☐

**D** I found it pretty rough going, actually. ☑ 1

**E** No, thanks. I'm just browsing. ☐

**F** Sorry, not yet—I'll do it now! ☐

**G** Did you renew our subscription to *World Weekly*? ☐

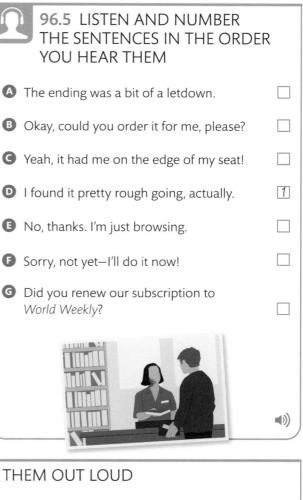

## 96.6 MATCH THE SENTENCES AND SAY THEM OUT LOUD

Did you renew our      a good vacation read?

**1** Can you recommend      *Fashion Monthly*?

**2** It's the best book      rough going, actually.

**3** Yeah, it had me on      I've read in ages.

**4** I found it pretty      subscription to *World Weekly*?

**5** Want a flip through      the edge of my seat!

# Answers

Audio recordings are available for you to listen to for all answers marked with the symbol 🔊. Please see pp.8–9 for more information on how to access all the supporting audio resources for this book.

## 01

### 1.7
- **A** 2
- **B** 6
- **C** 7
- **D** 3
- **E** 8
- **F** 4
- **G** 1
- **H** 5

### 1.8 🔊
1. How do you **do**?
2. **Good** evening.
3. It's nice to **meet** you.
4. Good **afternoon**.
5. Hey, Jay, how's it **going**?
6. **Hey**, everyone!
7. How are you **doing**?
8. Long **time** no see!

## 02

### 2.6 🔊
1. This is my friend, Kit.
2. I'd like to introduce my friend, Kit.
3. I'd like you to meet my friend, Kit.
4. This is my partner, Kit.
5. I'd like to introduce my partner, Kit.
6. I'd like you to meet my partner, Kit.
7. This is my colleague, Kit.
8. I'd like to introduce my colleague, Kit.
9. I'd like you to meet my colleague, Kit.

### 2.7 🔊
1. Of course. I'm Samantha, but you can **call** me Sam.
2. It's a pleasure to **meet** you, Mr. Ali.
3. I don't think so. **Great** to meet you!
4. **How's it going**? I'm Joe.

## 04

### 4.4
- **A** 6
- **B** 4
- **C** 1
- **D** 8
- **E** 7
- **F** 2
- **G** 3
- **H** 5

### 4.5 🔊
1. Sorry, my English **isn't great**.
2. Sorry, I didn't **catch that**.
3. I'm not quite sure **what you mean**.
4. Sorry, I'm not **following you**.
5. Can you repeat **that more slowly, please?**

### 4.6 🔊
1. Sorry? Could you say that again, please?
2. Sorry? Could you repeat that more slowly, please?
3. Sorry? Could you explain that one more time, please?
4. Sorry? Could you talk me through that again, please?
5. Excuse me? Could you say that again, please?
6. Excuse me? Could you repeat that more slowly, please?
7. Excuse me? Could you explain that one more time, please?
8. Excuse me? Could you talk me through that again, please?
9. Pardon? Could you say that again, please?
10. Pardon? Could you repeat that more slowly, please?
11. Pardon? Could you explain that one more time, please?
12. Pardon? Could you talk me through that again, please?

## 05

### 5.5 🔊
1. Yes, I'm really **into** it right now!
2. I absolutely **love** them!
3. I've **always** loved it.
4. I'm a big **fan**!
5. Yeah, it's **pretty** good!
6. It's so my **thing**!
7. This soup is **great**, isn't it?
8. What do you **think**?

### 5.6 🔊
1. I'm not much of **a sushi fan**.
2. Skateboarding isn't really **my thing**.
3. No way! I can't **stand them**.
4. I couldn't think of **anything worse!**

### 5.12
- **A** 4
- **B** 3
- **C** 8
- **D** 1
- **E** 2
- **F** 5
- **G** 10
- **H** 7
- **I** 9
- **J** 6

### 5.13 🔊
1. I'd prefer tacos.
2. I'd rather have tacos.
3. I'd much rather have tacos.
4. I'd definitely go for tacos.
5. I'd prefer pizza.
6. I'd rather have pizza.
7. I'd much rather have pizza.
8. I'd definitely go for pizza.

## 06

### 6.5 🔊
1. Yeah, I know what you mean.
2. Yeah, I hear you.
3. Yeah, I couldn't agree more.
4. Yeah, I totally agree.
5. Absolutely, I know what you mean.
6. Absolutely, I hear you.
7. Absolutely, I couldn't agree more.
8. Absolutely, I totally agree.
9. Exactly, I know what you mean.
10. Exactly, I hear you.
11. Exactly, I couldn't agree more.
12. Exactly, I totally agree.

### 6.6 🔊
1. Absolutely, I couldn't **agree more.**
2. I don't think **so either.**
3. I know **what you mean.**
4. We might have to agree **to disagree on this!**
5. Sorry, I'm not **with you on this one.**

## 07

**7.6** 🔊
1. **Why** don't we bike to the park?
2. I **think** I'll give it a pass.
3. **Count** me in!
4. I know! **Let's** go swimming!
5. **Sure** thing!
6. I'm not that **interested**, to be honest.
7. **Sounds** good.
8. I don't really **feel** like it, sorry.

**7.7** 🔊
1. Is anyone going to Juan's party tomorrow?
2. Is anyone going to the beach tomorrow?
3. Is anyone going to the castle tomorrow?
4. How about hitting Juan's party tomorrow?
5. How about hitting the beach tomorrow?
6. How about hitting the castle tomorrow?
7. Are you up for Juan's party tomorrow?
8. Are you up for the beach tomorrow?
9. Are you up for the castle tomorrow?

## 08

**8.4**
| | |
|---|---|
| A 2 | E 6 |
| B 8 | F 5 |
| C 1 | G 3 |
| D 7 | H 4 |

**8.5** 🔊
1. Don't **mention** it.
2. Thank you so **much**!
3. My **pleasure**!
4. I can't thank you **enough**!
5. Thank you, I really **appreciate** it.

## 09

**9.5**
| | |
|---|---|
| A 7 | E 5 |
| B 2 | F 8 |
| C 1 | G 3 |
| D 6 | H 4 |

**9.6** 🔊
1. Thanks, I appreciate **you saying that**.
2. That's okay, **it was nothing**.
3. I'm really sorry **I forgot your birthday!**
4. Thank you, that **means a lot**.

## 10

**10.4**
| | |
|---|---|
| A 4 | E 6 |
| B 1 | F 8 |
| C 7 | G 3 |
| D 5 | H 2 |

**10.5** 🔊
1. Thank you **for your time**.
2. It was a pleasure **meeting you**.
3. Good talking **with you**.
4. Speak to **you soon**.
5. Bye! Have **a safe trip!**
6. Great to **catch up!**

**10.6** 🔊
1. It was a pleasure meeting you.
2. It was great meeting you.
3. It was good meeting you.
4. It was a pleasure to see you.
5. It was great to see you.
6. It was good to see you.
7. It was a pleasure talking with you.
8. It was great talking with you.
9. It was good talking with you.

## 12

**12.4** 🔊
1. Could we do Sunday instead?
2. Let's make it quarter after, just to be sure.
3. Friday works for me.
4. It's at 10.

**12.6** 🔊
1. Which day **suits** you for lunch this week?
2. Friday **works** for me.
3. Sunday is **good** with us!
4. Hey, are you free for a drink **on Tuesday**?
5. Sorry, we can't come over **next** Saturday.
6. Keep it **free**!
7. We've set the date for **May 31st** of next year!

## 13

**13.6**
| | |
|---|---|
| A 4 | E 5 |
| B 1 | F 6 |
| C 3 | G 8 |
| D 2 | H 7 |

**13.7** 🔊
1. It's really windy today, isn't it?
2. It's freezing today, isn't it?
3. It's boiling today, isn't it?
4. It's a little chilly today, isn't it?
5. It's lovely weather today, isn't it?
6. It's really windy out there!
7. It's freezing out there!
8. It's boiling out there!
9. It's a little chilly out there!
10. It's lovely weather out there!

## 15

**15.4**
| | |
|---|---|
| A 5 | D 2 |
| B 1 | E 4 |
| C 6 | F 3 |

**15.6** 🔊
1. Yes, I have a **brother and two stepsisters**.
2. I'm an **only child**.
3. I have two **younger sisters**.
4. We grew up **in Springfield**.

## 16

**16.5**
| | |
|---|---|
| A 6 | F 1 |
| B 2 | G 4 |
| C 3 | H 5 |
| D 8 | I 10 |
| E 7 | J 9 |

**16.6** 🔊
1. **Happy** birthday!
2. I hear **congratulations** are in order?
3. We're really **proud** of you!
4. All the **best** for your retirement.
5. Well **done**!
6. I'll **miss** you all!

## 17

**17.3** 🔊
1. I'm good! How are things with you?
2. I didn't know you were coming!
3. At a thrift store—for 10 dollars!
4. I'm an English teacher. How about you?

## 18

**18.6** 🔊
1. Interested in going for coffee this Saturday?
2. Interested in going for coffee next Friday?
3. Interested in going for coffee sometime?
4. Interested in going out this Saturday?
5. Interested in going out next Friday?
6. Interested in going out sometime?
7. I was wondering if you'd like to go for coffee this Saturday?
8. I was wondering if you'd like to go for coffee next Friday?
9. I was wondering if you'd like to go for coffee sometime?
10. I was wondering if you'd like to go out this Saturday?
11. I was wondering if you'd like to go out next Friday?
12. I was wondering if you'd like to go out sometime?

**18.7** 🔊
1. I was hoping **you'd ask me.**
2. You took **your time!**
3. That would be **really nice.**
4. I just like you **as a friend.**

**18.12**
A 7      F 6
B 1      G 2
C 3      H 10
D 4      I 5
E 8      J 9

**18.13** 🔊
1. It was nice to **hang** out with you.
2. What kind of things are you **into**?
3. I'd really like to see you **again**.
4. I'd better **head** off. Early start tomorrow!
5. How long have you been **single**?
6. I'm just **booking** a ride.

## 19

**19.4**
A 5      E 2
B 1      F 7
C 6      G 4
D 3

**19.6** 🔊
1. Anything you need, just **ask**.
2. Let me know if I can do **anything**.
3. I know things are **tough**, but we're here for you.
4. You've been a lot of **help**.
5. That's really **sweet**. I will!
6. I'm very **grateful**.
7. I know this hasn't been **easy**.
8. Thank you, I really **appreciate** it.

## 21

**21.3**
1. A
2. B
3. B
4. A
5. B
6. A

## 22

**22.5**
A 3      D 6
B 1      E 2
C 4      F 5

**22.6** 🔊
1. Want to get curry **takeout** tonight?
2. Two burgers to **go**, please.
3. I'll **pick** it up on my way home.
4. Okay, I'll **order** it on the app.
5. We have no food. **Let's** get pizza!
6. Our fried chicken order still hasn't **arrived**.
7. Let me **check** what's happening.
8. Do you **want** fries with that?

## 23

**23.6**
A 5      E 6
B 3      F 8
C 7      G 2
D 1      H 4

**23.7** 🔊
1. Can I get a **beer**, please?
2. Do you serve **mocktails**?
3. A glass of **wine** for me, please!
4. What **cocktails** can you recommend?
5. What **soft drinks** are there?

## 24

**24.7**
A 2      D 6
B 3      E 4
C 1      F 5

**24.8** 🔊
1. I'll bring you the **menu**.
2. I'll have the **steak**, please.
3. Could you bring us a **pitcher of water**, please
4. I think I'll go for the **fish**.
5. I'll bring you the **black pepper**.
6. Could I have the **salad**?

**24.13**
1. A
2. B
3. B
4. A

**24.14** 🔊
1. Nothing **special**, to be honest.
2. No, I'll **get this**.
3. It's a bit too salty, **actually**.
4. **Really tasty**. How's yours?

**24.15** 🔊
1. This chicken is a bit too salty, actually.
2. This chicken is a bit too cold, actually.
3. This chicken is nothing special, actually.
4. This chicken is really tasty, actually.
5. This chicken is a bit too salty, to be honest.
6. This chicken is a bit too cold, to be hones
7. This chicken is nothing special, to be hone
8. This chicken is really tasty, to be honest.

## 25

### 5.5
- 4
- D 5
- 3
- E 6
- 1
- F 2

### 5.7 🔊
- I'll start **weighing** the flour.
- **Chop** the butter into cubes.
- **Preheat** the oven to 475°F (250°C).
- Turn it down and **simmer** for 20 minutes.
- I'm **roasting** a chicken for lunch.
- **Mix** the ingredients together.
- I've **baked** you a birthday cake!
- Okay, I'll **set** the timer!

### 5.13
- 4
- E 8
- 5
- F 6
- 1
- G 3
- 2
- H 7

### 5.14 🔊
- I think I'll start **with a mushroom kebab.**
- I'd love **a bit of everything!**
- I'm allergic **to shellfish.**
- Should I make some **garlic bread to** with it?
- Thanks for **having us over.**
- Something **smells good!**

### 5.15 🔊
- This is so delicious.
- This is really delicious.
- This is absolutely delicious.
- This is so amazing!
- This is really amazing!
- This is absolutely amazing!
- This is so fantastic!
- This is really fantastic!
- This is absolutely fantastic!
- This is so yummy.
- This is really yummy.
- This is absolutely yummy.

## 27

### 27.6
- A 5
- D 2
- B 1
- E 6
- C 3
- F 4

### 27.7 🔊
1. The **3D glasses** made it so realistic!
2. Which **screen** is it showing at?
3. Can we have **seats** at the back?
4. I wasn't **happy** about the ending.
5. Is there time to get **popcorn**?
6. How long is the **movie**?
7. Is this the **subtitled** screening?
8. Is the movie okay for **kids** under 10?

## 28

### 28.6
1. A
2. B
3. A
4. A
5. B
6. B

### 28.7 🔊
1. I've booked seats **in the front row.**
2. Is there **an intermission?**
3. Can I see **your tickets, please?**
4. Where is **the cloakroom?**

### 28.8 🔊
1. Follow me. You're in the front row.
2. Follow me. You're in the back row.
3. Follow me. You're in Box 5.
4. I've booked seats in the front row.
5. I've booked seats in the back row.
6. I've booked seats in Box 5.

## 29

### 29.5
- A 4
- E 1
- B 2
- F 7
- C 5
- G 3
- D 6
- H 8

### 29.6 🔊
1. Here's **the lineup** for the whole weekend.
2. I'll meet you back in **the main arena.**
3. No, we can just **turn up.**
4. 9 p.m., but the opening band has just **come on.**
5. What an amazing **performance!**

## 30

### 30.6
- A 3
- E 8
- B 5
- F 2
- C 1
- G 7
- D 4
- H 6

### 30.7 🔊
1. Have you been to this yoga class before?
2. Have you been to this Pilates class before?
3. Have you been to this fitness class before?
4. Have you been to this spin class before?
5. Have you been to this dance class before?

## 31

### 31.4 🔊
1. Yes, we run them on Saturdays.
2. Of course. What time would you like?
3. Over here!
4. No, I sprained my ankle last week!

### 31.6 🔊
1. Wanna join us for a game of **badminton**?
2. Are you coming to **ice hockey** practice?
3. Do you give **golf** lessons here?
4. I'd like to book a **tennis** lesson, please.
5. We run **soccer** practice on Mondays.

## 32

### 32.5
- A 6
- D 5
- B 1
- E 2
- C 4
- F 3

## 32.6 🔊
1 Any seats left for the golf tournament today?
2 Any seats left for the tennis final today?
3 Any seats left for track and field today?
4 Any seats left for the soccer game today?
5 Want to go to the golf tournament today?
6 Want to go to the tennis final today?
7 Want to go to track and field today?
8 Want to go to the soccer game today?

# 33

## 33.4
1 B
2 A
3 B
4 A
5 B

## 33.5 🔊
1 I'm giving **pottery** a try!
2 I've taken up **knitting** recently.
3 I only started learning **karate** a year ago.
4 I usually play **tennis** on weekends.
5 I've just started learning the **piano**.
6 I've been playing the **guitar** for six years.

## 33.6 🔊
1 I've been doing karate for two years.
2 I've been playing the guitar for two years.
3 I've been learning the piano for two years.
4 I've been playing tennis for two years.
5 I've been doing karate since I was 12.
6 I've been playing the guitar since I was 12.
7 I've been learning the piano since I was 12.
8 I've been playing tennis since I was 12.

# 35

## 35.6
1 A
2 A
3 A
4 B
5 A

## 35.7 🔊
1 Can I have a jar of honey, please?
2 Can I have a bunch of grapes, please?
3 Can I have a loaf of bread, please?
4 Can I have a punnet of strawberries, please?
5 Can I have a carton of eggs, please?
6 Could I have a jar of honey, please?
7 Could I have a bunch of grapes, please?
8 Could I have a loaf of bread, please?
9 Could I have a punnet of strawberries, please?
10 Could I have a carton of eggs, please?

# 36

## 36.2
A 3    D 6
B 5    E 2
C 1    F 4

## 36.3
1 B
2 A
3 B
4 B
5 B
6 A

## 36.9
A 3    D 5
B 6    E 4
C 1    F 2

## 36.10 🔊
1 Excuse me, where's the **frozen food** aisle?
2 Would you like to use the **self-checkout**?
3 Where can I find the **pet food**?
4 Do you have **baby products** here?
5 I can't find the **fruit** and **vegetables**.

# 37

## 37.5
A 2    D 3
B 1    E 6
C 4    F 5

## 37.6 🔊
1 Will it **survive** the winter?
2 When is the best time to plant these **seeds**?
3 How much **sunlight** do they need?
4 Does it need much **looking** after?
5 How often should I **feed** it?
6 How do I get rid of **weeds**?

## 37.7 🔊
1 We need some advice **on starting a vegetable garden.**
2 What's a good **compost to use?**
3 I don't really mind, but **my apartment doesn't get much light.**
4 What kind of houseplants **are you looking for?**
5 How do I **get rid of weeds?**

# 38

## 38.6
A 5    F 4
B 7    G 6
C 1    H 3
D 8    I 10
E 2    J 9

## 38.7 🔊
1 I'm looking for a **screwdriver**.
2 Where can I find a **hammer**?
3 Do you have any **drills**?
4 Who can I ask about **saws**?
5 What kind of **nails** do you sell?
6 Where are the **screws**?

## 38.8 🔊
1 What do I need for plastering walls?
2 What would you recommend for plastering walls?
3 What's best for plastering walls?
4 What do I need for tiling my bathroom?
5 What would you recommend for tiling my bathroom?
6 What's best for tiling my bathroom?
7 What do I need for filling a crack?
8 What would you recommend for filling a crack?
9 What's best for filling a crack?

# 39

## 39.4
| | |
|---|---|
| Ⓐ 1 | Ⓓ 2 |
| Ⓑ 6 | Ⓔ 4 |
| Ⓒ 3 | Ⓕ 5 |

## 39.6 🔊
Ⓐ Do you have this sweater in a size 10, please?
Ⓑ Do you have this jacket in a size 10, please?
Ⓒ Do you have this suit in a size 10, please?
Ⓓ Do you have this shirt in a size 10, please?
Ⓔ Do you have this sweater in a larger size, please?
Ⓕ Do you have this jacket in a larger size, please?
Ⓖ Do you have this suit in a larger size, please?
Ⓗ Do you have this shirt in a larger size, please?
Ⓘ Do you have this sweater in the next size down, please?
Ⓙ Do you have this jacket in the next size down, please?
Ⓚ Do you have this suit in the next size down, please?
Ⓛ Do you have this shirt in the next size down, please?

# 40

## 40.5 🔊
Ⓐ The **boots** are too tight.
Ⓑ Where can I return these **shoes**?
Ⓒ This **dress** is too small.
Ⓓ I have to return this, but I lost my **receipt**.
Ⓔ The **pants** don't fit right.
Ⓕ I need to return this **bag**.

# 41

## 41.6 🔊
Ⓐ Can you do **Thursday at 3 p.m.?**
Ⓑ Is Saturday afternoon **any good?**
Ⓒ I just need **a quick trim.**
Ⓓ Sorry, we're fully **booked on Thursday.**
Ⓔ Can you come in **on Monday?**

## 41.7 🔊
❶ Can you fit me in on Monday?
❷ Can you fit me in on Tuesday afternoon?
❸ Can you fit me in on Wednesday morning?
❹ Can you fit me in on Thursday at 3 p.m.?
❺ Can you do Monday?
❻ Can you do Tuesday afternoon?
❼ Can you do Wednesday morning?
❽ Can you do Thursday at 3 p.m.?

## 41.11
| | |
|---|---|
| Ⓐ 5 | Ⓕ 7 |
| Ⓑ 1 | Ⓖ 2 |
| Ⓒ 8 | Ⓗ 6 |
| Ⓓ 9 | Ⓘ 3 |
| Ⓔ 4 | |

## 41.12 🔊
❶ I feel like a change, but I don't know what to **go for.**
❷ Just **my usual,** I think.
❸ I'll have some **gel** on it, please.
❹ What color would be **best** for me?
❺ Could you cut the bangs **a bit more?**
❻ I think a shorter style would really **suit you.**
❼ Leave it longer **on top,** please.

## 41.13 🔊
❶ What style would be best for me?
❷ What color would be best for me?
❸ What highlights would be best for me?
❹ What style would suit me?
❺ What color would suit me?
❻ What highlights would suit me?
❼ What style should I go for?
❽ What color should I go for?
❾ What highlights should I go for?

# 42

## 42.6
| | |
|---|---|
| Ⓐ 3 | Ⓓ 5 |
| Ⓑ 1 | Ⓔ 6 |
| Ⓒ 2 | Ⓕ 4 |

## 42.7 🔊
❶ How many would you **like?**
❷ Can you **put** it on the scale, please?
❸ How much does it **cost** to send this to Japan?
❹ I'm here to **pick up** a package.
❺ Can you **sign** for this, please?
❻ How soon will my package **arrive?**
❼ Can I **send** this letter to France?
❽ Sure. I've been **waiting** for it to arrive!

# 43

## 43.5
❶ A
❷ B
❸ A
❹ B

## 43.6 🔊
❶ I'd like to open a bank account, please.
❷ I'd like to withdraw $300 in cash, please.
❸ I'd like to open a savings account, please.
❹ I'd like to transfer money into my bank account, please.
❺ I'd like to deposit money into my savings account, please.

## 43.12 🔊
❶ You can transfer **your share later.**
❷ I've just ordered **our vacation money!**
❸ The ATM just **swallowed my card!**
❹ Should we split it **three ways?**
❺ Let me know **your bank details.**

# 44

## 44.5
| | |
|---|---|
| Ⓐ 1 | Ⓓ 2 |
| Ⓑ 5 | Ⓔ 3 |
| Ⓒ 4 | Ⓕ 6 |

## 44.6 🔊
❶ Do you run computer **courses** here?
❷ Do you have this as an **audiobook?**
❸ I need to renew these **books,** please.
❹ How do I join the **library?**
❺ Where is the children's **section?**
❻ Can I see your **newspaper** archive?

## 46

**46.7**
1. A
2. A
3. A
4. B

**46.8** ◀))
1. Is there a math club?
2. Is there a science club?
3. Is there a history club?
4. Is there an after-school club?
5. Is there an art club?

## 47

**47.6**
- A. 4
- B. 1
- C. 6
- D. 3
- E. 2
- F. 5

**47.7** ◀))
1. What are your entry **requirements**?
2. Sure, it's a two-year, **full-time** program.
3. I've just signed up for the French **class**.
4. The **teacher** is amazing!
5. The **website** also has lots of information.
6. What **qualifications** do I need?
7. Is there a chance to study **abroad**?
8. Students work once a week in a **salon**.

**47.12**
- A. 2
- B. 5
- C. 1
- D. 4
- E. 6
- F. 3

**47.13** ◀))
1. Do you know where the art school is?
2. Do you know where the humanities department is?
3. Do you know where the physics lecture is?
4. Do you know where the coffee shop is?
5. Can you tell me where the art school is?
6. Can you tell me where the humanities department is?
7. Can you tell me where the physics lecture is?
8. Can you tell me where the coffee shop is?
9. Any idea where the art school is?

10. Any idea where the humanities department is?
11. Any idea where the physics lecture is?
12. Any idea where the coffee shop is?

**47.19**
1. A
2. B
3. B
4. A

**47.20** ◀))
1. I'm finding it hard to **make friends**.
2. I'd **rather not**, actually.
3. Not **too bad**!
4. I'd be **up for that**!

**47.21** ◀))
1. How are you finding **your first week**?
2. I'm feeling **a bit homesick**.
3. I think I'll **pass**.
4. Sounds like **fun!**

## 48

**48.5**
- A. 2
- B. 4
- C. 3
- D. 5
- E. 6
- F. 1
- G. 7

**48.6** ◀))
1. Okay, let me get some **details** about you.
2. This **job** looks interesting …
3. I'm looking for a **part-time** sales job.
4. What **hours** can you work?
5. Have you used this job search **website**?
6. Yes, could you email us your **resume**?
7. What **skills** do you have?
8. Is the job in the **window** still open?

## 49

**49.5**
1. A
2. B
3. B

**49.6** ◀))
1. I really want to apply for **this job.**
2. I just need to fill in **my personal details and it'll be ready.**
3. Don't forget to send **your cover letter, too!**
4. Have you finished **your application yet?**

## 50

**50.5** ◀))
1. I'm used to working under pressure.
2. I'm a quick learner.
3. I enjoy solving problems.
4. I'm really eager to use my planning skills.

**50.6** ◀))
1. What can you bring to our **company**?
2. What **salary** are you expecting?
3. What's the **notice** period in your current job?
4. How soon could you **start**?
5. I'm used to **working** under pressure.
6. I'm good with **customers**.

**50.7** ◀))
1. I have the experience you're looking for.
2. I have the skills you're looking for.
3. I have the qualifications you're looking for.
4. I have the enthusiasm you're looking for.
5. I have the strengths you're looking for.

## 51

**51.7**
- A. 3
- B. 1
- C. 5
- D. 7
- E. 2
- F. 4
- G. 6

**51.8** ◀))
1. Your first **break** is at 12:30.
2. And always wear your **hard hat!**
3. It's great to have you on the **team**.
4. I've set up your **email** account.
5. Want to grab some **lunch**?
6. How's your **morning** been?
7. Do you have **everything** you need?
8. Can you type in a **password**?

## 52

### 52.5
1 A
2 A
3 B
4 A

### 52.6 🔊
1 It's in half an hour. **How about** yours?
2 Not again! Okay, **let's call** the supervisor.
3 I'm **scheduled for** the morning shift.
4 Thanks. I'll **put it in** my calendar.

## 53

### 53.4
A 3
B 1
C 4
D 2
E 8
F 6
G 5
H 7

### 53.5 🔊
1 Now let's turn to **the subject of …**
2 The focus of **my presentation is …**
3 Last, **I'd like to finish by saying …**
4 Does anyone have **anything to add?**
5 Now I'd like to **talk about …**
6 First, **I'd like to begin by saying …**

### 53.6 🔊
1 Today, I'd like to talk about …
2 First, I'd like to talk about …
3 Now I'd like to talk about …
4 Last, I'd like to talk about …
5 Finally, I'd like to talk about …
6 Today, I'm going to talk about …
7 First, I'm going to talk about …
8 Now I'm going to talk about …
9 Last, I'm going to talk about …
10 Finally, I'm going to talk about …

## 54

### 54.5 🔊
1 Can I jump in? **I totally agree.**
2 If I can just add … **It will be a slow process.**
3 So that's the situation. **Let's hear your thoughts.**

4 Just to clarify … **Which changes exactly?**
5 May I go first? **For me, these changes are important.**

### 54.7 🔊
1 Let's hear from James on this **point.**
2 I think we're all here, so let's get **started.**
3 If you **ask** me, it's a nonstarter.
4 I see where you're **coming** from, so …
5 Can I **jump** in? I totally agree.
6 Just to **clarify** … Which changes exactly?
7 Let's go around the table and see where we all **stand.**

### 54.11
A 5
B 4
C 1
D 8
E 7
F 2
G 6
H 3

### 54.12 🔊
1 You, too. Let's stay **in touch.**
2 That's right. Sorry, I didn't catch **your name.**
3 Me, too. Let's **follow up** in the office.

## 55

### 55.6
A 6
B 5
C 4
D 1
E 3
F 7
G 2

### 55.7 🔊
1 Sorry for interrupting, **please keep going.**
2 Should we schedule **another meeting?**
3 My connection **keeps dropping.**
4 Would you like to **speak first?**
5 Can you enlarge it **on your screen?**
6 Great! I'll run through **the key points.**

## 57

### 57.7 🔊
1 We'd need to **put in a new kitchen.**
2 I want a property **close to the subway.**
3 I really like **the layout.**
4 I think **it's too small for us.**

### 57.8 🔊
1 We'd like a house with a yard.
2 We'd like an apartment with a yard.
3 We'd like a property with a yard.
4 We'd like a house close to the subway.
5 We'd like an apartment close to the subway.
6 We'd like a property close to the subway.
7 We'd like a house near a school.
8 We'd like an apartment near a school.
9 We'd like a property near a school.

### 57.13
A 3
B 1
C 6
D 5
E 2
F 4

### 57.14 🔊
1 How much is the **rent**?
2 Are **utility bills** included?
3 Can I put this **picture** up?
4 The **washing machine** is leaking.
5 Are **pets** allowed?
6 As soon as you've signed the **rental agreement!**

### 57.15 🔊
1 Can I have a **roommate**?
2 One year, with an option to **renew.**
3 Are utility **bills** included?
4 Do you need a **deposit**?
5 Do I **pay** the rent monthly?
6 What **references** do you need?

## 58

### 58.5
A 1
B 3
C 4
D 5
E 6
F 2

### 58.6 🔊
1 Is everything packed and **ready**?
2 Hope **the move** goes well!
3 Do you have any spare **boxes**?
4 I've told everyone our **moving** date.
5 We have to move out by the **weekend.**
6 I've **packed** up the bedroom.
7 Let's **load** the moving van!
8 We can **unpack** in the morning.

**58.7** 🔊
1. Hope the move **goes well!**
2. Let's load **the moving van!**
3. Where do you want us **to start?**
4. I've packed up **the bedroom.**
5. I'm here to pick up **the keys to my house.**

## 59

**59.7**
A 3　　E 8
B 4　　F 6
C 1　　G 2
D 7　　H 5

**59.8** 🔊
1. Are you free for drinks later?
2. Are you free for lunch later?
3. Are you free for coffee later?
4. Are you free for drinks tomorrow?
5. Are you free for lunch tomorrow?
6. Are you free for coffee tomorrow?
7. Are you free for drinks on Sunday?
8. Are you free for lunch on Sunday?
9. Are you free for coffee on Sunday?

## 60

**60.5**
1. A
2. B
3. B
4. A

**60.6** 🔊
1. Whose turn is it to empty **the dishwasher?**
2. I've cleaned the counters **and the oven.**
3. Great job! The kitchen **was in a bad state.**
4. Phew! That was **a major spring-clean!**

## 61

**61.5**
A 7　　F 9
B 6　　G 4
C 1　　H 5
D 3　　I 8
E 2

**61.6** 🔊
1. Could you give us a quote for fixing our fence?
2. Could you give us a quote for hanging some shelves?
3. Could you give us a quote for laying a carpet?
4. Could you give us a quote for painting our kitchen walls?
5. Are you able to give us a quote for fixing our fence?
6. Are you able to give us a quote for hanging some shelves?
7. Are you able to give us a quote for laying a carpet?
8. Are you able to give us a quote for painting our kitchen walls?

## 62

**62.7**
A 1　　D 5
B 4　　E 3
C 2　　F 6

**62.8** 🔊
1. Is she good **with children?**
2. I think he has **a broken leg.**
3. She's lost weight **and stopped eating.**
4. Hi, I'd like to **adopt a cat.**
5. We have to get him microchipped **and book his vaccinations!**

## 63

**63.6**
A 4　　E 8
B 5　　F 2
C 7　　G 3
D 1　　H 6

**63.7** 🔊
1. The power has **gone off.**
2. The power is **back on!**
3. The faucet has been **dripping** for days.
4. When was the furnace last **serviced?**

## 64

**64.6**
A 2　　E 3
B 1　　F 6
C 5　　G 8
D 4　　H 7

**64.7** 🔊
1. Should we play **the next level?**
2. Can you turn on **the subtitles?**
3. Is the console **plugged in?**
4. What should we **watch tonight?**

## 66

**66.5** 🔊
1. We're almost there—it's the next stop.
2. Yes, via the railway station.
3. Yes, they're right at the back.
4. Yup, just log on to our network.

**66.6** 🔊
1. Excuse me, does this bus go to the library
2. Excuse me, are we nearly at the library?
3. Excuse me, is this the right stop for the library?
4. Excuse me, does this bus go to the town center?
5. Excuse me, are we nearly at the town center?
6. Excuse me, is this the right stop for the town center?
7. Excuse me, does this bus go to the shopping center?
8. Excuse me, are we nearly at the shopping center?
9. Excuse me, is this the right stop for the shopping center?

## 67

**67.7**
A 6　　D 1
B 4　　E 2
C 3　　F 5

**67.8** 🔊
1. Can I reserve a **seat**?
2. What time is the next Nashville **service**?
3. There's a really long **line** for tickets!
4. Does this train **stop** at Birmingham?
5. Let's wait in the **waiting** area.
6. Hello. Can we **book** two round-trip tickets to Tampa, please?
7. Do I **tap** in at the turnstile?

**67.13**
1. 3
2. 1
3. 4
4. 5
5. 2

**67.14** 🔊
1. Excuse me, how do I get to Tampa?
2. Excuse me, how many stops is it to Tampa?
3. Excuse me, how much is a round-trip ticket to Tampa?
4. Excuse me, how much is a one-way ticket to Tampa?
5. Excuse me, how do I get to Atlanta?
6. Excuse me, how many stops is it to Atlanta?
7. Excuse me, how much is a round-trip ticket to Atlanta?
8. Excuse me, how much is a one-way ticket to Atlanta?

## 68

**68.4** 🔊
1. What **time** is boarding?
2. Can I change to a window **seat**?
3. What's the gate **number**?
4. How long is the **delay**?
5. Any chance I can **upgrade**?
6. What time does the **gate** close?
7. Place your bag in the **bin**, please!
8. Where is the **check-in** desk?

**68.9**
- A 6
- B 1
- C 5
- D 3
- E 4
- F 2

**68.10**
- A 3
- B 4
- C 5
- D 1
- E 6
- F 2

**68.11** 🔊
1. I'll put our stuff **in the overhead bin.**
2. Please switch your digital devices **to "airplane" mode.**
3. We'll shortly be passing through **the cabin with snacks and drinks.**
4. Your tray tables **should be securely fastened.**
5. Make sure your seat **is in the upright position.**

**68.14**
1. B
2. A
3. B
4. A

**68.16** 🔊
1. Where do we meet our **taxi**?
2. I can't see our **suitcases** anywhere!
3. It's carousel 3. I'll grab a **cart**.
4. Yes, I need to exchange some **Euros**.
5. I'm here to pick up a rental **car**.

## 69

**69.6** 🔊
1. For getting around town, mainly.
2. You just need to download the app!
3. There are bike docks all over town!
4. The brakes are loose.

**69.7**
- A 6
- B 5
- C 3
- D 1
- E 4
- F 2

**69.8** 🔊
1. What type of **bike** do you want?
2. The **battery** needs charging.
3. The front **tire** is flat.
4. Would you like a **test ride**?
5. I need a bike to get to and from **work**.
6. There are bike **docks** all over town!
7. You just need to download the **app**!
8. The **brakes** are loose.

## 70

**70.5**
- A 7
- B 4
- C 1
- D 8
- E 6
- F 3
- G 2
- H 5

**70.6** 🔊
1. Hello. Can I **book** a taxi from the airport?
2. How soon will the **cab** be here?
3. Can you **drop** me here, please?
4. I'm traveling with my service **dog**.
5. I left my laptop in one of your **taxis**.
6. Can you take me to this **address**?
7. How **long** will it take to get there?
8. Can I **pay** with contactless?

## 71

**71.6**
1. A
2. A
3. B
4. A

**71.7** 🔊
1. The windshield is **cracked.**
2. The steering wheel is **jammed.**
3. The tire keeps **going flat.**
4. The oil needs **to be changed.**

## 73

**73.4**
- A 2
- B 3
- C 1
- D 4
- E 6
- F 5

**73.5** 🔊
1. Do I need **a visa?**
2. Can I bring my **guide dog?**
3. Is it suitable **for young children?**
4. What's your **cancelation policy?**

**73.6** 🔊

1 Is this cruise all-inclusive?
2 Is this beach vacation all-inclusive?
3 Is this city break all-inclusive?
4 Is this safari all-inclusive?
5 Is this cruise adults only?
6 Is this beach vacation adults only?
7 Is this city break adults only?
8 Is this safari adults only?
9 Is this cruise suitable for young children?
10 Is this beach vacation suitable for young children?
11 Is this city break suitable for young children?
12 Is this safari suitable for young children?

# 74

**74.4**

1 A
2 A
3 A
4 B
5 A
6 B

**74.10**

| | | | |
|---|---|---|---|
| A 4 | | D 2 |
| B 1 | | E 5 |
| C 6 | | F 3 |

**74.11** 🔊

1 I'd like **a 7 a.m. wake-up call.**
2 The room **is too hot.**
3 The shower **is leaking.**
4 The Wi-Fi password **is wrong.**
5 I'd like a hair dryer **brought to my room.**

**74.12** 🔊

1 Could I have a hair dryer sent up, please?
2 Could I have some fresh towels sent up, please?
3 Could I have a club sandwich sent up, please?
4 Could I have two extra pillows sent up, please?
5 Could I have a hair dryer brought to my room, please?
6 Could I have some fresh towels brought to my room, please?

7 Could I have a club sandwich brought to my room, please?
8 Could I have two extra pillows brought to my room, please?

**74.16** 🔊

1 Did you enjoy **your stay?**
2 Yes, and help yourselves **to the buffet.**
3 Here's your bill **if you'd like to check it.**
4 Is it possible to **stay an extra night?**
5 Can I get **your room number?**

**74.17** 🔊

1 Could I have some more **coffee**?
2 Are you paying by **card**?
3 Could you call me a **cab**, please?
4 The **bed** was a little hard.
5 Can I leave my **luggage** here?

**74.18** 🔊

1 Can I see your **passport**, please?
2 What time is **checkout**?
3 We'd like a room with **queen beds**, please.
4 The **room** was a bit noisy.
5 Dinner was **delicious**.
6 Do you have a **king** bed available?
7 The **restaurant** serves dinner until 10 p.m.
8 Your room is on the second **floor**.

# 75

**75.5**

1 B
2 B
3 A
4 A

**75.7** 🔊

1 Want to get off **at the next stop?**
2 Quick! **Take a picture!**
3 Is there **wheelchair access?**
4 What are **your opening times?**
5 How much is **the entrance fee?**

# 76

**76.5**

| | | | |
|---|---|---|---|
| A 3 | | E 6 |
| B 1 | | F 5 |
| C 2 | | G 4 |
| D 7 | | H 8 |

**76.6** 🔊

1 Can we pitch our tent over in that field?
2 Can we set up camp over in that field?
3 Can we park our camper over in that field?
4 Can we pitch our tent near the shower block?
5 Can we set up camp near the shower block?
6 Can we park our camper near the shower block?
7 Can we pitch our tent across from the trailers?
8 Can we set up camp across from the trailers?
9 Can we park our camper across from the trailers?

# 77

**77.4**

| | | | |
|---|---|---|---|
| A 5 | | E 1 |
| B 8 | | F 2 |
| C 7 | | G 6 |
| D 4 | | H 3 |

**77.5** 🔊

1 Can we hire a **paddleboard** here?
2 How much is a **sun lounger** for the day?
3 Where can we buy a **beach ball?**
4 Can we hire a **paddleboat** for the day?
5 Do you do **surfing** lessons?

**77.6** 🔊

1 Can we hire **a paddleboat here?**
2 Is it safe **to swim today?**
3 Yes, but you must **stay between the flags**
4 Do you do **surfing lessons?**

## 78.4

| | |
|---|---|
| Ⓐ 4 | Ⓓ 2 |
| Ⓑ 1 | Ⓔ 3 |
| Ⓒ 6 | Ⓕ 5 |

## 78.5 🔊

1. Excuse me, do you know **the way** to the bus station?
2. Can you tell me how to **get to** the museum?
3. Yes, **go straight** ahead and it's on your left.
4. Take the **first right** after the library.
5. No, you need to **go past** the church …
6. … then **cross** the road …
7. It's just **next to** the hospital.

## 78.6 🔊

1. Excuse me, do you know the way to the church?
2. Excuse me, can you tell me how to get to the church?
3. Excuse me, do you know the way to the museum?
4. Excuse me, can you tell me how to get to the museum?
5. Excuse me, do you know the way to the bus station?
6. Excuse me, can you tell me how to get to the bus station?
7. Excuse me, do you know the way to the bank?
8. Excuse me, can you tell me how to get to the bank?

## 79.6

| | |
|---|---|
| Ⓐ 2 | Ⓕ 8 |
| Ⓑ 5 | Ⓖ 3 |
| Ⓒ 1 | Ⓗ 7 |
| Ⓓ 6 | Ⓘ 4 |
| Ⓔ 9 | |

## 79.7 🔊

1. The train is canceled **due to lack of available train crew.**
2. Yeah, I won't make the beach. **I have a stomach bug!**
3. Look at the board. **Our train has been canceled!**
4. Your insurance should cover you **if you get a doctor's note.**

## 81.4

| | |
|---|---|
| Ⓐ 6 | Ⓓ 3 |
| Ⓑ 2 | Ⓔ 4 |
| Ⓒ 1 | Ⓕ 5 |

## 81.6 🔊

1. I have a really sore throat.
2. I have a really bad headache.
3. I have a really itchy rash.
4. I have a really sore ear.
5. I have a really itchy eye.

## 81.10 🔊

1. Yes, I'm taking antibiotics.
2. How often should I take it?
3. For about a week.
4. Yes, I also have a runny nose.
5. Hmm … it looks like an allergy.

## 81.11

| | |
|---|---|
| Ⓐ 8 | Ⓕ 9 |
| Ⓑ 5 | Ⓖ 6 |
| Ⓒ 1 | Ⓗ 2 |
| Ⓓ 7 | Ⓘ 4 |
| Ⓔ 3 | |

## 81.12 🔊

1. I have a really sore **eye**.
2. I also have a runny **nose**.
3. My **hand** really hurts.
4. I have an itchy rash on my **foot**.
5. My **ear** is killing me.

## 82.6 🔊

1. I need to see the primary care **nurse**.
2. Hi there, I'd like to book an appointment with **Doctor** Cole.
3. Can I **reschedule** my appointment?
4. Can I book an **appointment** for my daughter?
5. Do you have **anything** sooner?
6. When's the next **available** slot?
7. If you need an urgent appointment, we'll place you on the **triage** list …
8. I think I might have an **eye** infection.

## 82.7 🔊

1. I'd like to book an appointment with the doctor.
2. I'd like to reschedule an appointment with the doctor.
3. I'd like to book a checkup with the doctor.
4. I'd like to cancel an appointment with the doctor.
5. I'd like to book an appointment with the dentist.
6. I'd like to reschedule an appointment with the dentist.
7. I'd like to book a checkup with the dentist.
8. I'd like to cancel an appointment with the dentist.
9. I'd like to book an appointment for my daughter.
10. I'd like to reschedule an appointment for my daughter.
11. I'd like to book a checkup for my daughter.
12. I'd like to cancel an appointment for my daughter.

## 83.7

| | |
|---|---|
| Ⓐ 3 | Ⓔ 4 |
| Ⓑ 1 | Ⓕ 7 |
| Ⓒ 8 | Ⓖ 6 |
| Ⓓ 5 | Ⓗ 2 |

**83.8** 🔊
1. I've had a bad cough for a week **and it's getting worse.**
2. I've been **vomiting all night.**
3. I'm due for **a checkup.**
4. I've been under **the weather.**

# 84

**84.5** 🔊
1. I need a **doctor immediately.**
2. I burned my hand on the **stove. It's really painful.**
3. I'll grab **some tissues.**
4. My husband has **severe chest pains.**
5. He's having **a seizure.**

**84.6**
1. B
2. A
3. A
4. B

**84.7** 🔊
1. It looks like she may need **stitches.**
2. Hold this cold pack over the **swelling.**
3. My husband has severe chest **pains.**
4. That's a nasty **scrape.**

# 85

**85.3**
A. 4
B. 3
C. 5
D. 2
E. 1

**85.4** 🔊
1. I need to see someone as soon as **possible.**
2. We have a **medical** emergency.
3. How soon will I be seen by a **doctor?**
4. I have a **checkup** with the nurse at 4:30.
5. Do I need to have **surgery?**
6. I'm going to need to **examine** you.

**85.10**
A. 7     E. 2
B. 8     F. 3
C. 6     G. 1
D. 4     H. 5

**85.11** 🔊
1. I'll just take your blood **pressure** first.
2. Still a bit **groggy.**
3. Don't worry. We'll have you up and **about** in no time.
4. I'll just check your **temperature** and pulse …
5. You may feel lightheaded as the **anesthetic** takes effect.
6. How long will I be **under** for?
7. Now count **backward** from 5 …
8. There were no **complications.**

# 86

**86.6**
A. 1     D. 2
B. 6     E. 3
C. 4     F. 5

**86.7**
A. 6     F. 10
B. 2     G. 9
C. 1     H. 4
D. 7     I. 3
E. 8     J. 5

**86.8** 🔊
1. I brush my teeth **twice a day.**
2. I need to see **the hygienist.**
3. I think my crown **has come loose.**
4. Can I have **my teeth whitened?**
5. My son's first teeth **are coming through.**

# 87

**87.7** 🔊
1. I've been feeling a bit low this week.
2. I've been feeling very low this week.
3. I've been feeling really low this week.
4. I've been feeling a bit anxious this week.
5. I've been feeling very anxious this week.
6. I've been feeling really anxious this week.
7. I've been feeling a bit depressed this week.
8. I've been feeling very depressed this week.
9. I've been feeling really depressed this week.
10. I've been feeling a bit up and down this week.
11. I've been feeling very up and down this week.
12. I've been feeling really up and down this week.

**87.8** 🔊
1. How is this **affecting** you?
2. These sessions are really **helping** me.
3. I'm finding it hard to **cope.**
4. Your feelings are **valid.**
5. How did that make you **feel?**
6. That's a real **trigger** for me.
7. Can we **explore** this more?
8. I'm doing **better** this week.

# 89

**89.8**
A. 4     E. 7
B. 1     F. 6
C. 8     G. 5
D. 3     H. 2

**89.9** 🔊
1. We'll need to check our system **and get back to you.**
2. Is there anything else **I can help you with?**
3. He knows where **to reach me.**
4. Hello, I wonder **if you can help me …**
5. Thank you so much **for calling.**

# 90

**90.7** 🔊
1. Sorry, I can't **talk** now.
2. I can't remember my **PIN.**
3. I'll **message** you back.
4. I'll put you on **speaker.**
5. My phone has **died.**
6. I've been **locked** out.
7. My **screen** has frozen.

**0.8** 🔊

Hello? You're **breaking** up—the signal is terrible.

Sounds perfect. **See** you then!

Good, thank you. I'm just **checking** about tonight.

Okay. We can **fix** it for you.

## 91

**1.5**

| | |
|---|---|
| 5 | **D** 1 |
| 2 | **E** 4 |
| 6 | **F** 3 |

**1.6** 🔊

Choose "free Wi-Fi" from the **menu**, then you can register.

Go to "settings," then tap "**security**".

You can join my **hot spot** if you like.

Yeah, that URL seems dicey. Let's try another **site**.

**1.11**

| | |
|---|---|
| 6 | **D** 3 |
| 1 | **E** 2 |
| 4 | **F** 5 |

**1.12** 🔊

I'm **booking** a doctor's appointment.

I need to **check** my emails …

I have a **webinar** this afternoon.

I'm **streaming** a new series.

… and sign up for that **online** training course.

I'm **ordering** more cat food.

I'm **scrolling** through my socials.

I'm just **tracking** the grocery delivery.

**1.13** 🔊

I'm downloading **our tickets for today.**

I'll share yours with you **on our group chat.**

I'm setting up an online account **for our energy bills.**

I'm just uploading my essay … **then I have a webinar this afternoon.**

## 92

**92.5**

| | |
|---|---|
| **A** 6 | **D** 3 |
| **B** 5 | **E** 4 |
| **C** 2 | **F** 1 |

**92.6** 🔊

1. It's asking me to set up **authentication on my account.**
2. I'm trying to get tickets, **but the website keeps crashing.**
3. My screen has **completely frozen.**
4. You could try **restarting the computer …**
5. … or you could connect **from a different device.**

## 93

**93.6**

1. A
2. A
3. B
4. B
5. A
6. B

**93.7** 🔊

1. Check your **trash**. Maybe it's still there.
2. Okay, let's have a look at your **filters**.
3. Yeah, I'll **forward** you her message.
4. It looks suspicious—I wouldn't **download** it.

## 94

**94.6**

| | |
|---|---|
| **A** 7 | **F** 8 |
| **B** 1 | **G** 6 |
| **C** 5 | **H** 2 |
| **D** 3 | **I** 4 |
| **E** 9 | |

**94.7** 🔊

1. I'm just **clicking** on it now.
2. **IDK**, will have to see how I feel TBH
3. I can, sweetheart! Can you **see** me?
4. I know, right? **LOL**

## 95

**95.6** 🔊

1. I saw! I think you've broken the Internet.
2. Or how about a monthly podcast?
3. Not him! Just block him.

**95.7** 🔊

1. Or how about a monthly **podcast**?
2. That's just a **troll**. I'm blocking them.
3. I saw! I think you've broken the **Internet**.
4. There are tons of **comments** on my post!
5. They're all up on my **profile**.
6. More video **content** would help.

## 96

**96.5**

| | |
|---|---|
| **A** 7 | **E** 6 |
| **B** 2 | **F** 4 |
| **C** 5 | **G** 3 |
| **D** 1 | |

**96.6** 🔊

1. Can you recommend **a good vacation read?**
2. It's the best book **I've read in ages.**
3. Yeah, it had me on **the edge of my seat!**
4. I found it pretty **rough going, actually.**
5. Want a flip through *Fashion Monthly*?

# Index

Main topics are shown in **bold** module numbers.

# Acknowledgments

**The publisher would like to thank:**
Sophie Adam and Elizabeth Blakemore for editorial assistance; Amy Child, Mark Lloyd, and Collette Sadler for design assistance; Jane Ewart for project management support; Sonia Charbonnier for fonts; Oliver Drake for proofreading; Elizabeth Wise for indexing; Christine Stroyan for audio recording management; and ID Audio for audio recording and production.

All images are copyright DK. For more information, please visit **www.dkimages.com**.